Shaping Power for Good
Wayfinding to Right Relationship
Dr. Amanda Aguilera

RIGHT USE OF POWER
- PUBLISHING -

Right Use of Power Publishing

Book Cover by Jorde Matthews, Be Someone Design Co.

Illustrations by Dr. Amanda Aguilera

1st edition 2025

This book is dedicated to Dr. Cedar Barstow
and the Right Use of Power community –

*for your tireless dedication to
standing in your strength & staying in your heart.*

"And one of the great problems of history is that the concepts of love and power have usually been contrasted as opposites, polar opposites, so that love is identified with a resignation of power, and power with the denial of love...What is needed is a realization that power without love is reckless and abusive, and that love without power is sentimental and anemic. Power at its best is love implementing the demands of justice, and justice at its best is power correcting everything that stands against love...It is precisely this collision of immoral power with powerless morality which constitutes the major crisis of our times."

- Dr. Marting Luther King, Jr.

Last presidential address to the Southern Christian Leadership Conference, August 16, 1967

Foreword

It's not every day you meet someone who not only studies power but lives it—intentionally, humbly, and with unwavering clarity. Dr. Amanda Aguilera is that kind of person. As the Founder of Right Use of Power Institute, and Amanda's colleague, mentor, friend, and collaborator, I've had the privilege of working closely with her since 2006, and I continue to be inspired by her ability to approach complex topics with both intellectual depth and heartfelt presence.

Shaping Power for Good: Wayfinding to Right Relationship is a remarkable title—and this is a remarkable book. It declares two essential truths: that power can be shaped, and that it can be shaped for good. Isn't this precisely what we need? To understand that there is an alternative to the traumatic abuses and misuses of power that dominate our headlines, workplaces, and communities—and linger in our bodies and minds? In this timely, original, and much-needed exploration of power—what it is, how it operates in our lives, and how we can relate to it in conscious, ethical, and transformative ways—Amanda offers a clear and steady light focusing on the good that is possible in the use of power.

Amanda introduces the concept of power consciousness—an invitation to become more aware of the ways power moves through individuals, relationships, and systems. She doesn't shy away from hard truths, nor does she settle for simple answers. Instead, she builds a nuanced, multidimensional framework that empowers us to engage with power more honestly and courageously. She also introduces wayfinding as the ancient practice of navigating the sea by the stars translated into wayfinding as the powerful and engaging practice of navigating power dynamics into right-relationship with others.

What sets this book apart is that it's not just theoretical—it's deeply practical and deeply human. Amanda's lived experience, combined with years of professional practice, informs every chapter. She writes as someone who has done the inner work, navigated difficult conversations, and stood in the tension between compassion and accountability. She makes the complex feel accessible without oversimplifying.

Imagine what becomes possible—for organizations, communities, and individuals—when people develop power consciousness. When they understand both the nature and shadow of power. When they recognize that healthy uses of power require not just good intentions, but skill and self-awareness. When they say "yes" to their power—personal and professional—and with intention and care, shape it as a force for healing, justice, and connection.

This book is a stand-alone guide and also a brilliant sequel to the Right Use of Power: The Heart of Ethics, the book that is the foundation of Right Use of Power Institute. Amanda deepens the exploration of personal and status power and adds essential dimensions—collective, systemic, and universal power—to our typology. Her frameworks and visuals make complex ideas strikingly accessible.

This book is important because it gives us the vocabulary, frameworks, and tools to do the work of change—individually and collectively. Whether you are a leader, therapist, educator, activist, or someone seeking to live more ethically in the world, Amanda's voice will guide you and you will come away with both new concepts and actionable steps for using your power-consciousness to shape power for good.

—

Dr. Cedar Barstow, CHT, DPI

Hakomi Trainer and Therapist,
Author of *Right Use of Power: The Heart of Ethics,*
and Founder of the Right Use of Power Institute.
www.rightuseofpower.org

Preface

Initially, this book was not supposed to be about wayfinding or "right-relationship." I thought I would write more about the science and observations on power, given my affinity for the topic, my interest in research, and my love of a good-sized appendix. And then I began writing, and it started to unfold in a different way than I had anticipated (as books and creative works tend to do). Despite much of my own resistance, it finally developed into its own thing—beyond the plans I had for it. But I suppose that is the way of things when you open yourself up to creative sources. I finally surrendered to its insistence.

One of the most surprising influences in this book was actually initiated from a children's movie, of all places. And it was so influential that it prompted me to revise the manuscript towards the end of writing it. I took my kids to watch Moana 2 in the movie theater. The movie is about a young Polynesian wayfinder who follows the call of her ancestors. She recruits people from her community to go on a journey to ultimately unite people from different islands. I was excited to see the continuation of the first movie and to be with my kids to watch it. I had settled in with some popcorn, and then about five minutes into the movie, I started crying—and I didn't stop until one hour after the movie was over! I'm a crier—so more often than not I will cry in movies even if they aren't sad. But this seemed excessive, even for me. And the crying wasn't, "oh, that was touching." It was a deep grief with a kind of achiness that also felt like longing. Initially, I couldn't figure out what was going on. I was mystified by my reaction, but I knew enough to pay attention.

After processing it internally, in therapy, and through my own study of the subject of wayfinding, I realized that the themes of the movie and my reaction to it were deeply related to the book I was writing—and my own unique calling in this life. I also realized that my reaction was tied to the collective grief that many are experiencing at this point in time in 2025 in the United States. The movie and my reaction highlighted for me the profound disconnection many of us have from the natural world, from the elements, from each other, from our calling, from finding out who we really are, from community, from our ancestors, even from grief itself.

While all of these things are related to what I write in this book, it was wayfinding specifically that became a new focus for how I talk about navigating social power dynamics. I remember at one point in the movie, one of the characters, Matangi, said incredulously to Moana, "You think you can only get somewhere if you know the way?. . .A true wayfinder doesn't know the path at all. That's the whole point!" Something clicked for me then. The principles I was trying to apply to power had already been laid out in this ancient art form that human beings have relied on for thousands of years. We can know as much about power as we want, but participating in power well or finding right-relationship can't be put on a map—or perhaps even in a book. You can see why this discovery was troubling for me, as I was nearing the end of my manuscript.

I also had doubts about my ability to translate the concept of wayfinding well, given I have never studied wayfinding, apprenticed with an elder, nor grown up in a culture that imparted deep ancestral wayfinding practices. Surfing that doubt and uncertainty was a valuable process (one that I'm familiar with as a queer, cisgender, white woman). What came during the many hours of listening and reflection that followed were two insights that convinced me to move forward. One is that wayfinding has been a part of the human experience in different ways for thousands of years, in virtually every society in the world. And almost every Western society in modernity has sacrificed that knowledge in the name of progress and technology.

The second was that I felt wayfinding in my bones, calling me to orient toward place, intuition, relationship, and the unknown. Those who know me well know that I am often the first to get the newest technology—whether it's a new app, innovative software, or a device. As a neurodivergent person, I rely heavily on technology to assist me in the areas where my executive functioning often fails. And as an Enneagram 5 with an obsession with information, I appreciate having immediate answers to all my many questions with the touch of a button. And yet, here I was, being called to loosen my grip on knowledge and surrender to what I didn't know. While this is wildly uncomfortable for me, when I do that, a different kind of knowing arises. I knew I had to follow this calling into the unknown—and I knew that it needed to be a guiding force in the book. I realized that I needed to "wayfind" my way to wayfinding itself—and offer my own interpretation and integration of it in the context of power. And, of course, I still struggle with the inherent problematic nature of a white person in the United States offering a text about wayfinding to power. But this is a struggle I continue to embrace, as I think it is an important one. My hope is that my struggle and offerings in this book do not result in harm to others. If it does, I would welcome the opportunity to repair that harm in some way. If you feel generous enough to offer feedback,

I would welcome it as a gift.

The truth is, this book came about as something needing to be birthed through me. It is an expression of both my mind and soul and an attempt to stay connected to Spirit and my well-ancestors as I typed. This is all to say that the book is an intimate sharing and has a spiritual undertone. And because modernity has become increasingly avoidant of or polarized around the spiritual, it is necessary to give a fair warning of this unusual arrangement before you begin reading. As I am presenting a new model of power, I had to cover a vast amount of information, so sometimes it reads like a textbook with a lot of footnotes (especially in Parts One and Two). And then the spiritual undertone throughout the book and the spiritual overtone in Part Three will make it feel... a lot less like a textbook. So if you prefer textbooks or spiritual self-help books, you'll get a little of each. Perhaps it will spread out the discomfort.

Finally, I use a lot of images, maps, and models throughout the book because I think visually, and it helps me to understand the world. I also think images can represent more than words can even attempt (except, maybe, poetry, which I also include where I can). Conversely, I will often break things down into pieces and categorize them, not to dissect or get away from feeling (ok, maybe sometimes I do that), but rather to understand the pieces so we can put them back together in new ways. As someone on the spectrum, I tend to present in a direct and matter-of-fact way. But please know that I do not intend to convey that I have all the answers. You can view the book more as a proposal or single perspective that comes through particular identities. There are, of course, limitations to any of the models I present in this book. As the British statistician, George Box, said, "Remember that all models are wrong; the practical question is how wrong do they have to be to not be useful." I would add that even when they are useful, models are only helpful for a short time until they inevitably need to shift, grow, or be replaced. So, the models I present throughout this book are always evolving. Also, models can start to look an awful lot like fingers pointing to the moon,[1] so don't get too attached to the models. They are meant to serve relationships, not to serve "being right." In the words of one of the world's foremost systems analysts, Donella H. Meadows:

"Everything we think we know about the world is a model. Every word and every language is a model. All maps and statistics, books and databases, equations and computer programs are models. So are the ways I picture the world in my head—my mental models. None of these is or ever will be the real world…We know a tremendous amount about how the world works, but not nearly enough. Our knowledge is amazing; our ignorance even more so. We can improve our understanding, but we can't make it perfect."[2]

Here you will find a book full of imperfect models that many of my students and colleagues have suggested I publish. May they be of benefit.

---

1. In Zen Buddhism, the metaphor of the finger pointing to the moon is often used to illustrate the importance of directly experiencing reality rather than relying on secondhand interpretations or clinging to conceptual frameworks. When the teacher points at the moon, the student can focus on the finger instead of what the finger is pointing to (the moon). The finger is a helpful guide, but the ultimate goal is to see the moon (reality) for oneself.

2. Meadows, D. H. (2008). *Thinking in Systems: A Primer.* Chelsea Green Publishing, p. 86-87.

Contents

1

Introduction

"To be fully alive, fully human, and completely awake is to be continually thrown out of the nest. To be comfortable is to be a bit of a jerk, and to be in discomfort is to be fully fledged." - Pema Chödrön

"You can't see what you don't understand. But what you think you already understand, you'll fail to notice." - Richard Powers

"Our wayfinding in life is an art that brings together intuition, consciousness, and our connection to the world around us." - Joanna Macy

In modern, Western societies, we've engineered a peculiar kind of misfortune: the increased effort and repeated aim to sidestep inconvenience, discomfort, and uncertainty. To most, this doesn't sound like misfortune at all—it sounds like progress. After all, much of our cultural evolution has been driven by the production of new and varied ways to alleviate suffering in one form or another. However, even the alleviation of suffering could be considered a form of avoidance. There is a lot that we avoid about being human.

I name this focus on avoidance as a misfortune because my own experiences of suffering, discomfort, and especially uncertainty have led me to the greatest gifts I have received in my life.

Of course, this is often an unwelcome realization until it is in hindsight. In fact, we do almost everything in our power to avoid these experiences when they arise. We have invented a variety of addictions, distractions, and psychological obstacles to attempt to prevent the uncomfortable parts of being human. Unfortunately, this avoidance leads us further away from the innate power we were born with—and closer to harming ourselves and others.

We have essentially used all the power we have access to to distance ourselves from the experience of vulnerability. And the further we get from the vulnerability of our humanness and the struggle of being human, the further we get from accessing the kinds of power that can help us to find "right-relationship."[1] The curious part is that vulnerability leads to *more* access to power, not less. While this may seem counterintuitive now, this book serves as a guide to becoming familiar with the various kinds of power human beings access and how they bring us closer to—or further away from—right-relationship.

Over the years, I have observed some things about how people generally understand power. One is that people assume they already know what power is, and so they spend little time investigating it. And even when they do investigate it, they tend to fall into the common misconceptions about power (which we will cover in the first chapter). The second thing I realized is that it rarely changes a situation when people talk about power. Not because it isn't helpful to talk about it, but because the way people talk about power tends to lack nuance and specificity.

Power is a dynamic that exists in *all* relationships. The health of each relationship depends on the fundamental energy that exists

---

1. In the next chapter we will define what "right-relationship" is but I'm curious if you have an intuitive guess?

between and through us—and how we engage with that energy is *power*. Simply put, power is a dynamic that *connects* us. Unfortunately, most of us haven't been socialized to look at it that way. We are generally taught the opposite: that power is something to possess, fear, or want—something to use for personal gain. This disconnected understanding of power has led to great devastation and harm.

Without deserving it, I have repeatedly benefited from others' generosity in helping me to turn toward the devastation and harm caused by my and others' unconscious participation in power dynamics. Their generosity led me to learn how to grieve, to work through guilt, and to heal. I have spent a great deal of time working with darkness and shadow, trying to find discernment and the thread of soul and spirit that runs through my life. I have had many mentors along the way in this apprenticeship – some haven't even realized they were mentoring me. I call all of these mentors my "Lineage of Influence," a map I created and continue to add to as a reflection and a way to honor those who have helped me grow.

I still regularly get lost, though. I lose my way and then return to the thread again. The thread represents connection: to our own power, to others, and to that which is bigger than all of us and includes all of us. This book is about returning to that thread of connection again and again. It's about learning how power is much more nuanced and complex than we've been taught —or are willing to admit. And it is an attempt to answer the question: How do we access and shape power toward right-relationship?

After using this question as my mantra for months, I was led to the ancient practice of wayfinding. Traditionally, wayfinding has been used to navigate one's physical environment, whether in a desert, on the sea, at an airport, in a savannah, in a mall, or in the Arctic. Unlike other, more technical navigation methods, wayfinding relies on an active, conscious relationship with place, an ability to adapt and access intuition, and an emphasis on the quality of the journey, not just the destination. Like many other humans, I believe the wayfinding approach can also be applied to one's internal landscape, as well as the environments of relationships, groups, and organizations. Like wayfinding, becoming power-conscious, learning the art of shaping power, and finding right-relationship cannot happen without discomfort or uncertainty.

If you want to be more conscious of how you show up in relationships or participate in power, are dedicated to positive social outcomes, and have a willingness to experience discomfort and uncertainty, this book is for you! I have gone to great lengths to provide more nuance and to re-examine common ideas about power. No matter what your beliefs about power are, I will likely challenge them at some point in the book. Healthy doses of curiosity and courage are recommended, as well as some patience to get through the denser parts!

This book has three primary aims: 1) to support your understanding of the complexities of social power dynamics[2] ; 2) to provide insights for becoming more power-conscious so you can shape power for good; and 3) to explore ways of bringing about right-relationship more often in your life by utilizing wayfinding principles.

As you may have already noticed, I have included some definitions in the appendix as well as call-out boxes and footnotes throughout the book. I like to make up words, and sometimes I use

---

2. *Social power dynamics* – *the complex interplay of power in relationships between individuals and groups within a social system. It encompasses the ways in which power is distributed, exercised, contested, and resisted within a society or system.* While there are power dynamics present throughout existence, I will primarily be focusing on social power dynamics and human relationships.

words with slightly different definitions than you might be used to—so I recommend taking a moment to read those. This book consists of three parts, each designed to build upon the previous one. Part One builds the groundwork for the rest of the book. Part Two is the most information-heavy, but it provides more nuance. Part Three builds on the first two parts of the book; however, you can skip directly to that section if you prefer to focus on the more actionable steps. Let's begin with a brief introduction to each part of the book.

Part one: Understanding Power

"The mature person becomes able to differentiate feelings into as many nuances, strong and passionate experiences, or delicate and sensitive ones, as in the different passages of music in a symphony. Unfortunately, many of us have feelings limited like notes in a bugle call." - Rollo May

I recall when I first learned about Nonviolent Communication and came across this quotation from Rollo May. I felt a resonance with it. I didn't grow up with the encouragement to feel or talk about my feelings, so communicating about feelings didn't exactly come naturally to me. When I was studying to become a therapist, I felt like a bugle horn among other, more delicate instruments, like the flute or cello. Over time, I realized that what helped me identify and distinguish my feelings was having a framework and language to understand and talk about them. This had a profound impact on me and my relationships.

At the start of my journey to understand power, I realized that this very same dynamic applied: I had no framework or language for understanding power. I could generally feel it, and I knew it was around, but I couldn't point to it, nor did I have the words to talk about it. I felt either powerless or guilty about the power I did have. And I participated in power dynamics in the way I observed others do so. Unfortunately, that led me to misuse the power I had access to and to ignore the power dynamics I didn't understand. Fortunately, those misuses of power led me to look a little deeper at power, and I came across the work of Dr. Cedar Barstow called the Right Use of Power™. Dr. Barstow created a language and framework for discussing power that I found captured the nuance other models lacked. It felt like I started to hear a symphony—or perhaps jazz is a more appropriate metaphor (more on this later). Having a framework for understanding the complexity of power and a language that captures its nuances has been a revolutionary experience for me and many of Dr. Barstow's other students around the world.

Over the years, in partnership with Dr. Barstow and many other RUP facilitators, I have expanded the Right Use of Power curriculum to include additional types of power. I have been lucky enough to remain in close contact with Dr. Barstow and now lead her nonprofit organization, The Right Use of Power Institute. The ideas from the expanded curriculum offered by the Institute are outlined in this first part of the book.

Before we get into power, I first offer a chapter on right-relationship. I explain what I mean by this term "right-relationship" and why I've made it central to this book. The second chapter covers how we define power and how our definitions and ways we understand power shape how we participate in its dynamics. I will outline how power is understood in dominant culture and the importance of expanding our understanding of power. Then I will walk you through some common misconceptions about power. The remainder of Part One is a deep dive into the different types of power, each with its own chapter.

As I mentioned in the preface, this section will read more like a textbook, with definitions and conceptual outlines. I do not claim to offer a comprehensive view of power—just a contribution toward approaching its complexity. Ultimately, what I have outlined in Part One is an expanded language and framework for power that is aimed at supporting our ability to become more power-conscious.

Part Two: Becoming Power-Conscious

"Intentional living is the art of making our own choices before others' choices make us." - Richie Norton

Whenever I teach or write, I almost always light a candle and burn palo santo wood. It is a kind of ritual that helps me connect with what is beyond my ego or small self. I find that teaching is more impactful when ego is not driving the proverbial bus. However, for most of my life, I was averse to rituals. Apart from the Christian church I grew up in and the standard American cultural rituals (weddings, funerals, etc.), I wasn't taught the purpose and importance of ritual in daily life. My neurodivergent brain and introverted nature also made communal rituals hard to relate to and mostly overwhelming. Even throughout my travels in other countries, I appreciated rituals that conveyed cultural nuance, but they felt hard to connect with and not "mine." It wasn't until I reached my forties that I began to understand that I could create my own rituals—for myself and within my interpersonal relationships. And they didn't have to involve incense and chanting. In fact, they didn't necessarily have to be religious or spiritual at all. What rituals do for me is help me to be intentional about how I show up in my life, relationships, and communities. They help me cultivate the habit of choosing how I live, and of being connected to myself and to something larger than myself.

Part of living intentionally and being intentional in my relationships means being able to see and be with what *is*. Because power is the dynamic present in every relationship, becoming power-conscious is necessary for finding right-relationship. Part Two of the book explores how we can cultivate power-consciousness and shape our participation in power on personal, interpersonal, collective, and systemic levels. We look at the intersections of the types of power and how we are shaped in different ways by different kinds of systems. In this part of the book, we'll get into the complexities of power differentials and how they manifest in dominant culture. Touching on the neurobiology of power, we will look at how the brain and body respond in power dynamics and how we can become more aware of and respond to them more consciously. We will then identify the Phases of Power-Consciousness and strategies for moving from one phase to the next.

Part Three: Wayfinding

"Wayfinders go beyond the known, and journey on voyages of discovery to new horizons. Central to the wayfinding approach is seeing what is really going on—discerning the detail and seeing the whole." - Spiller, Barclay-Kerr, and Panoho

There is so much wisdom in the world and beautiful examples of how we can live well together. Unfortunately, that wisdom gets drowned out by the incessant information competing for our attention, or it gets ignored, invisibilized, or replaced. We have become colonized away from ancient wisdom and time-tested ways of living well together. This has left us with a deep discontent in modern cultures—a pervasive anxiety. I could only really see it and feel it after spending some time deep in the jungles of Peru with a Shipibo tribe. There was no electricity or running water. The tribe's people ate whatever they caught or harvested that day. They got up with the sun and went to bed after sunset. They lived with the rhythm of the Earth. I was fortunate to live among them for a brief time. Despite having packed sturdy hiking shoes and hand sanitizer, after a while, shoes didn't make sense, and dirt didn't feel dirty anymore. It felt like my sense of self had returned to its natural state in that environment.

Then I returned to the United States, and there it was—a constant hum of anxiety all around me. I was taken aback by how physical that anxious energy felt and how disruptive it was to my sense of self. When I investigated this energy, I realized that those of us in the Western world had lost our connection to natural rhythms, ancestral wisdom, and right relations. To be clear, this book is not an attempt to idealize, co-opt, or return us to indigenous or ancient ways, but an attempt to question our modern, western understanding of relationship and power by looking both backwards and forwards.

One of the ways I challenge our dominant culture's approach to power and relationship, is through a power-conscious wayfinding model and steps for how we can practice our power-consciousness in a sustainable way. Wayfinding is an imperfect, fundamentally human approach to orienting ourselves and moving through the world that relies on our willingness to be vulnerably present with one another. Wayfinding is about going beyond what we know so that we can discover new ways of being in relationship. The journey toward power-conscious right-relationship is as much about intentionally connecting with ourselves and our environment as it is about the quality of our connection with others.

I wrote this book in the hopes that it will ignite a spark in you that leads to more intentional living in the world, where shaping power toward right-relationship becomes more of a norm than a rarity. In these times where many of the world's leaders lack ethics or a sense of collective responsibility, we need every person to use the power they have with wisdom, skill, and compassion. Social Psychologist, Dr. Dacher Keltner said, "Every time we experience power—a recurrent feeling in our everyday interactions—we find ourselves at a moment, a fork in the road, where we must confront perhaps the most important choice we will make in life, yet one we make on a daily basis." In our daily decisions about how to participate in power dynamics and how to show up in our relationships, we have a choice about how we use the power we have access to. Can we make the choice to shape power toward right-relationship? What will it take for us to make that choice continuously, though imperfectly? How do we become aware of the power dynamics in our relationships, communities, and organizations? Do we know how to find right-relationship across difference? Will we have the courage to rely on power-conscious wayfinding in the moments that matter?

2

Right Relationship

"Without community, there is no liberation... But community must not mean a shedding of our differences, nor the pathetic pretense that these differences do not exist." - Audre Lorde

"The times are urgent; let us slow down. What if the way we respond to crisis is part of the crisis?" - Bayo Akomolaf

Right-Relationship: A temporary state that is reached when everyone in the relationship experiences an active honoring of their rooted personal power[1] and when there is an honest acknowledgment by all of the other types of power at play in the relationship.

It is important that we begin with what our journey is pointed to, which is right-relationship. The whole point of this book is not to talk about power for power's sake—it's about how we can use the power we have access to so that we can show up differently in our relationships and in the world. If we aren't trying to make our way toward right-relationship, learning about power, from my

---

1. We go into the meaning of the phrase "rooted personal power" in the Personal Power chapter.

perspective, is pointless at best—dangerous at worst. At the same time, we can't make it to right-relationship without understanding social power dynamics and becoming power-conscious. For example, if I do not understand, or at least try to understand, the oppression you experience and the ways I unconsciously participate in that, you and I cannot be in right-relationship—no matter how well-intentioned I am. The same is true for all of us.

Right-relationship is the place we come to when we are continuously aiming toward connection and that we are honoring the dignity of life in whomever we are connecting with—with ourselves, with each other, with the more-than-human beings (plants, animals, insects and all the living organisms who were here before human beings), and with that which is Greater (however you define that – God, the Universe, Source, Great Mystery, Collective Consciousness, the Divine, the Higher Self, etc.). Right relationship demands something more courageous: the simultaneous honoring of personal dignity *and* the messy truth of how power actually moves between people. It is a call for discernment—even if it means consciously ending the relationship or creating clearer boundaries. Boundaries—whether leaving a job that erodes your dignity or ending a friendship steeped in misuses of power—are not failures of connection but *honest* ones. They create space for relationships that honor, rather than diminish, our humanity.

Ultimately, right-relationship is not a fixed destination, but a way of traveling—a commitment to move through the world with eyes wide open to both our own power and the invisible currents shaping every interaction. It asks us to hold two truths at once: *I matter*, and *I am not the only one who matters*. This delicate balance is where real connection begins—not in the absence of power dynamics, but in their honest acknowledgment.

Why does this matter? Because *our relationships and the power dy-*

namics within them create our world. This is the potential of right-relationship: relationships that bring *justice and liberation* alive—as both a personal practice and a collective lifeline. In a world fractured by domination—over people, land, and even life itself—it offers a way forward: not through power's elimination, but through its *ethical engagement.*

So how do we find right-relationship? This book is an attempt to respond to this question—not to give a complete or right "answer" but to investigate it in the context of power. I will offer two foundational aspects here about how we find it, and the rest of the book can delve further into the nuances. The first is that right-relationship is something more to be discovered and remembered rather than created. And the second is that I've never gotten close to right-relationship when I'm in a hurry. In a world that prizes speed and productivity, we often rush through interactions, decisions, and even conflicts without pausing to notice the invisible threads of connection that exist between us. Right-relationship can't be rushed. It requires the kind of attentiveness that lets us see the employee hesitating to speak up in a meeting, the friend whose laughter doesn't quite reach their eyes, or the way a river's murky water tells a story of upstream pollution. Slowing down creates space to remember what we've been conditioned to forget: *that we belong to each other.*

At the heart of Indigenous wisdom is the understanding that right relationship is not an abstract ideal—it is the living practice of belonging. Unlike Western paradigms that often frame relationships in terms of transactions or hierarchies, Indigenous teachings root connection in kinship, where humans are not above nature, but *woven into it.* The Lakota phrase *Mitákuye Oyás'in* ("all my relations") and the Haudenosaunee Thanksgiving Address—which gives gratitude to water, plants, animals, and winds—are not poetic metaphors but ethical frameworks. They remind us that every action ripples outward, affecting ancestors, future generations, and the more-than-human world. When we pause long enough to listen—to the land, to histories of harm, to our own instincts, to our well-ancestors—we start to sense the web of relationships we're always navigating.

This remembering is radical. Colonial systems thrive on disconnection—on making us forget that the coffee in our cup is tied to the hands that harvested it, that the "news" we consume shapes how we see (or don't see) suffering oceans away. Right-relationship is the practice of asking, *"Who and what made this possible?"* before taking a bite, signing a contract, or casting a vote. Like a gardener who knows each plant's needs because they've knelt in the soil long enough to learn, right-relationship flourishes in patient presence. When we find this presence, we find that the path toward right-relationship wasn't ahead of us at all. It was beneath our feet all along, waiting for us to stop running and feel its pulse.

Remember by Joy Harjo (1951)

Remember the sky that you were born under,
    know each of the star's stories.
Remember the moon, know who she is.
Remember the sun's birth at dawn, that is the
strongest point of time. Remember sundown
and the giving away to night.
Remember your birth, how your mother struggled
to give you form and breath. You are evidence of
her life, and her mother's, and hers.
Remember your father. He is your life, also.

Remember the earth whose skin you are:
red earth, black earth, yellow earth, white earth
brown earth, we are earth.
Remember the plants, trees, animal life who all have their
tribes, their families, their histories, too. Talk to them,
listen to them. They are alive poems.
Remember the wind. Remember her voice. She knows the
origin of this universe.
Remember you are all people and all people
are you.
Remember you are this universe and this
universe is you.
Remember all is in motion, is growing, is you.
Remember language comes from this.
Remember the dance language is, that life is.
Remember.

-*Part One*-

Understanding Power

3

Defining Power

"The evocation of an alternative reality consists at least in part in the battle for language and the legitimization of a new rhetoric." - Walter Brueggemann

What is power? If you close your eyes and let all the associations, feelings, memories, and thoughts arise when you hear the word "power," what comes up for you? For many people, when they think about power, what arises is mostly negative: the experience of being on the receiving end of the misuse or abuse of power. For others, it is the desire for more power, or a fear of power, or simply a general avoidance or confusion. Alternatively, you may have already done some work around power and have some positive associations with the feeling of personal empowerment or collective power.

The context from which we have come and in which we are is hugely important for understanding the nature of how things manifest. This includes power. Robert Dahl said, "The concept of power is as ancient and ubiquitous as any that social theory can boast.[1] " He and many other men with influential platforms over the last several thousand years have defined, discussed, and

---

1. Dahl, R. (1957) The Concept of Power. Behavioral Science, 2, p. 201–215.

analyzed power, including Plato, Aristotle, Machiavelli, Nietzsche, Marx, and Weber. Western culture has been shaped by hundreds, if not thousands, of years of thought by a very small group of people—all of whom come from a very narrow section of identities that accompany particular forms of power.

While I don't want to spend time outlining every perspective on power in history, I do want to briefly point to how much influence a rather small number of intellectuals have had over the concept of power itself. Throughout Western history, power has been thought of as a force that could be possessed and used to effect change or influence. For most of them, the concept of "power-over" was at the forefront of their theories. Power-over is essentially how one person or group exerts control over another person or group. Machiavelli, a Florentine Diplomat in the Renaissance age, was perhaps the most influential in guiding the concept of power over the last 500 years. The Machiavellian perspective espouses advice like, "It is much safer to be feared than loved," and "If an injury has to be done to a man, it should be so severe that his vengeance need not be feared." Even today, one of the best-selling books on power is based on a Machiavellian framework.

Despite the slow evolution of the understanding of power in Western cultures, there have been many contributors from ancient Eastern cultures and some in more modern Western cultures who have addressed power in more expansive ways. Lao Tse (Laozi), the reputed author of the Tao Te Ching from ancient China, proposed that true power comes from aligning oneself with the Dao (the Way) and exercising power through humility, simplicity, and harmony with the natural order. Laozi believed that the best leaders are those who are least visible, allowing things to occur naturally and letting people grow and develop without imposing authority. He suggested that forceful and heavy-handed use of power is counterproductive and ultimately self-defeating. While Confucius saw power as something that should be exercised in accordance with a hierarchical social order, where each person respects their roles and responsibilities, he believed that harmony could be achieved when rulers lead with benevolence and adhere to moral principles.

In the late 1800s and the early 1900s, the concept of power in the West began to evolve with thoughtful mentions from John Stuart Mill and Bertrand Russell, followed by dedicated thoughts from Mary Parker Follett, Hannah Arendt, Michel Foucault, and many others. All of these contributors started to create a more nuanced understanding of power in the West. Although the concept of a collaborative approach to power dates back to Aristotle, the similar concept of "power-with," as mentioned by John Stuart Mill and further elucidated by Mary Parker Follett, is the idea that power can be shared through collaboration and relationships.

With the evolution of our understanding of power has also come an evolution in diversity, equal rights, cross-cultural relationships, and innovative workplaces. As we've been exposed to different cultures and ways of being in relationships, as our understanding of our identities and capacities has expanded and evolved (race, gender, etc.), we have had to reckon with outdated definitions of power. And, if we do not continue to evolve our understanding of power, we will get stuck in rigid ways of being in relationship - ways that cause harm to the majority of us (the majority including the more-than-human beings as well).

Defining power intentionally is essential because how we understand it directly influences how we participate in it. If we define power as "power-over," then what is the natural result? Power will be used for the purposes of control. What about power-with? When we consider this other understanding of power, we experience an expansion into the realm of relationship and collaboration. The language we use around power fundamentally shapes how we understand and participate in it. Fred Kofman said:

> "[Language] can serve as a medium through which we can create new understandings and new realities as we begin to talk about them. In fact, we don't talk about what we see; we see only what we can talk about. Our perspectives on the world depend on the interaction of our nervous system and our language—both act as filters through which we perceive our world...The language and information systems of an organization are not an objective means of describing an outside reality—they fundamentally structure the perceptions and actions of its members. To reshape the measurement and communication systems of a [society] is to reshape all potential interactions at the most fundamental level. Language...as an articulation of reality is more primordial than strategy, structure, or...culture."

Simply put, if we don't have the language to talk about the nuances of power, we will be unable to change them. Even more importantly, the language we use about power directly primes its manifestation. As we will see, our perception of power is inherently tied to how we participate in it. Power, of course, is something easier to feel than to define. We have all felt a sense of power in a room, person, or group. As palpable as power can be, it can also be invisible. The problem is that when power is just a feeling or when it is invisible, it is difficult to point to, name, challenge, or work with. Part of my aim is to make social power dynamics more visible and accessible so that we can witness the exchanges in relationships that fundamentally shape how we live our lives.

I'd like to contribute to the expansion of our understanding of power beyond the traditional see-saw of power-over and power-with approaches, particularly to uncover the nuances and complexities present in social power dynamics. I do this not by engaging in "the battle for language," as Brueggemann suggests, but by creating space for both a wider view and a very detailed one. Part of the challenge of seeing power in all of its dimensions lies in the ability to hold complexity in a sustained way. But before we can get to the complex, we need to start with the basics. And power's most fundamental definition is:

Power – *the ability to have an effect or influence*

In the Right Use of Power, and even in many dictionary definitions, we view the concept of power as fundamentally neutral: the ability to have an effect or influence. I appreciate starting with the simplicity and openness of this definition so that we can invite more complexity later. The inherent neutrality of power is also worth noting. Like fire, the outcome of power dynamics is directly related to how we use it. It can be life-giving, providing light and warmth, or it can be used for control and destruction. Due to our numerous associations with power, we tend to think of it based on our past experiences. We may cast it in a negative light, or think that it only belongs to certain groups of people. When we start with power as fundamentally neutral, we can be free to see the nuances that may help us to engage in relationships with more consciousness.

Common Misconceptions of Power

Before we explore the Types of Power, I'd like to pause and address some common misconceptions about power that can hinder our understanding of it. As power has been defined and written about over time, some common ideas about power have persisted in and pervaded dominant culture. However, I have found that the most common ideas about power are misleading. I believe these misconceptions about power have influenced many of the misuses of power we see in our world. It feels important to address these misconceptions up-front so that you can get a glimpse of what we're missing when it comes to power. And, they might be hard to read. You may have resistances come up because I'm going to talk about something that perhaps you have assumed you know, in a way that maybe you haven't considered. Throughout the book, we will examine the origins of these misconceptions and why they have persisted over time.

Misconception #1: Power is a singular thing.

This is the most common misconception, one that has been challenged in various ways over time. Power has many different types and dimensions. To reduce them all to a single word, "power," is similar to reducing the complexity of human emotions to a single feeling. Just as emotions can range from joy to sorrow, anxiety to anger, power manifests in various forms. These different forms have been put into categories like political power, social influence, economic control, and personal empowerment. There are multiple models of power that people have created over time and have used more nuanced terms such as coercive power, reward power, legitimate power, referent power, and social power.

While the types and dimensions of power I will outline in this book are different from other models, each type of power, no matter the model used, operates within its own context, shaped by cultural, historical, and situational factors. By acknowledging the multifaceted nature of power, we can better understand its impacts on relationships, institutions, and society as a whole. This nuanced perspective allows for more effective strategies in addressing various social issues, as we recognize that power dynamics are not linear nor monolithic but rather a complex web of interactions and influences.

Beyond there being multiple types of power, I'd like for us to shift our entire understanding of power as a "thing" to a *dynamic* that is present in every relationship—whether that is the relationship we have with ourselves, other individuals, or with and between groups. Bertrand Russell said, "The fundamental concept in social science is power, in the same sense in which energy is the fundamental concept in physics." In everyday language, we might refer to energy as if it were a tangible object, but in reality, it is an abstract concept that describes a property of systems. For example, we might say someone is "energetic," but this describes their behavior rather than a physical quantity. While we can measure energy and observe its effects, it's best understood as a fundamental aspect of how the physical world operates rather than a singular entity. Similar to energy, power is not an entity in itself; rather, it is a concept that describes a dynamic present in every relationship. Power is a fundamental dynamic aspect of how the social world operates.

Misconception #2: Power is a finite resource that you can possess.

In dominant culture, where capitalism reigns, we tend to think in terms of owning or possessing. Everything is categorized as "mine" or "yours," "ours" or "theirs." It makes sense to extend this idea of possession to power, especially if you view it as a "thing." Even among modern scholars of power, there is still this misconception that power is a game of getting, maintaining, and using it. Like most "things," power has been commodified. In economic terms, where commodities are the materials of exchange for wealth, it is scarcity that gives them value. So scarcity, or the perception of scarcity, becomes a target for those who possess or want to sell certain commodities. In other words, when things are scarce, they are more valuable in dominant culture.

When we think of power as a commodity, we get caught in the game of scarcity. Studies show that a scarcity mindset can have numerous negative effects for human beings, including stress, anxiety, poor decision-making, limited creativity and problem-solving, strained relationships, reduced ability to recognize opportunities, neglect of self-care, and decreased focus. When we apply these negative effects to the use of power, we can see where a lot of the misuses and abuses of power come from! Ultimately, a scarcity mindset is a psychological perspective where individuals focus on what they *lack* rather than what they *have*. When people talk about power, we tend to emphasize the power we *don't* have access to, rather than the power we *do* have access to. This is a result of the scarcity mindset and considering power as a finite resource.

When we think of power in terms of it being a singular thing, we are more likely to consider it a finite resource. If there is only so much power to go around, we are more likely to engage in greedy behavior and hoard it just like we may do with any other finite resource. Treating power like a finite resource is like treating love like a finite resource. It impacts how we engage with it—ultimately becoming transactional. bell hooks said, "The word 'love' is most often defined as a noun, yet all the more astute theorists of love acknowledge that we would all love better if we used it as a verb." There is a different kind of responsibility that arises naturally when we view love as a verb. It is suddenly active and we have to choose to participate in it. Whereas love, as a noun, is all about possession and loss. It is similar with power. When we understand power as a verb rather than a noun, we can participate more intentionally in power dynamics. To put it simply, you cannot possess power, but you can participate in it—and *how* you participate in the dynamics of power is how you shape it.

Misconception #3: Power is something only some people have.

Building on misconception #2 where power is viewed as a finite resource, it makes sense that we might believe that only some people have access to power. While it is certainly true that there are people who have access to certain types of power while others do not, it is *not* true that any person is completely powerless. To assume so is to make them so. Alice Walker said, "The most common way people give up their power is by thinking they don't have any." When we think of ourselves as powerless, we cannot choose to show up in social power dynamics intentionally. And when we assume other people are powerless, we engage with them differently.

Referring back to Kofman's reference to language and its power to shape how we think and act, it is important that we are intentional and careful with our words. All-or-nothing (dualistic) thinking and using power as a noun rather than a verb, makes words like "powerless" and "powerful" feel real. But to name someone as powerless is to say that they have no ability to have an effect or influence—ever. This is simply not true—even when we think of the most vulnerable among us. For example, when we think of human babies it might come to mind that they are completely helpless. But what happens when that baby cries? It certainly has an effect and influence on those around the baby!

Many people will think of examples to prove me wrong on this. Surely, there are people who have absolutely NO power! In one way, they are right (because we can't possess power), but in the way they mean it, it is simply a particular power paradigm at work (which we will explore in the Systemic Power chapter). There is power that is given by others (which is only given to certain people) and then there is the power that is sourced internally that cannot be touched by others. I think of Nelson Mandela or Viktor Frankl, who, at some point in their lives, had every type of externally sourced power stripped from them, yet neither of them considered themselves powerless—and both had considerable influence despite their imprisonment. The kind of power they accessed is the subject of an entire chapter of this book and is the key to shaping power for good.

We could flip the coin and also say that no one has absolute power. I would get equal push-back with that statement. We will talk more about this and personal power later, but essentially, these are extremes that we have normalized because of the ways particular power paradigms have socialized us. Part of the work of liberation is to recognize these paradigms and free ourselves from their social-ization—to the degree that we are able. While I argue that no one is completely powerless or completely powerful, we can indeed *feel* powerless or powerful, which brings us to Misconception #4.

Misconception #4: How powerful you feel is equal to the power you have access to.

This is an important nuance that I feel compelled to highlight here: there is a difference between how powerful you *feel* (which is called "felt power") and the power *you actually have access to*. The term "felt power" was popularized by sociologist and philosopher Alfred Schütz who used the term in his work to describe the subjective experience of power by individuals in social contexts. Felt power refers to how people perceive and experience their own power and agency in various social situations. It is inherently personal and based on an individual's beliefs, feelings, and experiences. Felt power is internally focused and relates to a person's perception of agency and sense of confidence rather than the external structures or rules established by systemic power. As we will see, Systemic Power plays an enormous role in our felt power and manifests in a variety of ways depending on where we are positioned in the system. For example, forms of felt power can arise from , and directly impact how we participate in social power dynamics.

There are many cases in which Systems assign a great deal of access to particular types of power to particular individuals who may simultaneously *feel* powerless. And it is also true that those who don't have access to many types of externally-sourced power, still *feel* quite powerful. The social psychologist, Amy Cuddy, conducted research on forms of felt power through what she calls "power poses." She explores the intriguing idea that adopting certain body postures can influence our feelings and behaviors. According to her studies, taking expansive, open postures—like the "wonder woman" pose with hands on hips—can boost confidence and even affect our physical stress hormone levels. We will go deeper into the neurobiology of power in later chapters, but it is important to understand that while felt power doesn't always coincide with how relationships are set up in systems, it certainly has an enormous impact on our intrapersonal experience which directly impacts how we show up in those relationships.

Misconception #5: Talking about power can harm organiza-

tions or relationships.

This one comes from years of experience that Right Use of Power facilitators have had in supporting leaders and organizations navigate interpersonal difficulties, ethical breaches, staff turnover, and internal culture issues. As executive coaches, consultants and trusted advisors who understand power, we often get called into organizations to help with whatever intractable challenge or conflict they may be experiencing. Inevitably, the underlying issue is related to power dynamics, and yet the people involved in shaping those dynamics are either surprised by this or want to deny it. Often those that have access to externally-sourced power, such as leaders of an organization, are reluctant to even talk about power.

Unfortunately, talking about and addressing power is taboo in many modern Western cultures. Criticizing those in power can have consequences, from social ostracism to legal repercussions. This is why many employees will not speak up—even when it impacts their productivity and satisfaction with their work. Systems with rigid hierarchies often discourage open discussion of power imbalances, as such discussions could challenge the established order. Even organizations that prioritize goals like diversity and equity are reluctant to have honest conversations about social power dynamics.

Talking about power can also touch on sensitive topics like oppression, exploitation, and inequity. The potential to cause offense or re-traumatize individuals makes some hesitant to engage in these conversations. However, when you have a language and framework for understanding and talking about power, our ability to address the nuance of power in ways that preserve the dignity of all is possible. Put simply, you can't change what you can't talk about.

There are some courageous people and organizations who are

willing to look honestly at their internal dynamics, recognize their shortcomings, and dedicate the appropriate resources, time and energy to ensuring that they co-create a culture of belonging by talking honestly about power. Here are the benefits they experience:

Increased self-awareness: Openly discussing power dynamics helps individuals understand their own position within power structures, their influence on others, and how others' power might affect them.

Improved relationships: Actively acknowledging power dynamics in relationships can foster greater trust and transparency. Honest communication about expectations, boundaries, and needs can lead to stronger, healthier connections.

Conflict Positivity: While initially uncomfortable, addressing power imbalances directly can prevent resentment and help to make conflicts less frequent and more generative. Regular communication can mitigate misunderstandings and create a more equitable dynamic.

Greater accountability: When power is discussed openly, we are generally more accountable for our actions and decisions. Transparency can reduce the potential for abuse and corruption.

Enhanced collaboration: Understanding power dynamics within a group or organization can improve collaboration. By acknowledging individual strengths, responsibilities, and vulnerabilities, teams can work more effectively towards shared goals.

Improved decision-making: Honest discussions about power and considering diverse perspectives can lead to more informed and inclusive decision-making processes.

Misconception #6: Power is static and difficult to change

Along with the first five misconceptions comes another popular idea that power is fairly fixed. While many people believe there are some exceptions, it is largely considered the rule that power is static. From the perspective of the "haves" and "have-nots," this is understandable. Typically, those who are in power maintain that power. Groups with the most access to power design and maintain systems to ensure they will continue to have access to power.

However, because of the entrenched nature of systemic power, we often fail to see how we can shape power in the moment, in ourselves, and in relationships. In his book, *Belonging: The Science of Creating Connection and Bridging Divides*, Geoffrey Cohen talks about the importance of "situation crafting." The idea is that instead of merely reacting to existing circumstances, individuals can proactively create situations that foster positive outcomes by fostering "people's awareness of the situation, its impact on them, and their contribution to it."[2]

In other words, we can engage in the types of power we do have access to and use them intentionally to craft situations, even in seemingly minor ways, that influence our context, environment and even our own motivation, productivity, and emotional state. We will talk more about this in the Power for Social Change section, but I want to emphasize that power dynamics, in the moment, are pliable. Intentionally crafted moments can add up to changed relationships. Changed relationships can add up to collective power, which can change systemic power - but only if we start with clearly seeing power dynamics in the moment, its impact on us, and our contributions to it.

---

2. Cohen, G. L. (2022). *Belonging: The Science of Creating Connection and Bridging Divides*. W. W. Norton & Company, p.159.

Misconception #7: Power-Over is how power works

I have already outlined that power-over has been challenged over time with concepts like "power-with," and that power-over is still the dominant understanding of how power works. The unfortunate part of this misconception is that it discourages people who are trying to do good things in the world, and who have access to power, from participating in that power fully and intentionally. So many people are afraid of hurting people with the power they have access to. This is understandable given our history with the misuses and abuses of power we have experienced and witnessed in our lives. And yet, it leaves a lack of intentional participation in social power dynamics where wise participation in power is sorely needed. It also fundamentally ignores the responsibility we have when we have access to power. Ultimately, as my mentor, Dr. Barstow, has illustrated, this under-use of power is actually a misuse of power.

The other not-so-side effect of believing that power-over is how power works is that it prevents us from seeing power differently. I have witnessed more and more a divide in how different generations view power, as well as how they understand respect; it causes a great deal of turmoil in organizations worldwide. Part of the misunderstanding between the generations is this very misconception. Older generations see power as a necessary evil and have learned to cope with power-over hierarchical structures and their effects. Younger generations see power as an unnecessary evil and wish to do away with power and its structures altogether. Here we are caught in the either/or dualistic thinking again. In my work with organizations, I help staff from different generations work through these binary traps and expand their view, language, and framework of power so that they can meet each other without having to give up their power or necessarily destroy their structures (although sometimes they choose to consciously change or dismantle some of the structures together).

As we will see, these misconceptions work together to form a web that causes static around power - which makes it very difficult to navigate well. I will continue to address aspects of these misconceptions, but first I'd like to start outlining the different types of power so that we can begin to grasp the nuances of power.

4
Types of Power

"In the end, for nuanced translation, it's all about the details." – Walter Benjamin

In the evolution of Right Use of Power, we have identified six distinct types of power: Personal, Systemic, Role, Status, Collective, and Universal. Each of these different types of power contributes to a more nuanced picture of power so that our vocabulary can fit more closely to what is happening in terms of power in relationships. So let's look at each type of power and how they interact. I'll give some basic definitions of the types of power, and then we'll go more in-depth with each one in subsequent chapters.

Personal Power

In modern times, not many of us are taught that we are inherently powerful—that we are powerful beyond measure from the time we are born. Personal Power is our birthright. It is each individual's ability to have an effect or influence in the world. Personal power is internally sourced, innate, connected to Universal Power and can be developed over time.

In Right Use of Power we say that personal power is accompanied by the inherent human right to be treated with dignity, respect, and fairness. Personal power is always present, but we can be more or less aware of it and have more or less access to it. It can be limited by ourselves, others, and systems, but we can learn to retain our personal power even in the most challenging circumstances. We will discuss personal power in depth throughout the book because of its primary importance in navigating power because it mediates ALL of the other types of power in our experience.

There are two different types of personal power: socialized and rooted. **Socialized personal power** is the personal power that comes from the way systems have shaped us. The beliefs, strategies and elements of the way we influence others that is in line with the systemic paradigm that we are operating within.

Whereas **rooted personal power** is personal power that comes from, or is rooted in, something greater than the self and systems. This kind of personal power is not dependent upon external factors for its presence or growth.

Systemic Power

To fully comprehend the other types of power, we must first grasp the basic concept of systems and their power. There are an infinite number of systems, and we are part of more than we can think of—from government institutions to schools, to religions, and even our family of origin. In each system, there are structures that contain sets of rules: some are made explicit (like laws, policies, codes, etc.), and some are kept implicit (what is considered polite, beautiful, professional, etc.).

Systemic Power, with its pervasive influence, shapes everything we see and cannot see, what we are aware of and unaware of, the implicit and the explicit. Like our historical context, systems literally mold how we exist in the world, our relationships, our institutions, our textbooks and anything tangible or intangible inside of that system. And, even when we transition from one system to another, we still carry the imprint of the system we were originally socialized in, to some extent.

You can think of systemic power as a container. A container shapes everything in it: it provides limits and structure for its contents. Take a flower pot, for example. The shape and size of the pot influence root growth and the overall form of the plant. A tall, narrow pot encourages vertical root growth while a wide, shallow pot promotes lateral root development. The pot, or system, both supports and constrains growth in particular ways. Depending on the type of plant and what it needs, the type of container may be supportive of or inhibit its growth.

Deep roots from a tall container and wider roots in a shallow container.

It is important to note that systems create an environment that we are not always aware of, but that influence every aspect of our lives—even after we become aware of that influence. For example, a plant that has been put into a pot and left there to grow eventually grows bigger and needs to be re-potted into a bigger pot. But when we take the plant out of the pot it was in, we see that the plant, roots, soil, and other planting materials have taken the shape of that container. So even when we take it out of the container, everything in it still retains that shape. This is how systemic power works over time: it shapes us at a fundamental level, and it does so below the surface, often without us even realizing it. We'll talk more in the following chapters about healthy and unhealthy containers or expressions of systemic power.

The contents of the pot retain the shape of the container.

My current working definition of Systemic Power is **the widespread expression of a particular power paradigm on an institutional, national, or global level.** This power is generated and perpetuated over time through structural and subliminal norms, rules, laws, standards, values, policies, parameters, and other implicit and explicit guides. These elements are designed to shape and socialize everything within the system (behaviors, information, relationships, history, beliefs, etc.). Systemic Power creates the parameters in which power is expressed intrapersonally, interpersonally, and through groups. One way it does that is by creating role and status power.

Role Power

Role power is the influence derived from a position of authority. Role power only exists in relationship with one or more others. In this respect, I call role and status power "interpersonal types of power." Examples of role power include the additional influence someone has access to by occupying positions like teacher, doctor, police officer, president, therapist, supervisor, facilitator, CEO, etc.

Dr. Barstow calls role power an "add-on" type of power because it is always in addition to your personal power. It is important to note that role power is not a fixed state when we occupy it. With some exceptions, we enter and exit role power as we enter and exit a position. I may wake up each morning with my personal power, teach a class (entering role power along with my personal power) but when the class is over and I go have lunch with a friend, I exit the role. I am no longer in a teaching role because my friend is not my student. So, at lunch with a friend, I still have my personal power, but to use my role power as a teacher would be inappropriate in that relationship.

To reiterate, role power only exists when we are in relationship with someone who is related to our position. I am only a teacher when there is a student, a therapist only when there is a client, a doctor only when there is a patient. However, most of us know several people who identify as their role no matter if they are presently relating to someone who is down-power from them. The conflation of role and personal power, which happens frequently, is at the root of many misuses which we will explore later in the book.

Status Power

Like role power, status power has different types and similar origins, but instead of arising through a position, it comes from a value-based, extrinsic assessment. It can be culturally conferred or otherwise assigned according to the values of a particular system or a collective. Essentially, status power is how we are externally defined in terms of value. And when our characteristics, whether inborn or acquired, align with what is valued by those external to us, it carries a particular kind of influence (status power). This can look like financial wealth, race, gender, religion, ability, citizenship, and any number of other charateristics or dinstinctions that are either real or artificially created.

When a system creates norms and values based on its paradigm, status power manifests inherently. And sometimes status power is created intentionally by those who stand to gain from it. For example, the phenomenon of "whiteness" did not exist until the justification of enslaving black people became advantageous for those with lighter skin. So status power gets expressed through stories and solidified into norms, standards and sometimes even more concretely into rules and laws. Another form of status power is the social value of money (socioeconomic status). For systems in which the possession of money is highly valued, those who possess more money *in comparison to someone else* has access to more status power in that relationship (whomever they are relating to in that moment). This same dynamic can be applied to any other status (gender, ability, sexuality, etc.) that can be normed in a society.

Collective Power

Collective Power is power that comes from gathering personal, role and status power from multiple sources to effect change toward a common interest. Collective power refers to the enhanced strength and influence that groups of individuals can achieve by working together toward common goals. It is the idea that when people unite, their combined efforts and resources significantly amplify their ability to effect change compared to what they could accomplish alone.

This concept is foundational in social movements, where collective power is harnessed to advocate for political, social, or economic change. It also applies in organizational contexts, where teamwork and collaboration can lead to improved outcomes. However, collective power, like power in general, is fundamentally neutral. So collective power can be used for multiple ends.

Unions, flocks of birds, support groups, hate groups, schools of fish, associations, social movements, cooperatives, and armies are examples of collective power.

Universal Power

Universal power is the vast force beyond cognitive understanding that connects and encompasses all that exists. Ultimately, universal power is nonconceptual, so capturing it in words is quite challenging—and many more with greater minds than mine have written extensively on the subject (again, though the language and terms might be different). However, because of its inherent influence and importance to the discussion and transformation of our understanding of power, it cannot be left out.

Human beings have tried to describe this power as energy, the universe/cosmos, Source, life force, God, the More, the force of creation/destruction, dependent origination, the Great Mystery, etc. Every person has a different understanding of it and relationship with it. Those who choose to connect with it have different traditions, rituals, language and customs to engage with Universal Power, some more than others.

Similar to Systemic Power, Universal Power has an all-encompassing element that shapes everything we see and cannot see, what we are aware of and unaware of, the implicit and the explicit. But there are two fundamental and key differences that I want to point to which is that Universal Power is not created by human beings, and that universal power is not concrete or static.

Types of Power – Definitions

- **Personal Power:** *each individual's ability to have an effect or influence*

- **Systemic Power:** *the widespread expression of a particular power paradigm on an institutional, national, or global level*

- **Role Power:** *externally-sourced power that accompanies a position in a system or collective*

- **Status Power:** *externally-sourced power that is derived from values conferred by systems or collectives*

- **Collective Power:** *power that results from gathering strength and influence from multiple sources to promote a common interest*

- **Universal Power:** *the vast power that is beyond cognitive understanding and is the force that connects all that exists*

The Power Differential

Before we go deeper into these different types of power, it's important to name a fundamental aspect of social power dynamics: the power differential. Essentially, when there is a difference in the power between two people, we call that a **power differential.** In the Right Use of Power language, just for ease, we call the person who has more influence to be "up-power," and the person who doesn't have access to that type of power to be "down-power" in relation to the up-power person. This language is offered to indicate positionality in the relationship. For example, if someone is in up-role power, they might be a teacher, a doctor, a judge, a police officer, or someone who has been elected, awarded, or assigned a position that serves a particular function within the system.

Now, for *down-role* power, it's always in relationship to an up-power person. So if someone is a teacher, then there is also a student. Otherwise, the teacher would not exist. So the student, we would say, is down-role in relationship to the teacher. Another example would be a doctor and patient. The doctor would be considered to be up-role, and the patient would be in down-role from them.

For status power, we say someone who has particular qualities, characteristics, or identities that the system considers valuable in some way to have *up-status* power for that identity or characteristic in relation to someone who does not possess that identity or characteristic, who would be *down-status.* So, for example, in many systems someone who is identified as white would be considered to be in up-status power in relation to people of color who would be considered to be down-status. Another example is someone who is born transgender is typically down-status while cis-gender people are up-status. Depending on the system, it could be that a young person is up-status and an older person is down-status, or it could be the opposite.

I want to emphasize a few things here, all of which I will address more extensively later in the book. One is a reminder that interpersonal power is largely constructed and maintained by systems and collectives. Second, **down-power doesn't mean no power because we always have personal power.** Finally, I am intentionally not factoring in intersectionality in this moment, just for the sake of simplicity of this introduction. We will get to how different types of status power intersect along with the other types of power as well as discuss the complexities of the power differential and how to navigate them in later sections of this book. For now, understanding the language of "up-power" and "down-power" will help us to explore the types of power more effectively.

5

The Dynamic Forces of Power

"In all chaos there is a cosmos, in all disorder a secret order." - Carl Jung

There are many Right Use of Power facilitators who have contributed to substantial evolutions of the Right Use of Power curriculum. In fact, we have a circle in our sociocratic organization[1] called, "Rock-the-Boat." The sole objective of that circle is to challenge the Right Use of Power concepts and curriculum. In the process we challenge one another and have deep discussions about the principles. It allows us to examine our biases, question our assumptions, look at the impacts of our work, and ultimately evolve as an organization as we evolve our understanding of power. I've brought both my process and concepts from this book to that Circle[2] on several occassions and it has been invaluable.

One of the members of the circle, Thea Elijah, and I have regular conversations about power. One day she brought me an image that she crafted and it had two concepts in it that have contributed a

---

1. Sociocracy is a form of distributed governance that uses consent-based decision-making and nested, semi-autonomous groups called "circles," with each circle having specific aims and accountabilities.

2. A special "thank you" to the members of the Rock-the-Boat Circle: Sari Ajanko, Maya Shaw Gale, Veronica Borgonovi, Susan Skjei, Thea Elijah, Cedar Barstow, and Nelly Mercadet.

lot to my clarity about how the dynamics of power work across all the types of power. She illustrated how there are two fundamental dynamic forces at play: configuration and emergence. Similar to the opposing yet complementary forces of yin and yang, emergence and configuration play a huge part in social power dynamics.

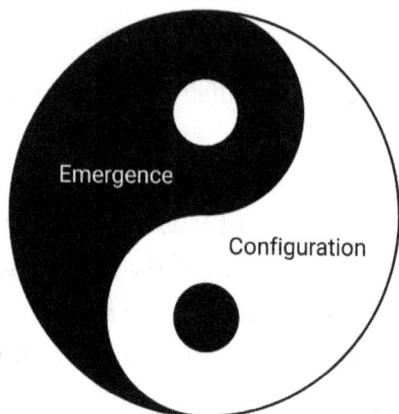

Emergence refers to the spontaneous, often unpredictable, and complex arising of new properties, patterns, or behaviors from the interactions of individuals. It is fluid, chaotic, and often driven by bottom-up processes. In social systems, emergence can be seen in the way new ideas, movements, or behaviors arise organically from the interactions and relationships between individuals.

Configuration refers to the structured arrangement, organization, or design of elements into a coherent and functional whole. It is characterized by order, intentionality, and often, but not always, driven by top-down processes. In social systems, configuration involves the deliberate structuring of institutions, organizations, or societal frameworks to achieve specific goals, maintain stability, and facilitate coordination.

Just as Yin arises from Yang and Yang arises from Yin, emergence and configuration are interdependent and constantly influencing each other in social systems. Emergence often arises from existing configurations, and new configurations can emerge from spontaneous, unstructured phenomena. For example, the labor movement in the late 19th and early 20th centuries emerged from the collective grievances of workers (emergence). Over time, this movement led to the creation of labor unions and labor laws (configuration), which structured the relationship between workers and employers. These structures, in turn, influenced the emergence of new labor movements and demands (emergence).

Some expressions of power are more configurative while others are more emergent and each of the types of power tend to express one force or the other—but all of them have some degree of both. Similar to the Taijitu or yin yang symbol[3] , there is a drop of each element in the other. These drops represent the fundamentally interdependent and transformative nature of these forces. They emphasize that balance is not about equal parts of Yin and Yang but about the harmonious interaction of both forces. The presence of each within the other ensures that neither becomes too dominant.

Similarly, configuration and emergence are both in a dynamic dance, dependent upon one another for balance and the ongoing dynamic of power. While configuration (e.g. systemic power) can create structure and stability, emergence (e.g. personal and collective power) is equally needed for creativity and change—to create opportunity for reconfiguration. This is how we evolve as humans and in our relationships. As dynamic forces with constant interaction, configuration and emergence essentially form a spiral. The

---

3. I think its interesting that in the West we don't call it by its actual name which refers to its entirety, but rather refer to the symbol as its parts, "Yin" and "Yang."

spiral represents progression rather than simple repetition. Each cycle of configuration and emergence builds upon the previous one, leading to growth and evolution.

This is all to say that the balance of power is not a fixed state but an ongoing process of adjustment and transformation. Each cycle of configuration and emergence brings new challenges and opportunities for balance. And the balance of power, while never fully achieved in the human world, is necessary to seek with regularity because it fosters stability, fairness, and sustainability across various domains. Whether in politics, nature, relationships, or personal well-being, balance prevents dominance, encourages cooperation, and ensures that no single force can disrupt the equilibrium. Without balance, systems become unstable, leading to conflict, exploitation, and eventual collapse. And sometimes the collapse is necessary. Sometimes the imbalances create an opportunity for reconfiguration.

Configuration and emergence form the dance of power. They are fundamental forces that are interconnected and interdependent—and yet somehow we attempt to separate them. Some of us will try to make configuration better than emergence or vice versa and then we'll resist the force of the other. But both are necessary for the full expression of power. We will be drawing on the concepts of emergence and configuration and the ways these forces interact throughout the book.

6

Systemic Power

"Systems thinking is a discipline for seeing wholes. It is a framework for seeing interrelationships rather than things, for seeing patterns of change rather than static snapshots." - Peter Senge

"Unfortunately, as numerous revolutionaries have discovered when they topple the oligarchs, our hatred is misplaced. The true culprit is much deeper and much more pervasive." - Charles Eisenstein

System - *a set of interconnected components that work together to achieve a specific purpose or function.*

Systemic Power - *the effect or influence of a system on its components and surrounding systems.*

There are many kinds of systems in existence, and they each play an integral part in the lives of human beings. Biological systems (organs, cells, the nervous system, etc.), information systems (social media, databases, etc.), mechanical systems (motor vehicles, elevators, clocks, etc.), environmental systems (ecosystems, agriculture, etc.), and social systems (families, schools, governments, etc.), each have profound effect on our lives—and yet the origins of those effects often go unnoticed or unacknowledged. For example, information systems like social media influence our ideas, beliefs, and social interactions, though many users may not recognize how deeply algorithms and data management shape us. As we are scrolling, we don't always have in the forefront of our minds how what we see was curated to reinforce our existing beliefs, keep us on the platform as long as possible, and convince us we need to engage in certain behaviors or buy certain things. Because we don't see or understand the algorithms while we are scrolling, we don't consider their impact—or the intention behind the impact created by that information system. This is part of the systemic *power* of social media.

The primary reason we don't consider systemic influences (systemic power) in our everyday lives is that systems are complex and not easily understood, so we tend to simplify and look at what is easier to understand instead. Unfortunately, this leads us right into the "Streetlight Effect," which comes from this short parable:

Once, a policeman was observing a man who was searching for something under a streetlight. The policeman approached and asked, "What are you looking for?" The man replied, "I lost my keys."

The officer joined the search, but after several minutes, he inquired, "Are you sure you lost them here?" The man responded, "No, I lost them in the park." Confused, the policeman asked, "Then why are you looking for them here?" The man replied, "Because this is where the light is."

Instead of looking where the problem originated, we look where it is easier to see. This is largely why systemic problems persist—we simply don't see them.

When I teach about systemic power, I like to use this brilliant political cartoon from INKINCT Cartoons, based in Australia. The cartoon depicts a clear-cut forest with a single koala hanging onto a stump and shaking with terror. There are two people in suits with a clipboard pointing at the koala and saying, "This young koala has a mental health problem."

Image by INKINCT Cartoons

From my view, one of the most confounding social issues of our time is when we try to make a systemic problem about individuals, specific groups of people, or interpersonal situations. This little koala, whose home has been clear-cut, is understandably distressed. But instead of stopping to look at the bigger picture, we point the finger and blame the easy target who is labeled as "the problem." Margaret Wheatley said, "… we act as if simple cause and effect is at work. We push to find the one simple reason things have gone wrong. We look for the one action, or the one person, that created this mess. As soon as we find someone to blame, we act as if we've solved the problem."

Does the koala need support in handling the loss of its home? Yes. But what is the underlying cause of its distress? If this question is asked at all, the response is usually related to the inherent badness of the person or group. In this case, mental health. But historically, it has been a number of other systemic byproducts. Meadows said,

> "Hunger, poverty, environmental degradation, economic instability, unemployment, chronic disease, drug addiction, and war, for example, persist in spite of the analytical ability and technical brilliance that have been directed toward eradicating them. No one deliberately creates those problems, no one wants them to persist, but they persist nonetheless. That is because they are intrinsically systems problems—undesirable behaviors characteristic of the system structures that produce them. They will yield only as we reclaim our intuition, stop casting blame, see the system as the source of its own problems, and find the courage and wisdom to restructure it."[1]

Systems are clearly capable of a lot of harm, and because we all participate in unhealthy systems, we participate in the perpetuation of that harm. We will talk about what we can do about this in the second and third parts of the book. For now, let's look a little more deeply into systemic power of social systems so that we can start to identify what originates from systems and how systemic power manifests. For the purposes of this book, we will largely look at social systems, but understanding how social systems interact with other larger and smaller systems are also important points in our

---

1. Meadows, D. H. (2008). Thinking in Systems: A Primer. Chelsea Green Publishing.

wayfinding toolbox.

To offer a more nuanced definition of systemic power (of social systems): *It is the widespread expression of a particular power paradigm on an institutional, national, or global level generated and perpetuated over time through structural and subliminal norms, rules, laws, standards, values, policies, parameters, and other implicit and explicit guides that are meant to shape everything within the system (behaviors, information, relationships, beliefs, etc.).*

I spent a lot of time trying to understand systemic power and, in the process, came up with some models to help me think through the perpetuation of social systems and the major systemic patterns that I see all around me. Before I get into the first model, which I call the Systemic Power Cycle, I'd like to outline a few of the fundamental attributes that I discovered about systemic power.

Systemic Power is Constructed and Configurative

Systemic power originates from an essential pattern that aims toward a particular purpose. For example, the genetic code of an acorn is its essential pattern. It encodes the DNA of the seed in a particular shape, which guides its growth toward that which it is meant to become—an oak tree. This particular configuration means that it cannot be an aspen tree or a maple. Everything within its construction guides it to become an oak tree.

In social systems, this pattern is a paradigm and purpose (a pattern of beliefs that serves a particular purpose) which is communicated through stories, which then manifest into structures and behaviors, all shaped to support the underlying paradigm and systemic purpose. Everything within the system— from the original paradigm down to the smallest behaviors of the system—is configured according to its essential pattern. Out of the configuration of a system, structures are designed and created to maintain its pattern and purpose. Systemic power in its most fundamental state is configurative. Unfortunately, many unhealthy social systems get constructed or reconstructed with the intention or sole focus on supporting the beliefs or purpose of the system, not necessarily the constituents. This leads me to another fundamental attribute.

Systemic Power is Invisible with Visible Consequences

A system is complex and pervasive, but its construction is largely invisible, or made invisible—often only seen by those who write the rules or suffer because of them. However, while the construction of systemic power is largely invisible-ized, its *consequences* are quite visible, especially if you are forced to experience them—or if you are willing to look. For it is systemic power consequences that make up our daily lives from what kind of shoes we wear to how we relate with ourselves and one another.

Like the old idiom, "A fish is the last to discover water," it can be challenging to view the context we inhabit because it is ever-present. It is "the way things have always been" or "just the way things are done." We are socialized not to look too closely. And, like in the Wizard of Oz, when we try to look behind the curtain to see what things are really made of—to make visible what has been hidden, the man behind the curtain yells, "Pay no attention to the man behind the curtain!" as he tries to maintain his disguise. It is like this with systems—a push/pull of the implicit and explicit. What is seen, what is hidden, what is looked for, and what is ignored is a significant part of the power of systems.

Systemic Power has Healthy and Unhealthy Mani-

festations

Depending on how a system is configured (and what informs or influences that configuration), systemic power can be healthy, unhealthy, or somewhere in between. Unfortunately, we tend to have more unhealthy examples of social systems in the dominant culture than healthy ones, but it is important to make the distinction between them because I believe it is possible for us to build and maintain healthy systems (and I believe our future and the Earth depend on that possibility).

At one end of the continuum, a healthy system has a configuration that facilitates each person's access to their personal power, which is rooted in universal power (what I have termed "rooted personal power"). That is, the support and constraint provided by a healthy system ultimately serve to ensure that each being has access to its innate wisdom, medicine, or inner genius. In healthy systems, there is an alignment that creates resonance from top to bottom or all around and inside. Thus, role and status power in healthy systems are also engaged to bring about the rooted personal power in everyone. A healthy system ultimately serves its constituents more, or at least as much as it serves to perpetuate itself.

On the other end of the continuum, an unhealthy system happens when its construction fails to support each person's access to personal power. Or when the focus becomes too heavy on sustaining the system at the sacrifice of supporting its constituents. This can happen when those in role or status power get distracted by socialization, ego, or a lack of self-care. There is an attempt to control or begin to shift the system into configurations that benefit the few. Or we become rigid and solidified into certain ways of being, failing to observe our impact. In unhealthy systems, we fail to ask: Does the construction of this system facilitate each person's access to their rooted personal power? And does the impact of role and/or status power in this system deepen or reduce each person's access to their rooted personal power? If status and/or role power within a system is creating a dynamic of privilege and oppression, the system is unhealthy.

So if unhealthy systems continue to exist, why do they keep getting perpetuated? This question led me to create the Systemic Power Cycle.

The Systemic Power Cycle

"If a factory is torn down but the rationality which produced it is left standing, then that rationality will simply produce another factory. If a revolution destroys a government, but the systematic patterns of thought that produced that government are left intact, then those patterns will repeat themselves…There's so much talk about the systems. And so little understanding." - Robert Pirsig

"A system is never the sum of its parts its the product of their interaction." – Russell Ackoff

Imagine a small village nestled in a valley. For generations, the villagers have practiced a unique form of farming, passed down through families. The oldest members, the "Elders," control the water source – the lifeblood of the village. According to their ancient and sacred traditions, the Elders distribute different amounts of water for each family in the village.

A young woman named Anya, raised within this system, accepts the tradition as the natural order of things. She learns from her parents, the Elders, and the community that this water distribution is just and fair. She grew up hearing the stories of tragedy when water was distributed differently and when their farming techniques were not as sophisticated. She is praised when she follows tradition and is promised an important role in the village as one of the water keepers when she gets older.

As she grows, Anya witnesses the struggles of families who receive less water, but she reminds herself of the Elders' explanation: these families are given less based on their farming methods, and this particular distribution is deemed best for the village. She is uneasy with the disparity in the water supply but trusts that there is a wisdom from the village tradition that, as the Elders suggest, is beyond her understanding.

Then, one year, a drought hits the village. Families traditionally disadvantaged with a smaller water supply, suffer terribly, some losing their crops entirely. Anya, now witnessing the suffering firsthand, begins to question the Elders' explanations. She observes that the Elders' families, despite receiving the most water, are not necessarily the most efficient or hardworking farmers, nor do they always follow the traditional farming methods that are considered so sacred to the village.

This village represents a social system. In it are people with varying degrees of power and access to resources. There is a belief system and historical traditions that influence the structures and roles in the village. Stories that are told ensure the preservation of these traditions. Despite the suffering of some of the villagers, the system has continued the way it is for generations. How and why does this happen?

Systemic power works in a cycle that is created and perpetuated through the process of socialization[2]. It starts with a paradigm, which is a belief or worldview that gets adopted or ingrained through a self-reinforcing cycle. The Systemic Power Cycle is made up of five fundamental parts: 1) Systemic Paradigm, 2) Stories, 3) Structures, 4) Behaviors, and 5) Collective Reality. Let's take a look at each part of the cycle and how they work together to perpetuate a system.

The Systemic Power Cycle

1. **Systems shape a paradigm**

2. **The paradigm shapes stories**

3. **Stories shape status and structures**

4. **Structures shape role power and direct/constrain behavior**

5. **Stories, Structures, and Behaviors cumulatively shape a**

---

2. For a detailed look at how the process of socialization works for an individual, I recommend looking at the *Cycle of Socialization* developed by Dr. Bobbie Harro.

shared reality that reinforces the paradigm

Systemic Paradigm

The word "paradigm" originates from the Greek word "paradeigma," which means "pattern" or "example." In ancient Greek, "paradeigma" was derived from the verb "paradeiknunai," which means "to show side by side" or "to compare." A systemic paradigm is the underlying belief system or ideology that forms a pattern of comparison between what is valued and not valued, according to its purpose. This could also be seen between what is important/not important, what is meaningful/not meaningful in the system achieving its purpose. Essentially, the systemic paradigm shapes or molds everything in the system, is inherently about relationships, and almost always relates to how power operates within a system.

You can think of the systemic paradigm like the original fractal that gets recreated throughout the system. A fractal is a complex pattern that exhibits self-similarity, meaning it repeats its basic shape at different scales. Fractals are created by repeatedly applying a simple rule or set of rules to a starting point. Each iteration builds upon the previous one, generating increasingly complex structures. As the process repeats, self-similarity arises naturally because the same basic rule is applied at every scale.

An example of a systemic paradigm might be that there are certain people with more inherent faculty than others and in order to achieve the purpose of a healthy village/kingdom/community/organization, those with more inherent faculty most take care of and decide things for those who have less faculty. Depending on the particular system, this could look like divine right, bloodlines, intelligence, skill, or wealth. This same idea gets recreated throughout the system so that the value comparison is consistently between those who have the inherent faculty and those who do not. In the village example above, those with more faculty are the Elders.

A contrasting example of a systemic paradigm might be that everything is connected to everything else. Depending on the particular system, this paradigm might be based in interdependence, ecology, or a holistic spirituality like many indigenous cosmologies or Taoism, for example. With this kind of paradigm, the value comparison is between those who live in accordance with interconnectedness and those who do not.

In both of these examples of paradigms, there is a governing idea that involves an inherent relationship between people. But each paradigm would produce a very different kind of system with very different relational structures. Whatever the systemic paradigm, it always becomes manifest through the process of socialization which is expressed in three phases, each phase lending itself to the next. These phases form a cycle that keeps the systemic wheel turning and, often, the systemic paradigm in place.

Socialization is the way in which individuals learn and internalize the norms, values, behaviors, and cultural narratives of a system. It is the method by which we learn how to be a part of the system—and it is largely done unconsciously. Unfortunately, many systems are created to benefit only the system or only those who have a lot of role and status power in that system. So being socialized into a harmful system is learning how to harm or be harmed.

One of the ways the paradigmatic shape of the system gets expressed is through stories.

Systemic Stories

The narratives that accompany the systemic paradigm not only tell us what is valuable and what is not, they also inform our very way of being. Charles Eisenstein said, "Stories bear tremendous creative power. Through them we coordinate human activity, focus attention and intention, define roles, and identify what is important and even what is real." We know what is *real* from systemic stories. Let that sink in for moment. In a social system, stories serve as powerful tools for cultural transmission, social cohesion, and identity formation. I chose to include stories for a reason: to point to the creative and imaginative quality of how systems build their momentum. These stories get told repeatedly to ensure everyone knows **how to *belong* in a system.** Because belonging is at the very heart of survival, systemic stories are the most powerful shapers of our beliefs. Stories are like the instructions for accessing belonging in a system. They tell us what behaviors are rewarded and which are punished. Geoffrey Cohen, Stanford Professor and belonging researcher said, "Feeing excluded is experienced in much the way physical pain is, with both activating many of the same neural networks in the brain. Psychologists call it "social pain" saying people are as motivated to alleviate it as they are to slake thirst and find shelter." We all need to feel we belong in the systems of which we are a part. This makes systemic stories some of the most powerful social tools there are for shaping a culture and the beliefs therein. These stories can be transmitted and reinforced verbally and nonverbally. They can be told through fairytales or history books, political speeches or hate speech, nursery rhymes, family values, or religious texts. They can be spread through jokes, sermons, gossip, lectures, and everyday behavior. In modernity, the spread of systemic stories is now faster than anything we've seen before with social media influencers, AI algorithms and chats, and virtually any information we want available to us at the touch of a button.

Overarching systemic stories usually have a catchphrase or word that reminds us of the underlying values of the system. Let's look at two examples of this to get a better idea of how powerful stories can shape a society.

Manifest Destiny

"Manifest Destiny" was a 19th-century story that American settlers were destined to expand across the North American continent. This narrative held that expansion was justified and inevitable, often seen as a divine right or duty. The story of Manifest Destiny was used to rationalize the territorial expansion of the United States, influencing actions like the annexation of Texas, the Oregon Trail, and the Mexican-American War. This colonizing story suggested that the settlers were culturally and racially superior and had a mission to spread democracy and capitalism. This led to imperialistic and ethnic-cleansing policies and the slaughter and violent removal of Native American people and culture.

Ubuntu

Ubuntu is a Nguni Bantu term that translates to "I am because we are." This narrative emphasizes community, interconnectedness, compassion, and mutual respect. It reflects a worldview that prioritizes collective well-being over individual achievement, stressing the importance of relationships and the idea that a person's humanity is tied to the humanity of others. Ubuntu has played a significant role in fostering reconciliation and nation-building, particularly in post-apartheid South Africa.

These are two very different stories. What do you suppose are the natural consequences of each of these stories being told over and over? In some systems, like the one in 19th century North America, stories create status power. Based on characteristics in line with the original paradigm, certain people are considered to be more valuable than others. We'll talk more about how this happens in the status power section. In addition to creating status power, stories also serve as the basis for systemic structures.

Systemic Structures

This is a broad category meant to capture a number of different structures that give form to systemic stories. Examples include norms, laws, institutions, language, standards, physical buildings, expectations, roles, and governance models. Once instituted, structures serve to direct and constrain behavior so that those within the system stay aligned with the systemic paradigm.

For example, laws mandating standardized testing in education reinforce a paradigm that values measurable skills over creativity and critical thinking. This structure directs behavior towards rote learning and standardized preparation, often suppressing other forms of learning. There are legal consequences for non-compliance and rewards (e.g., scholarships) linked to test scores that further incentivize conformity.

Another example of a structure is a standard of beauty promoted by the media and fashion industries, which influence behaviors related to body image, self-esteem, and consumer choices. This pervasive beauty standardization creates a metric that individuals compare themselves against. Conformity to those standards sidesteps negative social judgment and increases social and even economic capital.

Physical structures also carry out a system's beliefs. For example, the design of public spaces that are accessible to people with disabilities, including ramps, wide walkways, accessible restrooms, and public transportation systems that are fully accessible, reinforce what we view to be "normal," including those with different physical abilities. This particular physical design makes participation in community life possible for everyone, regardless of physical abilities, which fosters a sense of belonging for everyone—not just the majority.

In essence, systemic structures function as mechanisms of social influence and carriers of systemic paradigms. They subtly and overtly direct behavior by setting boundaries, providing incentives, and shaping perceptions of what is considered normal, appropriate, and desirable within a given system. This ensures that the actions of individuals align with the overarching paradigm, perpetuating the system's structure and beliefs.

Structures are also responsible for creating formal roles and their role power. How roles are structured and supported will directly impact how those roles are "played." Meaning, human beings will show up in a role in the way the system shapes it. Let's a look at a couple of contrasting examples with two different school systems and the role of "teacher."

Example 1: Traditional, Hierarchical School System

This first example is a school with a highly structured system with a clear hierarchy (principal, vice-principal, teachers, students). The teacher's role is defined by a curriculum they must follow, standardized testing requirements, and limited autonomy in their teaching methods. The teacher's power derives from their position within the hierarchy and their authority to assess and grade students.

In this system, teachers might primarily focus on delivering pre-determined content and preparing students for standardized tests. Their interaction with students might be more formal and authority-driven. Innovation and creativity in teaching methods might be limited due to the constraints of the system. The teacher's power is primarily top-down, focused on control and assessment.

Example 2: Progressive, Student-Centered School System

Example 2 is of a less hierarchical system where teachers and students collaborate more equally. Teachers have greater autonomy in designing their curricula and teaching methods, focusing on student-led learning and inquiry-based projects. Assessment methods are more diverse and focus on understanding rather than rote memorization.

In this system, the teacher acts more as a facilitator and mentor, guiding students in their learning process and supporting their individual needs. Teacher-student interactions are more collaborative and less formal: they have more freedom to experiment with different pedagogical approaches, fostering creativity and critical thinking. The teacher's power is more relational and shared, based on expertise and mentorship.

These examples illustrate how the structure of the education system profoundly impacts how teachers perform their roles. The formal structure (hierarchy, resource allocation, curriculum design, assessment methods) shapes the teacher's behavior, their relationship with students, and their ability to effectively implement their pedagogical approaches. The structure of the role itself directly shapes how the individual occupying that role behaves.

And, because role power carries with it significant influence on their down-power people, the way that role is shaped and then fulfilled directly shapes those who are down-power from that role. In the case of a teacher and their students, both the school system and the way that system shapes the teacher role ultimately shapes the student. So there are multiple layers of impact and those layers add up to influence the behaviors of the system's constituents.

Behaviors

"The system, to a large extent, causes its own behavior! An outside event may unleash that behavior, but the same outside event applied to a different system is likely to produce a different result." — *Donella H. Meadows*

The behavior of systems is a culmination of the behaviors, relationships, and interactions of the constituents of that system. And those behaviors, relationships, and interactions are directly influenced by the socialization of that same system. Fundamentally, behavior is anything an organism does. The more complex the organism, the more complex the behavior. Herbert Simon said, "Human beings, viewed as behaving systems, are quite simple. The apparent complexity of our behavior over time is largely a reflection of the complexity of the environment in which we find ourselves."

From the perspective of power, we could say that our behaviors are made manifest through our personal power. Behaviors can come from what I call our *socialized personal power*—which is how we enact systemic stories and structures. Behaviors, in this sense, are the expression of our socialization. Then there are the behaviors that come from our *rooted personal power*. They are internally sourced and connected to Universal Power. Behaviors from rooted personal power tend to come from our intuition or gut. When we act from our rooted personal power we are connected to something larger than ourselves.

We must navigate between sourcing our behaviors from our rooted personal power and sourcing from our socialized power. The problem is that sometimes, with internalized systemic stories and structures, we may believe we are aligning with our rooted personal power when really we are accessing internalized systemic socialization. The question is: how do we know where our behaviors are coming from? And why does it matter?

We will get into both of these questions later in the book. For now, it's important to know that the behaviors of the constituents as well as the system itself collectively form a shared reality. And that we always have a choice in how we behave, whereas we don't always have a choice in the stories and structures that are created in systems

Collective Reality

The Collective Reality aspect of the Systemic Power Cycle represents the shared understanding and experience of the system's constituents. It's the tangible manifestation of the paradigm, stories, structures, and behaviors—the way things actually are within the system, as perceived and experienced by those within it.

Collective Reality is not merely intellectual; it's deeply experiential. Individuals internalize the system's norms and expectations, shaping their behaviors and interactions accordingly. The consequences of acting within or outside of those norms become part of the shared experience.

The Collective Reality is what closes the self-reinforcing loop that supports the initial paradigm. In other words, the culmination of the stories, structures, and behaviors form a shared reality that ultimately reinforces the paradigm. But we aren't aware that this is happening—we generally don't realize that we are contributing to that collective reality, nor that we are reinforcing the paradigm. When the shared experience confirms the prevailing beliefs and values, it strengthens the system's legitimacy and perpetuates the cycle.

Collective Reality is the most powerful expression of systemic power. The way things are perceived and experienced by the majority reflects and maintains the power dynamics embedded within the system. This shared reality can be a source of stability or oppression, depending on the nature of the paradigm and the structures it supports.

Reflection Questions:

1. Can you think of a story or narrative that has influenced a system you're part of (family, school, organization, government)? How has that story influenced your own behaviors or the way the system operates?

2. Make a short (or long) list of systemic issues where the focus has been on individual blame rather than systemic change? How might we shift the conversation to address the system itself?

3. How might adopting a systems-thinking approach change the way you view problems or challenges in your life or community?

4. As an exercise, identify a paradigm that influences a system you're part of. How does that paradigm shape the stories, structures, and behaviors within that system?

7

Role Power

"We may not be able to choose our roles in life, but we can choose how we perform them." - Harold Kushner

Role - a set of behaviors, expectations, resources, and responsibilities that are associated with a particular position within a social system or group. Roles are typically awarded, elected, granted, assigned, or hired by a system or collective to an individual. Examples: doctor, facilitator, coach, judge, leader, etc.

Role Authority - the externally sourced access and privileges that accompany a role. Authority is granted by a system and accompanies the role no matter who occupies that role.

Role Power Differential - a relationship where there is a difference in power between someone who occupies a role that has authority (up-role power) and the person(s) subject to that authority (down-role power).

Role Power - the influence that exists as a direct result of the difference in formal authority between two people and the particular interpersonal relationship between the up-role and down-role person.

Every social group or system has loosely or clearly defined roles assigned to specific individuals. Most of us have had many roles throughout our lives—some that carry more or less role power. We have all been in a role power differential, even if it was only as a child with a caregiver, parent, or teacher. We know what it feels like to be told what to do—to experience rules and limits we had no part in creating. I haven't met a single person yet that hasn't been on the receiving end of some of kind of misuse or abuse of role power. Our experiences range in severity and in how they have shaped us, but we all have an embodied sense of what it feels like to be in the down-role position. I believe the reverse to be true as well: we have all experienced being on the receiving end of uses of power that helped us, that were inspiring and connected. We are shaped by those too.

Take a moment to reflect on those who have been up-role power from you in your life, like a parent, teacher, spiritual leader, coach, boss, mentor, etc. Who are the first few who come to mind? They are likely someone who used their power in a way that left a lasting positive or negative impact on you. This is the importance of understanding role power: we have all been fundamentally shaped by it and we are consistently shaping others in every role we play.

Before we get into role power, we must first understand—what are roles? In their most basic form, roles are a set of behaviors and expectations that are assigned in some way to an individual. Julie Diamond, author of *Power: A User's Guide*, describes roles as "a set of behaviors that carries social meaning" or "the enactment of social expectations."[1] If there are things that need to get done within a group of people, roles are useful for collaborative effort and/or for carrying out the purpose of the organization. They allow for specialization, coordination, clarity, accountability, structure,

---

1. . Diamond, J. (2016). *Power: A user's guide.* Belly Song Press, p. 28.

and expectations between people. Ultimately, roles help fulfill the purpose of a system or collective.

There are many different ways that roles manifest, are perceived, and are carried out. Depending on the shape of the system that created the role, and the rigidity of the structures of that system, how the role gets enacted will vary widely. Role power is the dynamic that exists in a role power differential—between the up-role power and down-role power person(s). Role power gets its influence from both the authority of the role itself *and* the interpersonal dynamic between the up-role and down-role people. Let's take a look at each of these aspects of role power.

Authority

Up-power roles have some degree of **authority** that is assigned to them. Role authority has to do with the privileges and responsibilities that are specifically related to the *duties* of the role. What gives privileges and responsibilities that are formally assigned to a role authority to the person who fills that role, is that they allow the up-role person to determine something for someone else (e.g., to make decisions, allocate resources, or enforce rules for other people). So when a person enters that role, they have access to that authority, no matter who that person is or how they show up in the role. For example, the role of a medical doctor in a hospital has the formal authority to determine the diagnosis and treatment of a patient, to write prescriptions, and perhaps to hire or influence the hiring decisions for other hospital staff. These are all a part of the authority of the role—which, itself, has little to do with the particular person occupying that role (assuming they are qualified for the role).

Role Power Differential

A role power differential arises when there is a difference in power between someone who occupies a role that has authority (up-role power) and the person(s) subject to that authority (down-role power). Let's use the example of a doctor in a hospital. The doctor steps into the role. Who is down-power from the doctor? There are patients, nurses, and support staff. Each of these relationships is different, but the doctor would be up-role power from all of those types of down-power people because they have been given some kind of authority over them. However, the particular authority (privileges and responsibilities) is different in each of those kinds of relationships. With a patient, the responsibility has to do with their care and treatment and they are given access to resources and privileges (like writing prescriptions) to accomplish that. With nurses, a doctor might have the responsibility to guide them in caring for the patient by assigning them tasks, and the privilege of setting priorities or to make the final decision about a patient's care.

When people think of role power, generally this is what they think of. However, role power is more than just the role power differential and the authority of the role. It is also has to do with what happens within the relationship itself. There is a lot more going on there in terms of social power dynamics. Let's take a closer look.

Role Power

Role power is the influence that exists as a direct result of the difference in formal authority between two people *and* the particular interpersonal relationship between the up-power person and whoever is down-power from them. In other words, role power dynamics exist the moment a role power differential exists, which means role power is inherently relational. Role power does not exist outside of a relationship. This is important. It means that role power differs from relationship to relationship and is predicated on how the up-power person behaves, the level of trust they develop, and ultimately how the up-power person is perceived by the down-power person.

Let's say that a hospital recently hired two doctors. Both doctors are hired in the same role with the same level of authority. They work in the same department and treat the same kinds of conditions. But Doctor 1 and Doctor 2 have very different experiences.

Doctor 1 takes the time to establish strong relationships with patients, nurses, administrative staff, and other doctors. They are known for recognizing the contributions of the nurses and support staff and they often acknowledges their expertise. They consult with other doctors on their cases and spend time with every patient, ensuring they understand their diagnosis and treatment plan. Doctor 1 maintains an open-door policy, encouraging feedback and makes a point to follow up with patients after significant treatments or procedures, checking in on their recovery.

Doctor 2 has high expectations and holds support staff accountable for their performance. They are highly regarded for their expertise, and they frequently showcase their medical knowledge and problem-solving skills, positioning themselves as the go-to person in complex cases. Doctor 2 prioritizes efficiency, making decisions quickly and conveying those decisions clearly to the team and to their patients. They keep their consultations short and to the point, focusing primarily on medical issues and clinical outcomes.

What is the obvious difference between Doctor 1 and Doctor 2? While both doctors carry out their role authority, the experience of those down-power from them will likely be very different. Doctor 2 views their role as carrying out their formal authority, while Doctor 1 views attending to relationships as equally important as the formal role responsibilities. This is the difference between awareness of one's role authority and awareness of one's role *power*.

The Role Power Differential *Relationship*

So, we have covered the differences between a role, the role's formal authority, the role power differential—and role power involving the sum of these. As we have said, role power is inherently *relational*. It is the dynamic that exists in relationship. The power differential relationship carries with it an additional layer of influence beyond the job duties. Everything from the down-power person's perception of the up-power person's authority, to the level of trust between them impacts the amount of role *power* or influence a person has in that relationship.

If, for example, the down-power person does not recognize or acknowledge the up-role person's authority, or they have little trust in the up-power person, the up-role person has very little role power (influence from the role) with that person. So if we want to use our role power well, we must not only pay attention to the privileges and responsibilities from the formal authority of the role, but also to the role power differential relationship itself.

Privileges of a role generally include the honors, status, resources, benefits, compensation, social capital, skill development, and access that accompany the role. When we accept a role we usually do so for the privileges or benefits. In the case of a doctor, the benefits might include the salary, the satisfaction from helping people, the status of the role (which is typically a higher rank amongst other roles in the hospital), the access they have to the hospital, their own office, and personally-related benefits which might be related to their specific passions, goals or values.

Then there are the formal role responsibilities. These are the responsibilities related to the duties of the role that are usually presented clearly and in detail. These are typically outlined in a job description or, at the very least, clarified in conversation. For a doctor, this would include seeing X number of patients a week, keeping notes on each patient, managing nurses and support staff, etc.

But there are also responsibilities related to the role power differential *relationship*. These include things like the awareness of the vulnerabilities of the person(s) down-role power from you, tracking for your impact, and understanding your role power shadow (all of which we will cover in Part Two of the book).

These kinds of relational responsibilities are typically not elucidated for people unless it is through HR rules or ethical guidelines—which can come with eye rolls and yawns. Who wants to sit through the mandatory HR training? Who actually reads the ethical guidelines? Often in modern Western culture, interpersonal role responsibilities are typically treated with disdain or at least indifference. Again, people tend to think they already know how "to be a good person." But role responsibilities aren't about being a good person, they are about understanding and navigating role power well.

Understanding the vulnerabilities of the people down-power from you is probably the most important relational responsibility of the role power differential. For example, a doctor might consider the vulnerabilities of a patient: they are subject to the doctor's diagnosis and treatment plan which can have an enormous impact on their wellbeing, there is emotional vulnerability in illness, injury and disability, there are financial consideration that the patient must navigate, etc. In their power differential relationship with nurses, doctors have a different set of vulnerabilities to consider: they are subject to the doctor's decision on their job duties and advancements, they experience a high workload and are subject to burnout, they may fear negative repercussions if they ask questions about a doctor's decision, etc.

We will cover some more of the down-role vulnerabilities in Part Two of the book, but I also recommend exploring *Right Use of Power: The Heart of Ethics* by Cedar Barstow and *Power: A User's Guide* by Julie Diamond for more direction on how to use your role power well. I also recommend taking a live Right Use of Power training to explore the relational aspects of role power through experiential and somatic exercises.

Other responsibilities of the role power differential relationship are understanding the systemic pressures on the relationship, as well as any status power differences that may be present in addition to the role power differential. It is the relational responsibilities where we typically see ignorance, resistance or denial. And unless *all* of the responsibilities are clear, confusion and conflict can arise. It is important to remember that accepting a role means accepting the benefits, the role-related responsibilities, *and* the relational responsibilities—otherwise we are likely to misuse our role power.

An additional note on role power

One of the ways I deviate from Dr. Barstow's original definition of role power is that it is **not** *earned*. You may earn a degree or gain experience and get hired or elected based on the things you earned. But ultimately, roles are created by and then assigned, elected or awarded by the system to certain individuals. This distinction is important for many reasons. Saying that we earned role power gives us the illusion that we had a part in creating it. This makes over-identification with role power more likely which, as we will see, tends to make us misuse or abuse our role power.

If we feel like we earned role power, we are likely to overlook the relational responsiblities of the role power differential. Continually building trust with our down-role people is where the real *earning* exists. More importantly, believing that we earned role power is that it gives us the illusion of control that we don't have. If you earned something, you would then own it and get to decide what to do with it. While it is true that you have many important choices within your role, it is limited within the confines of the system. Take the example of the traditional school system versus an alternative one that we used earlier. The way a teacher shows up in their role is directly related to the paradigm and goals of the system. Similarly, the system can decide to remove your role altogether or remove you from the role.

You don't earn a role and you don't create the role power within a relationship, but you can choose how you show up in both the role and the role power in relationship.

Reflection:

Role power is an accessible entry point for understanding power differentials in general. This is an important starting place for us because the dynamics present in role power differentials are very similar to dynamics in other power differentials. Pick an up-role position in your life and answer the following questions:

- What are the responsibilities that come from the formal authority of the role?

- What are the relational responsibilities of the role?

- Who is down power from you?

- What are their vulnerabilities?

- What are the systemic pressures on the role power differential relationship?

- Is there also a status power differential present in the role differential relationship?

8

Status Power

Status - the extrinsic valuation of an individual's attribute(s) or trait(s) that determines social standing within a given context. Status includes access to particular advantages associated with an attribute or trait that others without that attribute or trait do not have access to (although those others may have other valued attributes that carry advantages).

*Status Power - the influence derived from a **perceived** status of value within a social system or collective.*

A lot of what has been written in the book so far was provided, in part, so we can more clearly understand and talk more honestly about status power. Systemic power often creates the stories and structures that lead to status power, so its an essential preface. And role power dynamics are very similar in function as status power dynamics - but without as much charge (so it can be a helpful place to start). Status power is one of the most elusive and complex forms of power and it is where a great deal of misuses and abuses of power can happen. Understanding the nuance of how it manifests and how it works is critical for engaging in power dynamics wisely and moving toward right-relationship.

Starting with the definitions of status and status power, it's first important to note that status and status power are different, but related. Just like with roles and role power, status is the thing that is necessary for the dynamic of status power to exist. **Status is a social standing within a group or system derived from an extrinsic valuation.** To the degree that a person creates, recognizes or believes in the extrinsic valuations of themselves and another person, will determine how they will show up in the status power dynamic between them. **It is the individual's or group's adherence to that extrinsic value which creates status power dynamics.** Before we go deeper into status power dynamics, it's important to first understand: What is an extrinsic valuation and why is it an important part of understanding status power?

Extrinsic Valuation

In 1938, Mr. N.W. Ayer, an advertising executive in New York City, paced before a large map dotted with diamond mines in his office. He wasn't just selling rocks; he was selling dreams. His client, De Beers, held a near-monopoly on the world's diamond supply, but the public viewed diamonds as merely sparkly stones, not the symbols of eternal love they would soon become.

Mr. Ayer knew the key wasn't just advertising; it was storytelling. He envisioned a world where every proposal whispered a promise sealed with a brilliant diamond. He commissioned artists, writers, and filmmakers to weave this vision into compelling narratives. They crafted advertisements that read like short stories, filled with romantic intrigue and passionate declarations. These stories appeared in glossy magazines, captivating readers with tales of devoted lovers whose affections were solidified by a diamond's dazzling sparkle. The message was subtly woven into the fabric of popular culture; films portrayed engagements as incomplete without the radiant gleam of a diamond ring.

Gradually, the narrative took hold. The diamond, once a mere gem-

stone, transformed into a symbol of unwavering love. Society's norms shifted, influenced by this carefully constructed narrative. The diamond engagement ring, once a luxury, became an expectation, its value increasing not just in monetary terms but in cultural significance. The story, carefully crafted, had become reality.

This is a story about the skillful creation of extrinsic value, which is the key to understanding status power. Extrinsic value is the value assigned to something based on its relationship to something else, rather than its inherent qualities. It's derived from its utility, social significance, or its association with other things we value. So let's take a look at this example with the diamond to take a closer look at extrinsic value and how it might unfold.

Many people value a diamond more than any other gemstone because of this crafty manipulation told through stories repeated over and over until it became a norm, particularly for the engagement ring. Over time, several things happened. The norm became so established that both the price and demand of diamonds skyrocketed, leading to more mines being opened to satisfy the demand. Decades later, mined diamonds got the nickname "blood diamonds" as they became tied to unethical practices like conflict diamonds funding wars, human rights abuses, hazardous working conditions with low pay and child labor, and severe environmental damage. While the popularity of diamonds, particularly mined diamonds, may be experiencing a relative decline due to ethical concerns and evolving consumer preferences, it hasn't disappeared. The cultural legacy of diamonds continues, as well as their high price and perceived value.

All of this impact because someone manufactured the value of something through stories until it was *perceived* as valuable. Someone tells a story over and over until others tell the same or similar stories, and then somewhere along the way it becomes "reality." The perceived valuation is thus unconsciously adopted and applied by those within that system or collective. It is the perception of value that matters with status power, not its inherent worth. Someone who doesn't know of, believe in, acknowledge, or understand that extrinsic value, like my youngest daughter when she was a toddler, might just as well prefer a smooth pebble over a shiny diamond. In short, extrinsic value equals perceived value, often in comparison or relationship with something else.

Looking at status characteristics like race, gender, ability, or wealth, we must understand that these are *extrinsic valuations*. They originate from somewhere outside of the person being evaluated. And then that person is perceived through that valuation. A value gets assigned to them and becomes a part of our perception of them. **It's almost like the person gets wrapped in a particular kind of veil where the status is what you see first, and it becomes harder to see the actual person underneath.**

Stories That Create Status

As we have seen, extrinsic valuations that become status in a context come from stories. There are a few different types of narratives that typically create status: 1) Systemic Stories; 2) Reputations; 3) Associations.

Systemic Stories

Since we already covered systemic stories, I will be brief here on how they relate to status power. Since systemic stories typically result from a systemic paradigm, they are inherently related to that paradigm. Systemic stories then lead to structures that tend to preserve these stories (and the status they create) for longer periods of time. This makes this type of status particularly entrenched. Systemic stories act like a form of social contagion that can accumulate over generations. These systemic narratives can result in long-lasting extrinsic valuations that lead to things like socioeconomic privilege, gender bias, racial prejudice, and ableism.

Reputations

Another kind of story that can create status power is reputation. A person's reputation is just a narrative constructed over time, composed of various observations and interpretations of an individual's actions and character. This narrative is shared and circulated within a social network, shaping how others perceive and interact with that individual. This is where fame, acclaimed experts, mentors, and influencers come from.

We will explore more about the intersections of power in Part Two, but it's worth mentioning here that personal power can become reputation-based status power, and then status power and personal power can get conflated and confused. To be clear in recognizing status power in these cases, remember that status is an extrinsic or external valuation. Status power is based on others' perception of value. Even in a one-on-one interaction, you can create a story about a person, but they are usually informed by stories that we have absorbed over time through socialization. Your own valuation of a person is inherently extrinsic, and it is likely influenced by factors that are largely unconscious.

Nonverbal communication (without words) is 93% of what we understand in an interaction with another person. Between that and our socialization, what we understand of a person is often so nuanced that we can't put it into words. We have a relatively immediate feeling about them, or we may immediately like or dislike someone. Within minutes, or even seconds, we put a veil over the person based on our extrinsic valuation of them. We do this so automatically and so immediately that we often don't reconsider that valuation or try to lift the veil to see the person underneath.

Associations

It might be a stretch to consider associations (a mental link between two things) as stories, but they do inherently imply a narrative. The very existence of a link suggests a relationship, experience, or reason for that connection. For instance, a person who graduated from an Ivy League university creates an association that leads to a particular kind of status in some circles. A story is created about the person because of their association with the school, and that story creates status. Or if you live in an expensive neighborhood, being associated with that neighborhood gives you a particular status. Associations that are a basis for status can be with any number of different things, people, or places that already have some status. For example, if you don't have the status of "popular" but you start to hang out with popular people, you may also gain that status by association (or that is the hope for them). Unfortunately, this can bring about a lot of performative behavior and inauthentic ways of being.

Associations can also be subtle or even consciously imperceptible. Or it may feel like something you can't quite put into words, but you still feel it strongly. You might "get the ick" about someone and not understand why. Then the status they were associated with previously disappears—you can no longer perceive it.

Comparisons are another form of association. While a general association is a passive or automatic mental link between two concepts, comparison involves a more deliberate and evaluative process. Comparison is fundamental to determining *relative* value. We assess the value of something by comparing it to alternatives. This process of comparison creates a hierarchy of value, influencing how we relate with others. This is an enormous part of the status power dynamic in relationships—its all relative.

Creators of Status Stories

Who creates the stories that lead to status and status power? Some envision powerful evil people manipulating stories for the construction of their evil empire (perhaps with an evil laugh at the end?). While I don't believe anyone is inherently evil, I do believe that people create stories for selfish gain—and that it is a slippery slope.

Do you know the story of *The Sneeches* by Dr. Seuss? In this children's story, the Sneetches are a species divided into two groups: those with stars on their bellies and those without. The Sneetches with stars consider themselves superior. One day, a traveling businessman, Sylvester McMonkey McBean, arrives with a machine that can put stars on the star-less Sneetches, and then stars on bellies were much more common. This is what happens next:

"Good grief!" groaned the ones who had stars at the first. "We're still the best Sneetches, and they are the worst. But, now, how in the world will we know," they all frowned, "If which kind is what, or the other way round?"

Then up came McBean with a very sly wink. And he said, "Things are not quite as bad as you think. So you don't know who's who. That's perfectly true. But come with me, friends. Do you know what I'll do? I'll make you, again, the best Sneetches on beaches And all it will cost you is ten dollars eaches."

"Belly stars are no longer in style," said McBean. "What you need is a trip through my Star-Off machine. This wondrous contraption will take off your stars. So you won't look like Sneetches who have them on thars."

McBean keeps adding new machines to meet new demands and make even more money, creating an escalating cycle of star-adding and star-removing. Eventually, the Sneetches realize they've wasted their money chasing arbitrary status symbols. The cycle ends when McBean, having made a huge profit, leaves.

While this is an overly simplified (but clever) story of status power, it reveals everyone's responsibility in the cycle of status power dynamics. Certainly, McBean is responsible for exploiting the status-seeking nature of the Sneetches, but he didn't create the initial story of stars being good and starless being bad. Unlike the history of diamonds, it's often impossible to point back to an exact origin of a status story. Nevertheless, the story gets perpetuated by the Original Star-Bellied Sneetches, desiring to continue to feel superior. They did not want to let go of their status, nor the advantages that came along with it. Since the story only allowed for the binary of "superior" or "inferior"—starred or starless—they couldn't allow themselves to fall into the other "inferior" group. This opened up an opportunity for McBean to make up a new story, "Belly stars are no longer in style." And how does this story get spread—through the Sneetches themselves with very little work on the part of McBean.

The unfortunate truth is that, consciously or unconsciously, we all create or co-create stories, repeat or recreate stories that lead to status power dynamics. We seem to have an innate need to stack up and compare ourselves and each other, and typically we put ourselves in the category of "good" or even "better than." And we do this in relatively simple ways without even thinking about it.

I was recently a presenter at a conference, and I also had a display booth. When I went to the registration table to collect my badge, the person at the table handed me my badge and a lanyard with a badge holder. As I walked away from the registration table, I noticed that the badge holder she gave me said "First Time Attendee." I immediately turned around, went to the front of the long line, and interrupted the next person in line to let the volunteer behind the table know that not only was this my fourth time at this conference, but that I was also a presenter and needed the "Speaker" badge holder (thank you very much). The conference had its own status system and, by God, I was going to reinforce it.

This all happened in the span of about a minute and I didn't even think about the status power implications in the moment. Did the conference status system have a purpose to help attendees connect with one another? Yes. Does it also serve to stratify for the purposes of ego satisfaction? Also yes. And I played right into it so much so that I engaged in rude behavior to make sure I was labeled correctly.

This tendency to create stories that lead to status—the tendency to compare ourselves to others and then judge ourselves more favorably—is thanks to a number of different cognitive biases. And if you have a human brain, you have also been under the influence of these tricky survival adaptations. Cognitive biases are essentially mental shortcuts our brains use to simplify complex information processing. While these shortcuts are often efficient, they can lead to inaccurate judgments and illogical decisions. These biases are largely implicit, hidden from those who carry them, though they can be quite apparent to others. It's not a matter of some individuals having them and others not, but rather a matter of degree and the influence of various individual and contextual factors. While we will go deeper into how our brains disrupt right-relationship later in the book, here are a couple of examples of cognitive biases:

Illusory Superiority Bias: This term directly addresses the tendency to view oneself as superior to others. It's a cognitive bias where we overestimate our own abilities and accomplishments relative to those of others. Driving is a good example of this. Most drivers rate themselves as above-average drivers, even though this is statistically impossible. People tend to focus on their own safe driving experiences while overlooking instances where they might have made errors.

Self-Serving Bias: This refers to the tendency to attribute positive outcomes to internal factors (e.g., skill, ability) and negative outcomes to external factors (e.g., bad luck, unfair circumstances). This bias contributes to a self-enhancing perception, sometimes leading to the judgment of oneself as superior. For example, a student who gets a good grade on a test might attribute it to their intelligence and hard work ("I studied hard, and I'm smart"). However, if they get a bad grade, they might blame the teacher ("The test was unfair"), the difficulty of the material ("It was too hard"), or external factors ("I didn't sleep well").

These biases point to our need to see ourselves in a good light, to protect our ego and sense of self. It is a natural thing to do. The problem is that in the process, we tend to create or perpetuate status valuations. We label others as "bad" or inferior so that we can preserve the image of ourselves as "good" or superior in some way. By differentiating ourselves from those deemed "bad," we reinforce our self-image as morally upright and virtuous. This reinforces a positive self-identity. This also happens at the group level. Labeling out-group members as "bad" strengthens in-group cohesion. By defining ourselves as morally superior to an out-group, we solidify our identity and strengthen our bonds with our own group.

Status Attributes

We have covered the different origins of status; now, let's look at status attributes themselves. Status is context-dependent and it can be based on a variety of different traits and attributes. I have identified three different layers to status that change how status power dynamics operate: changeability, distribution, and visibility. I want to take a moment to highlight again our tendency to compare ourselves with each other. We do this with our down-status attributes as well. We either like to compete with those who have more status or those who have the least. By outlining these different status attributes, I am not intending to provide fuel for the oppression olympics, but rather to note the different kinds of status.

Changeability

Some attributes are unchangeable—what we are born with (**inborn traits**), others change over time (**shifting attributes**), and still others could fall in either category (**flexible attributes**). For example, inborn traits are characteristics such as skin color, handedness, and genetic predispositions. Shifting attributes that can change over time include things like reputation, education level, or weight. And then there are those flexible attributes that we may be born into but can also change over time, like wealth, ability, or citizenship.

Distribution

Not only can status change over time, it can also be more or less prevalent in different areas or contexts. This is the layer that I call distribution. Certain attributes are more common than others. There are some status-based attributes that are less common and more localized. For example, if you are a competitor in a 4th grade spelling bee and you win first place, the status of that is highest in that particular competition, but then dissipates as the circle widens (less significant within the whole school, even less significant outside of school, etc.). Unless you walk around the rest of your life with your 1st place spelling bee medal, it is unlikely to have an impact on your status in most contexts.

However, distinctions such as age are universal, though their perceived value is based on the context. The perception of value of a particular trait can be local or global—it can be viewed similarly no matter where you go in the world, or could only carry value in specific areas or groups. Typically, status based on systemic stories about common attributes tends to be more widespread. For example, skin color and gender tend to be evaluated in terms of status similarly around the world, with some variations based on culture, presence of diversity, and the type of system. It is important to note that attributes that are more common and that have similar value across contexts carry with them a heavier status differential. Depending on where you fall within this type of status differential, the superiority or inferiority tends to be more entrenched and have a more lasting impact, especially when they are more visible, inborn traits.

Visibility

Another layer to status traits or attributes is their visibility—some are more visible than others. Attributes like skin tone and weight are immediately visible, while others, like intelligence, wealth, or ability, take time, demonstration and/or investigation to see. We may try to demonstrate or hide these based on the status we believe we get from it. We can up-play certain attributes in certain contexts and down-play the same attributes in other contexts. This is where we start to see strategies around status appear.

Status Power Strategies

Up to this point we have focused mostly on status, which is an important context for understanding status power dynamics. Now let's explore how status differences play out in relationship. Like role power, status power is inherently relational. It does not exist outside of relationship and it is always in association or comparison with something or someone else.

Apart from human beings, many other animal species demonstrate clear status power differences within their social groups. The status power dynamics are integral to their social order and influence things like access to resources and reproduction. Status power is primally alluring in social groups, and human beings are no exception. For those species that rely on one another for survival, social groups exist and status differences accompany them. We generally seek, consciously or unconsciously, good social standing within our social groups. And just like any other animal species, there are particular behaviors and strategies that we engage in within status power dynamics.

There are a couple of different status power strategies that human beings generally exhibit: 1) Status Influencing and 2) Status Assessment. These strategies happen so instantaneously and simultaneously that it can be difficult to distinguish between them. However, it is important to note their distinctions so that we understand what is actually happening and have the possibility of intervening in the process.

Status Influencing

The first strategy is **Status Influencing**. This is where we signal or hide attributes to manipulate others' status assessment. We may do this before or during a social interaction. So we may name-drop, drive a fancy car, dye our hair purple, or puff up our chest, to name just a few. And of course, there may be other reasons you drive a fancy car or dye your hair purple, but we also know that when we buy that car, or wear our hair a certain way, there is a certain status that comes with it. These are ways that we signal to other people about our status power because we are trying to appear valuable in some way to others in a system. And, as has been mentioned, context matters. A fancy car in one context may carry with it high status and in another may carry none.

The other behaviors we engage in this Status Influencing phase are hiding, masking, or code-switching. We tend to downplay the attributes that we know will put us at risk for rejection or even violence of some kind (based on research, both are experienced similarly in the body).[1] This is an important survival strategy and can result in exhaustion and even illness, depending on how frequently this strategy must be utilized. As someone on different spectrums of neurodivergence, I am constantly navigating between the degree of masking I need to do in a given situation and my energy level. This is one of the reasons I often prefer to be alone. Since most of my life, I didn't know I was different, I just constantly masked, not knowing there was an alternative. I survived by always having my nose in a book—a somewhat socially acceptable shield from social interactions. For those of us who need to employ a hiding strategy

---

1. Eisenberger, N. I., Lieberman, M. D., & Williams, K. D. (2003). Does rejection hurt? An fMRI study of social exclusion. *Science, 302*(5643), 290-292. & Smart Richman, L., & Leary, M. R. (2009). Reactions to discrimination, stigmatization, ostracism, and other forms of interpersonal rejection: A multimotive model. *Psychological Review, 116*(2), 365-383.

of some kind for a particular attribute, we feel most comfortable among those who are like us in that particular attribute. And, of course, due to intersectionality, this invisible labor only intensifies the more down-status attributes we have in a given context.

Status Assessments

The second status strategy is **Status Assessments.** The assessment happens when we are trying to understand how to relate to another person. Should we try to impress this person? Should we ignore this person? Should we be tough? Should we be gentle? Should we talk? Should we listen? No matter how authentic we want to be, most of us cannot help but make instantaneous adjustments to how we show up in relationship. Have you ever had a conversation with a random person and only later realized that they were a famous person or your new boss? We immediately replay the scenario and most likely would have modified our behavior in some way had we known a particular status we didn't know before.

Status assessments involve two primary functions: perception and assumption. First, we perceive the other person (remember 93% of an interaction being understood without their words), and then our assumptions immediately kick in. This process is filtered through our primary systemic lens, the context within which the interaction takes place, our cognitive biases, mood, past experiences, and even the particular structure of our brains.

This assessment of another person happens instantaneously. Studies show that first impressions can be formed in as little as milliseconds. For example, research has shown that individuals can make judgments about others' trustworthiness or attractiveness within 50 milliseconds of seeing their face. Other studies suggest that even a brief exposure of 100 to 500 milliseconds can be sufficient for individuals to form initial impressions regarding competence.[2]

Once formed, first impressions can be quite persistent. Initial judgments can influence subsequent interactions and perceptions, often leading individuals to maintain their first impressions even in the face of contradictory evidence.[3]

Status Power Engagement

Unfortunately, all of the influencing and assessment strategies can get in the way of us relating with the person underneath the veil of status. We spend our time and energy trying to assess each other and ourselves using either the metrics that systems or others have given us to use. This can keep us from being authentic, take us out of relationship with ourselves, and create barriers to relationships with others.

Status Power is an implicit game we play, and it is ultimately the game of belonging. Understanding that status is a social construction that influences our behavior with one another, frees us to make a conscious choice about how we engage. Do we conform to our socialization, or do we attempt to unveil the interaction? Do we prioritize comfort and hide, or do we courageously side-step our assumptions? The game of status power often results in an

2. Willis, J., & Todorov, A. (2006). First impressions: Making up your mind after a 100-ms exposure to a face. *Psychological Science, 17*(7), 592-598. https://doi.org/10.1111/j.1467-9280.2006.01750.x & Bar, M., Neta, M., & Linz, H. (2006). Very first impressions. *Emotion, 6*(2), 269-278.

3. Asch, S. E. (1946). Forming impressions of personality. *Journal of Abnormal and Social Psychology, 41*(3), 258-290. & Todorov, A., & Uleman, J. S. (2003). The efficiency of binding spontaneous trait inferences to actors' faces. *Journal of Experimental Social Psychology, 39*(6), 549-562.

incredible amount of social, emotional, and physical harm to any of us who are born without the attributes that the systems or groups we are a part of value. So when we don't fit the shape of the social container, of the system we are in, our survival is threatened.

So, are status power dynamics a good or bad thing? The answer is it could be either, depending on how we show up in them. Not seeing the status strategies or not understanding how status power works is the real problem. Participating in harm when we don't realize we are doing that is a problem. I can use the status I do have access to for supportive or selfish purposes.

The question is: How do we participate in status power dynamics in a way that brings us toward right-relationship? What responsibilities do we have in the status power dynamic? The key, I have found, is personal power.

Reflection Questions:

1. Think about the stories you've been told or have told yourself about status. How have these stories influenced your perception of yourself and others? Are there any stories you've unconsciously adopted that you want to question or challenge?

2. How do different contexts (work, social circles, family) affect the way status is assigned or perceived? Are there certain attributes that gain or lose value depending on the setting? How does this shape your behavior in different environments?

3. When you are in up-status, what responsibilities do you

think you have in navigating status power dynamics? How can you use your status to support others rather than reinforce existing hierarchies?

4. What does "right-relationship" look like to you in the context of status power? How can you actively work toward creating more equitable and compassionate interactions, both in your personal life and in the systems you're part of?

9

Personal Power

"To be rooted is perhaps the most important and least recognized need of the human soul." - *Simone Weil*

Personal Power: *the individual ability to have (or create) an effect or influence.*

Human beings are complex. We have a brain and consciousness that no one fully understands. We possess the ability to think critically and self-reflect, creating cultures and rules for living, and we have the capacity to create and influence the world around us. Along with all the other millions of species of living beings on the earth, we have been given life in some way, which is an inherently creative force. So how do we use that creative force within us? Rick Rubin, in his book, *The Creative Act*, said:

> *"To create is to bring something into existence that wasn't there before. It could be a conversation, the solution to a problem, a note to a friend, the rearrangement of furniture in a room, a new route home to avoid a traffic jam. What you make doesn't have to be witnessed, recorded, sold, or encased in glass for it to be a work of art. Through the ordinary state of being, we're already creators in the most profound*

way, creating our experience of reality and composing the
world we perceive."[1]

I love this description because it illustrates the ways in which
we create all the time—without even thinking about it. And it also
reminds us that we create our experience of reality. Very rarely
do we take responsibility for how we "compose the world we
perceive."

Personal power is our individual ability to have an impact on the
world, to create, to influence and even to be in relationship with
others. Up to this point in the book, we have explored systemic,
role and status power in depth. We've seen the pitfalls of power
and the harm it can cause. Personal power is a critical element
in any sustainable response to those pitfalls. For many of us, we
were not taught about personal power or how to recognize and
cultivate it. In dominant culture, we are generally taught that power
comes from what is external to us. It comes from systems, from
roles, or status. And so we put all of our focus on gaining power
from those sources—or we collapse into a sense of powerlessness.
Until we develop a sense of our personal power, we depend on
outside sources, and we can frequently abandon our own dignity
and internal sense of belonging.

Aspects of Personal Power

Many different parts and factors make up our personal power. I
created an image of personal power that includes its various aspects:
Inherent Belongingness, Influence, Felt Sense, Beliefs, Capabilities,
Access, Recognition, and Expression. There are entire books on

---

1. Rubin, R. (2023). *The creative act: A way of being.* Penguin Press, p. 1-2.

each of these areas that have been written, although they may use different language; so, I will try to keep these definitions brief. However, each aspect of personal power is important for understanding and accessing it.

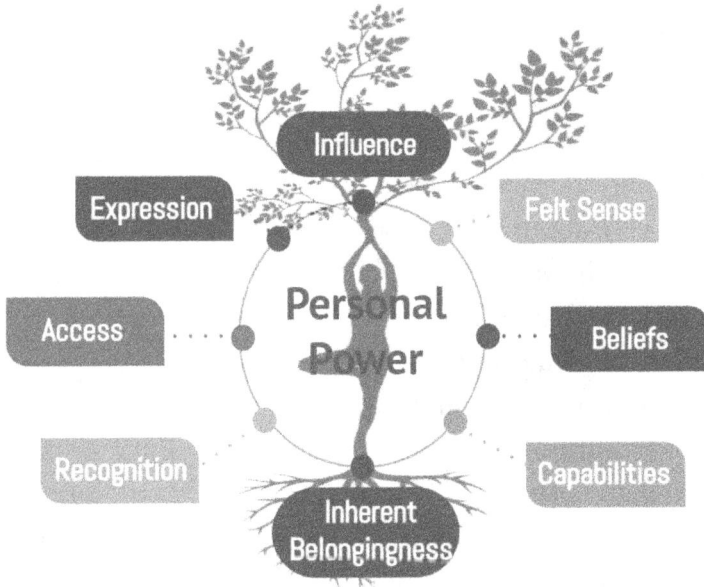

Influence

Like all of the other types of power, personal power is inherently neutral. We can choose to engage our personal power in multiple ways. How we influence the world with that engagement can be positive or negative; it can be self-serving or altruistic; it can be celebrated or hated. The resulting effect of our engagement with personal power is our influence. It is the achievement of our goals, the products of our creation, the growth or decline of our relationships, the insights we realize, or the ways that we hide from the world. How we use our personal power is a decision, whether we make it unconsciously or consciously. Ultimately, we are responsible for its resulting influence—whether it aligns with our intentions or not. So let's look at the factors that impact the influence we have in the world.

Inherent Belongingness

The ground of our personal power is what I call "inherent belongingness." Rather than internalizing how systems or others say we do or don't belong, we can become aware of the inherent belonging that we were all born with, regardless of who we are or how we are socialized. Inherent Belongingness is the immanence that comes with your birth on the planet. You inherently belong here. No matter what dominant culture says, or how you were raised, or what experiences you've had to make you believe otherwise, your birthright is that you inherently belong here on this earth. You were created to be here, whether you believe that is a function of nature, evolution, or a Creator. Perhaps take a moment to be still and notice how that statement lands with you - can you feel into the truth of your inherent belongingness? It is everyone's birthright to know - in our bones - that we inherently belong, as evidenced by the fact that *we are here.*

One way to think about inherent belongingness is that it is the origin of personal power. Just like roles are the source of role power and status is the source of status power, inherent belongingness is the origin of true personal power. Knowing this inherent belongingness, being in touch with it, is like having a strong root system. When you root into your Inherent Belongingness, you can also stretch out further with a greater reach. The stronger and deeper your roots are, the longer and thicker your branches can be. So, when you are rooted, you actually have the potential for greater influence. This is what I call "**rooted personal power.**" Rooted personal power is the internally sourced expression of your inherent belongingness. No matter how hard the wind blows or if a storm—or systems—threaten to tear you apart, you have the roots that will hold you strong. This is where our resilience comes from. In contrast, when we are not rooted or connected with our Inherent Belongingness, our personal power tends to become more shallow and can mimic our socialization. This is what I call "**socialized personal power.**" It is not that the roots are no longer there, because they exist all the time and for every person. Sometimes, there are "tornadoes" (i.e., a health crisis, oppression, assault, or poverty) that threaten to or actually uproot us. There are many moments and circumstances that turn our attention and orientation to what is happening around us—we get caught in the systemic pressures. But when we practice tapping into our roots, our Inherent Belongingness, it becomes much easier to navigate the world, even when the world is working against us. We will discuss socialized versus rooted personal power a little later in this chapter, but I wanted to differentiate between them here because they are closely tied to our sense of Inherent Belongingness.

Felt Sense

There is a felt sense of your personal power, and it exists in your body. It is a bodily awareness of your power that you can actually feel when you tune into your internal experience. You can try it now. Read through these instructions first and then try it out (it will only take a minute). *You can also scan the QR code to listen to a recording of this meditation:*

Close your eyes for just a moment and try to identify what you would consider to be your center. Where does the center of you exist within your body? Is it in your belly, your heart, your mind? Maybe your gut? Along your spine? The bottoms of your feet?

Once you have identified that place within you, now imagine that your roots extend out from the center of you and into the ground. Feel the stability of that. Your roots are the way you know that you inherently belong on this earth. Take a moment to feel that sense of inherent belongingness—that you belong here just like the trees and the grasses and the sky.

And now imagine that you have branches that reach up and outward from that center. The branches are balanced by the weight of your roots. You don't hesitate to reach as far as you can. That is your influence.

Now remember the sensation of your physical center and imagine a line of energy that runs through you—from your roots to your branches. Notice what that line of energy feels like, how it sustains you, how it nourishes you from your roots to your branches and back again.

Now - think of an activity you might be doing later today. It doesn't need to be a significant one - it could be anything from getting groceries to making a decision you've been weighing.

What does it feel like to imagine yourself doing this activity from this place of rooted personal power?

Do you notice anything about how you do this activity that might be different than if you are not engaging so deeply with your rooted personal power?

Now go back to your physical sensations, to your physical center. What does it feel like?

This is your felt sense of personal power.

When you feel the strength of your body, your heart, your mind, your emotions—you are tapping into the felt sense of your personal power. Some people don't or can't access that felt sense. This is common, so don't worry if it doesn't come to you right away. One of the consequences of living in a disconnected society is that we get disconnected from our bodies. We can get stuck living from the neck up, leading with our heads and ignoring our bodies' needs and desires. It may feel uncomfortable at first if you aren't used to paying attention to your sensations or internal experiences, but orienting to your felt sense is a crucial aspect of understanding your power. Practicing this exercise or your own way of accessing your felt sense of rooted personal power can help anchor you in moments of instability.

Amy Cuddy, a social psychologist, did a Ted Talk[2] in 2012 on the research she conducted on the physical experience of power. Cuddy, along with her colleagues, conducted a pivotal study[3] published in Psychological Science in 2010. This study suggested that individuals who engaged in high-power poses (expansive and open body language) experienced both psychological (increased feelings of power and a greater willingness to take risks) and even some physiological changes (including increased testosterone levels and decreased cortisol levels). This study suggests that our felt experience of power can have a significant impact both intrapersonally and interpersonally.

Another concept in the research is "felt power," which is different than your felt sense of personal power. Instead of the power you actually have access to, felt power is the subjective experience of feeling powerful or powerless in social interactions. Some people hold significant power in society, yet they often *feel* powerless. I

---

2. https://www.ted.com/talks/amy_cuddy_your_body_language_may_shape_who_yo u_are?trigger=5s

3. Cuddy, A. J. C., Wilmuth, C. A., Yap, A. J., & Carney, D. (2015). Preparatory power posing affects nonverbal presence and job interview performance. Journal of Applied Psychology, 100 4, 1286–1295.

believe that in these cases, the felt sense of their personal power is missing. Felt power can influence emotions, behaviors, and interpersonal dynamics, impacting how we interact with others and perceive our own capabilities. Research[4] has shown that individuals who feel powerful are more likely to engage in prosocial behaviors, such as helping others and providing support. Conversely, those who feel powerless may withdraw or exhibit defensive behaviors. Ultimately, your embodied, felt sense of your personal power, as well as your "felt power," has a dramatic impact on how you perceive and engage with the world—and it is intimately tied to your beliefs.

Beliefs

Our beliefs about our power originate from various sources and are shaped by multiple factors throughout life. Many of our beliefs about power stem from the systemic lens and socialization we experienced growing up, which means they are largely subconscious. These socialization experiences include our early family interactions and dynamics, media influences, cultural norms, school structures, and peer groups.

What have you been told about power? How have you experienced power, and how has that shaped your beliefs about it? Mahatma Gandhi said, "Your beliefs become your thoughts, your thoughts become your words, your words become your actions, your actions become your habits, your habits become your values, your values become your destiny." Beliefs about our power are taught explicitly or implicitly and then become internalized. When

4. Bombari, D., Mast, M. S., & Bachmann, M. (2017). Felt Power Explains the Link Between Position Power and Experienced Emotions. Emotion, 17, 55–66.

we don't take the time to examine our beliefs and their origins, it is akin to letting someone else direct our lives—it is a form of abandoning ourselves. Of course, examining our beliefs and adjusting them is easier said than done. We all have unconscious beliefs that shape how we think and act. But the more we can start to uncover and become curious about our beliefs, the more choices we have in how we live our lives.

One of the most impactful beliefs that we internalize is related to status power. We often take status power (an extrinsic valuation often originating from systems) and conflate it with our personal power. We essentially adopt the extrinsic valuation as an intrinsic one. And we do this on both sides of the status power differential. This is what is known as internalized oppression and internalized superiority. When status is assigned to us, especially based on in-born traits, we can internalize its value, which impacts our personal power. For example, lighter skin color is often associated with up-status power in many societies. When we unconsciously accept the superiority narratives that have been created and reinforced by those societies, it leads to a sense of entitlement and a lack of awareness or understanding. Similarly, if we find ourselves in a down-status position and internalize the narratives associated with that down-status, it can lead to self-hatred, low self-esteem, and a belief in our own inferiority. We might accept unfair treatment or even participate in our own marginalization. Whether it is inferiority or superiority, the internalization of extrinsic valuations can interrupt our access to our rooted personal power.

While there are narratives that are damaging to our personal power, we can also adopt beliefs that increase our connection to inherent belongingness. These are the beliefs that lift us up, create more personal agency, and connect us with our worth. Regardless of the kind of belief, it is essential to remember that it can change over time, and we can choose what we believe. So what do you choose to believe? And do your beliefs lead to rooted personal power or socialized personal power? We must heed Ghandi's warning and choose carefully, as beliefs ultimately determine how we show up in the world and how we experience life.

Capabilities

Your personal power is composed of all of the things you are capable of as a human being that you were either born with or have developed over time. Capabilities, in the context of power, refer to the opportunities individuals have to achieve what they value. They represent the potential and conditions that enable you to impact or influence the world, which can involve personality traits, skills, talents, characteristics, cognitive or physical abilities, or even aspects such as emotional maturity, integrity, somatic awareness, or spiritual connection.

As capability theorists, Amartya Sen and Martha Nussbaum point out, our life outcomes are not just about having the potential, but having the real freedom, resources, and environment to develop and exercise that potential. Sen and Nussbaum assess well-being based on people's real opportunities ("capabilities") to achieve what they value ("functionings"), emphasizing freedom and their unique aspirations. Functionings is an interesting concept that refers to the actual states of being and doing that a person achieves (e.g., being well-nourished, being healthy, being educated, participating in social life). Capabilities are the potential to achieve these functionings.

Ultimately, capabilities are what enable personal power. Having a wider range of capabilities directly enhances a person's agency. More options mean more freedom to choose and act in line with our values. Whereas a lack of capabilities restricts agency, limiting what we can realistically do.

It is essential to note (and this is an integral part of capability theory) that social justice is a crucial aspect of capability, as we cannot always determine the environments or resources to which we have access. Our capabilities are limited to the extent to which a system provides its constituents with the freedom, opportunity, and resources to develop those capabilities. If a system restricts these for some or all of the people in a system, their capabilities, thus their personal power, will also be restricted.

Recognition

Have you ever been skiing as an adult and seen a four-year-old zooming past you without poles? It's both a humbling experience and a reminder of the fearlessness of youth. When we are children, before we are socialized away from ourselves, we each have an inherent knowing of our rooted personal power, even if we didn't understand it or have the words to describe it. Children are creative and unrestricted by social convention and the fears that tether adults—they say and do the thing they want, even if it falls outside of social norms. Adults have the challenge of navigating socialization and the expectations and responsibilities that we inherit from systems, while also trying to maintain some connection to who we are and what we're meant to do in this life.

I used the word recognition intentionally because of its origin: "to know again." So how do we come to "know again" our personal power? In a given moment, do you recognize your personal power or not? Do other people recognize your personal power or not? And if someone recognizes your personal power or not, how does that influence your own capacity and your ability to access it?

When we are taught that we are powerless, for example, we may overlook that we still have the presence of personal power. Or if the person we are relating to in a given moment has a lot more role or status power than we do, we may focus on our lack of role or status power and then fail to recognize our personal power.

Access

You could have a huge toolbox of capabilities, but if you don't have access to them, then, in effect, it doesn't matter. Brene Brown talks about how shame is like a tornado or hurricane that sweeps away whatever toolbox of skills we have to address challenges. You can have a fantastic toolbox of skills, but when shame comes through, it just takes away your ability to access your personal power. So things like shame, isolation, and being excluded, oppressed, or ostracized influence our ability to access our capabilities.

It is also important to note that being in an abusive or oppressive relationship can not only prevent the development of our capabilities but also our ability to access them. Even being ignored or dismissed can have a profound effect on a person's access to personal power. Research, including the work of Kluger & DeNisi (1996), demonstrates that when an audience is disengaged or instructed to ignore a presenter, it creates a feedback vacuum that undermines the presenter's performance.[5] Positive feedback—such as an engaged audience—can significantly improve performance and self-efficacy. When an audience is actively engaged—through eye contact, nodding, questions, or affirmations—it signals approval and validation, which can increase the presenter's confidence, re-

---

5. Kluger, A. N., & DeNisi, A. (1996). The effects of feedback interventions on performance: A historical review, a meta-analysis, and a preliminary feedback intervention theory. Psychological Bulletin, 119(2), 254-284. DOI: 10.1037/0033-2909.119.2.254

duce anxiety, and enhance their ability to communicate effectively. Conversely, negative or absent feedback, such as a disengaged or distracted audience, can hinder performance by creating self-doubt, reducing motivation, and impairing cognitive functioning. This feedback-performance loop highlights how others' engagement with us can either amplify or diminish our access to personal power.

What prevents you from accessing your personal power? And how do the relationships and systems you are in enhance or inhibit access to your personal power?

Expression

And then finally there's expression. Expression is the unique way each of us manifests our personal power. How we express our personal power looks different for each individual. An introverted person's expression might look really different than an extroverted person's. However, it is even more than that, as we possess a unique combination of capabilities, varying degrees of access at different times, and diverse ways in which we choose to express our personal power in the world.

Contrary to how dominant culture or systems would have us think, there is no right or wrong in our expression of personal power. I see so many women enter high leadership positions and manifest in very masculine ways. Because men have been given more access to role power (due to their gender's status), we think that the way men have occupied leadership is what leadership looks like—what *power* looks like. Part of the beauty of personal power is that we get to discover our own unique expression of it. Again, from Rubin: "Attuned choice by attuned choice, your entire life is a form of self-expression. You exist as a creative being in a creative universe. A singular work of art."[6] What is your unique expression of *your* personal power?

Types of Personal Power

Personal power is both inborn and can be developed over time. As it develops, there are two distinct manifestations of it. I think of it growing down and in, and growing up and out—two different directions of growth that are equally important. The two types of personal power I've mentioned previously are rooted personal power and socialized personal power.

Depending on where we look or what we focus on, personal power—our influence — can be sourced from two different places. We can be focused on what is outside of ourselves or what is happening internally. In the context of personal power, being internally or externally referenced refers to the sources from which we derive our sense of control, motivation, and decision-making. Being internally referenced, we tend to access our rooted personal power, and when we are externally referenced, we tend to access our socialized personal power.

Socialized Personal Power

When we are externally referenced, we derive our sense of agency from external sources, such as societal norms, expectations from others, or external rewards. It is from this place that we follow the rules and pay attention to how we are "fitting in." From an externally referenced place, our actions and decisions are often influenced by how we perceive others will evaluate us or by the

---

6. Rubin, R. (2023). The creative act: A way of being. Penguin Press, p. 3.

standards set by external authorities. When we are accessing our socialized power, we often compare ourselves to others, which can lead to a focus on meeting external expectations rather than pursuing our personal goals.

However, just as we need our ego, our socialized personal power is necessary for navigating the world. Through socialization we can learn how to share our toys, eat the right foods, and manage our money. This socialized personal power supports us in living in relationship with others and surviving the communities and environments we live in. The problem arises when we become overly reliant on socialized personal power or believe that the knowledge and experiences of others are the sole source of our personal power. When we fail to look inside, to discover the wisdom we were born with, we miss one of the most important aspects of what it means to be alive.

Rooted Personal Power

When our influence in the world comes from an internally referenced place, we are turning toward our inner connection and our inherent belongingness. This is where "the still, small voice" is found—you could call it intuition, instinct, gut feelings, or sixth sense. When we are internally referenced, we rely on our own beliefs, values, and standards to guide our actions and decisions. This means that our sense of agency is derived from internal factors such as self-efficacy, personal goals, core values, spiritual connection, and intrinsic motivation. When we engage our rooted personal power, we tend to be more resilient in the face of challenges and view setbacks as opportunities for learning and growth.

However, our inner guidance or inner knowing doesn't always align with what is outside of ourselves. My friend and colleague,

Thea Elijah, recently introduced me to the work of Herman Witkin, an American psychologist. Witkin's research[7] focused on individual differences in how people perceive their environment. He discovered that individuals who are "field dependent" (externally referenced) tend to rely heavily on the surrounding visual field when judging an object's orientation. The overall context influences them, and they struggle to distinguish an object from its background. Whereas individuals who are "field independent" (internally referenced) are better able to separate an object from its background and judge its orientation independently of the surrounding context—they are less influenced by the overall field.

This concept was illustrated by Witkin in the slanted room experiment. I was immediately drawn to the concept because of its ability to illustrate how I understand the distinction between rooted and socialized personal power. In the experiment, participants were invited into a room that was tilted at an angle. The participants were asked to sit in a chair in a way they perceived as the "true" upright position. Field-dependent (externally referenced) individuals tended to rely on external cues, such as the tilt of the room, and sat in the chair aligned with the room's tilt. Field-independent (internally referenced) individuals relied more on their internal sense of balance and body orientation and sat in the chair upright.

I love this somatic metaphor for what it is like when we are accessing our rooted versus our socialized personal power. Are we primarily orienting ourselves according to cues from our environment and the systems we are in? Or are we coming from an internal sense of knowing? The truth is that we need both types of knowing

---

7. For further reading on Witkin's contributions, you can refer to:- Witkin, H. A., & Goodenough, D. R. (1981). "Cognitive Styles: Essence and Origins." Psychological Issues. & Witkin, H. A., Oltman, P. K., Raskin, E., & Karp, S. (1971). "Cognitive Styles: A Review and Integration." Psychological Bulletin.

and both types of personal power. The question is: are you aware of where you are coming from in a given moment? And do you regularly use both to inform how you show up in the world?

Reflection Questions:

1. Can you think of a moment when you felt a strong sense of personal power? What did that feel like? What sensations or emotions arise when you connect with your rooted personal power? How might this practice help you navigate challenging situations?

2. What beliefs do you hold about power? Where do these beliefs come from (e.g., family, culture, systems)? Are there any beliefs that limit your sense of personal power? How might you challenge or reframe these beliefs to align more closely with your rooted personal power?

3. How do you uniquely express your personal power? Are there ways you feel pressured to conform to external expectations rather than expressing your authentic self? How can you embrace your unique expression of personal power more fully?

4. Can you identify moments when you've relied on socialized personal power versus rooted personal power? How do these two types of power show up in your life, and how can you balance them?

5. What barriers (internal or external) prevent you from ful-

ly accessing your personal power? How can you address these barriers to create more opportunities for growth and expression?

10

Collective Power

"*Never doubt that a small group of thoughtful, committed citizens can change the world; indeed, it's the only thing that ever has.*" - Margaret Mead

"*Collective power relies on everyone using the power they have.*" - Ted Rau

"*Emergence is what happens when the properties of the parts of a system do not fully explain the properties of the whole.*" - Peter Corning

Collective - *a community that forms for a specific purpose*

Collective Power - *power that comes from gathering strength and influence from multiple*
sources to promote a common interest.

I was just listening to a song called *Beautiful Day* by Amos Lee, and it reminded me of a concert I went to with my partner and our friends, Ames and Kyla. It was a double concert with the Indigo Girls and Amos Lee. I had never seen Amos Lee in concert, and I hadn't really listened to a lot of his music (I went for the Indigo

Girls, who I've seen in concert at least a dozen times). What impressed me most about Amos wasn't just the music, which was good. It was the way that he showed up on stage in relation to the other band members. In my experience, a band will feature the lead singer, especially in a concert in the United States. All of your attention goes to the lead singer(s), and the rest of the band is kind of in the background. But with Amos Lee, he featured each of the musicians on the stage as much as he did himself. I've never had that experience before at a concert, where I had a distinct sense of each person on the stage and what they brought to the music *throughout the concert.* I had a sense of each individual's distinct musical genius or brilliance. It was an incredible experience and a beautiful expression of how to do power-with or how to show up differently so that everyone in the group, whether you're on stage, at work, or in any group, has a distinct sense of each person.

This experience also made me realize that when each person in a music group is able to fully tap into their power, something emerges from the music that wasn't predetermined or pre-planned. I think jazz illustrates this perfectly. I'm no expert in jazz music, but from what I understand, jazz is a dynamic art form with a unique emergent quality. Each musician possesses deep expertise of their instrument, but the magic of jazz happens through active listening and the spontaneous response to one another. While they may begin with a predetermined melody or chord progression, that structure melts away, replaced by a shared consciousness—a collective intuition that guides the music to unexpected places. Improvisation takes center stage, with each musician contributing their unique voice, reacting to and building upon the contributions of others. This creates a complex interplay where no single player dominates, but rather, all voices contribute to a dynamic, evolving whole. The result is what Kurt Koffka called a "whole that is *other* than the sum of its parts." The beauty of jazz lies in this unpredictable journey, where the music takes on a life of its own, driven by the power of collaboration and the freedom of individual expression. It's a powerful illustration of emergence and collectives: individual mastery, active listening, and collaborative engagement giving rise to something entirely new.

Music groups are a compelling example of collectives and collective power because they demonstrate how individuals can achieve more together than they could alone. In this chapter, we will explore the characteristics of collectives and how they contribute to the manifestation of collective power. I often use the metaphor of a music group as a neutral entry (who doesn't like music?) to illustrate this important aspect of human culture. Collectives are not only necessary for our functioning as human beings, but they are also fundamentally attractive to us (even to those of us who are introverted). Collectives are also invaluable as they tend to form around what is emergent, which is fundamental to the health of systems.

What is a collective?

Essentially, a collective is a community with a purpose. Collectives are comprised of a number of individuals who cooperatively combine their personal, status, and/or role power to further a mutual cause or agenda. Sometimes that mutual cause or agenda is in response to systemic power. The most obvious examples of this are unions, social or political movements, voting, and community organizing, all of which are dedicated to changing or improving systems. Other examples of collective power occur within the context of a system or in an effort to coexist alongside a system. In collectives like scientific or artistic collaborations, religious movements, professional organizations, fan communities, or open-source software development, there is a common interest that forms a sub-culture or even counter-culture that seeks to create or improve what already exists, as well as satisfy social needs. The common thread among these diverse examples is the collaborative effort of individuals or groups to achieve shared objectives, often resulting in significant impact that transcends individual capabilities and helps to evolve what has already been configured.

What is Collective Power?

The effect or influence that collectives create happens through collective power. Collective power refers to the ability of individuals to come together and achieve shared goals through unity, collaboration, and a shared purpose. It is a transformative force that can drive social, political, and cultural change, amplifying the voices of marginalized groups and creating resilience in the face of challenges.

The most potent effect of collectives is the influence that comes from gathering different types of power from diverse sources. This influence can be used to create support for communities, promote an idea, or inspire innovation or creativity. However, it can also be used to promote hate, marginalize others, manipulate public opinion, or incite violence. Or they can simply form to maintain the status quo and reinforce stasis. The influence of collectives can be used for many different ends. Hate groups form alongside support groups, self-serving cults are just as likely to form as spiritual movements that espouse altruism. Lynch mobs, homeowner's associations, and protests are all expressions of collective power.

Collective power can also be used to create balance in systems and keep systemic power in check. In fact, collective power is the only type of power that can change systems. Individuals may have a big impact, like Mahatma Ghandi or Martin Luther King, Jr., but these individuals alone did not change systems. What they were good at was leading and inspiring the formation of collectives that could, and did, change systems in significant ways. As Margaret Meade suggests in the opening quote, even small, dedicated collectives can have a huge impact. In fact, the biggest systemic changes have often come about with very little formal power. Dacher Keltner said, "Many of the most significant changes in our history—the adoption of women's suffrage, civil rights legislation, the free speech movement and its influence upon the protests against the Vietnam War, the overthrow of apartheid, the rise of gay rights—were brought about by people who lacked economic, political, and military might; they changed the world without coercive force."[1] By organizing effectively, collectives can change systems slowly over time or in a short burst of time—and they don't need permission from systems.

Collective Power as Emergence

What allows collective power to keep systems in balance is that it is fundamentally emergent. It might be organized or take time to develop, but collective power typically emerges in response to its environment (which is often configured by systems). The emergence aspect of collective power can be a spontaneous burst of creativity or it could be a slow boil of rage. It can look like a social movement that reaches a boiling point, like the Black Lives Matter or #MeToo movements. Or it can look like the emergence

---

1. Keltner, D. (2016). The power paradox: How we gain and lose influence. Penguin Press, p. 20.

of Hip Hop, which began as a grassroots movement, with young people using music, dance, and graffiti to express their experiences and resist oppression. Perhaps one of the most powerful examples of emergent collective power is mutual aid. It is a form of grassroots, community-based support where people come together to meet each other's needs, often in the absence of adequate government or institutional assistance. Based on principles of solidarity, reciprocity, and collective care, it emerges in moments of crisis when existing systems fail to provide for people's basic needs. The magic in collective power is that it has the freedom to respond to whatever is arising and shift the over-reliance on systems.

Directions of Collective Power

What I've described so far is what I call externally focused collective power, which is usually related to the purpose of the collective. The externally focused collective power refers to the impact the collective has on the world. Most people hyperfocus on this kind of collective power, often to the detriment of the collective itself. Collectives with a strong purpose in the world may become so focused on external influences that they forget to tend to the internal influences within the collective. I see this a lot in my consulting work. There is limited time, energy, and resources, and it all gets used up toward their mission. The collective care, communication, and interpersonal relationships become neglected, and internal conflict and division take over, threatening the sustainability of the group.

Collective power includes the influence that the collective has on itself and its members. This is the collective power that happens internally among the members. How is the collective impacting the group's members? Are the individual members closer to their personal power or further away from it when they are inside the collective? The most extreme example of this happens in cults, which ultimately separate people from their personal power.

There are numerous books, articles, videos, and similar resources on collectives and externally focused collective power; however, I would like to highlight a few characteristics of collectives that influence *internal* collective power dynamics. It is one thing to form a collective, and quite another to sustain it long enough to bring about real change. Here are some of the characteristics of internal collective power: Collaboration and the Division of Responsibilities, Collective Identity, The Interpersonal Playout (Wisdom and folly), The Common Ground, and Personal Power Access.

Collaboration and the Division of Responsibilities

I have the challenging position of being the Executive Director of a small nonprofit that must wear many hats. I am also a recovering perfectionist who holds high standards for herself. This is not a good combination. I often find myself reluctant to collaborate or delegate because I am afraid that it won't be done well. Or the thought of teaching others how to do a task seems like it would take longer than just doing it myself. But I cannot do all of the things myself—nor should I. I have to actively remind myself to loosen my grip and turn toward the reality that collaboration can bring more creative excellence than any one person could accomplish—no matter how high their standards.

For example, in a music group, each member brings unique skills (e.g., singing, playing various instruments, songwriting) that complement one another. While some musicians are multi-talented and can play any of the roles, they can rarely do so simultaneously. And no matter how creative or talented their mind is, it is only one mind, with only one set of experiences and identities. When you bring multiple people together, you create a synergy of talents that produces a richer, more complex result than any individual could achieve alone.

When we have roles that are specialized (e.g., lead singer, drummer, guitarist), you allow for deep expertise and a division of responsibilities that can lead the group to function efficiently and focus on its strengths. And, when the responsibilities are shared, they don't feel as heavy. This is one of the beautiful things about collaboration. However, there must be a shared vision and collective identity for the various roles to come together as a collective.

Collective Identity

Collective identity and a shared vision are not just abstract concepts; they are practical tools that enable groups to function effectively, mobilize resources, and achieve their goals. They transform a collection of individuals into a powerful, cohesive force capable of driving change and expressing collective power. A strong sense of "us" fosters trust, cooperation, and commitment among members. This shared identity helps to overcome individual differences and motivates individuals to work towards common goals. It also helps define the boundaries of the group, clarifying who is included and who is not.

Similarly, a clearly defined and inspiring shared vision provides direction and purpose. It aligns individual efforts, ensuring that everyone is working towards the same objectives. A shared vision also helps to attract and retain members, as people are drawn to be part of something meaningful and impactful. Music groups often form around a common purpose, such as creating art, expressing ideas, or entertaining audiences. This shared vision unites members and drives their collective efforts. If one group member primarily wants to entertain, while another primarily wants to convey a deeper message through their music, they each need to be clear about their objectives to see if they can develop a shared vision that includes both, or if they need to look for another more suitable group.

The Dynamics of Wisdom and Folly

The next characteristic is that all collectives are subject to both **collective wisdom and collective folly,** which plays out not only on the interpersonal level but also at the level of the collective. I got these terms from the book, *The Power of Collective Wisdom and the Trap of Collective Folly*, by Briskin, Erickson, Ott and Callanan, which I highly recommend. They said,

> "While some writers speak of collective intelligence, we use the term collective wisdom to reflect a quality of group understanding that is neither of the intellect alone nor of any individual alone. When this knowing and sense of right action emerges, it does so from deep within the individual participants, from within the collective awareness of the group, and from within the larger field of spiritual, cultural and institutional forces that surround any group actvitiy."[2]

The feeling of connection, room for generative conflict, willingness to be in the unknown, trust, and psychological safety are some of the things that come to mind for me when I think of collective

---

2. Briskin, A., Erickson, S., Ott, J., & Callanan, T. (2009). *The power of collective wisdom and the trap of collective folly*. Berrett-Koehler Publishers, p. 27.

wisdom. What are some other things that come to mind in your experience—when you have experienced collective wisdom? How do you know when you're in collective wisdom?

One of the things I appreciate most about their book is the certainty that any group is capable of finding collective wisdom—if they are willing to find it *together*. It is just as possible as collective folly, which stands in the way of our living in wisdom. We know when collective wisdom is present and when collective wisdom has been pushed out. And often, the thing that is most evident when collective wisdom is no longer present is a sense of 'us versus them' or 'me versus you.' When we fall into collective folly, there are certain patterns that emerge. One is separation and fragmentation. This can manifest as splitting or polarization, which is so evident in our world today. Briskin et al. said this division "often arises from unexamined assumptions that take on the qualities of truth. . .or hidden under the veil of false unity."[3]

This leads us to the most subversive manifestation of collective folly, which they describe as false agreement and the appearance of unity. This arises from what the collective is unwilling to acknowledge, which usually results in some kind of detriment to the group. In Buddhism, this is called "willful ignorance," which refers to the deliberate choice to ignore or avoid information, facts, or evidence that could challenge one's beliefs, opinions, or actions. It is a conscious decision to remain uninformed, maintain comfort, avoid cognitive dissonance, or protect one's worldview. Unlike ignorance that arises from a lack of access to information, willful ignorance is an active refusal to engage with knowledge that might require a change in perspective or behavior. In the case

---

3. Briskin, A., Erickson, S., Ott, J., & Callanan, T. (2009). *The power of collective wisdom and the trap of collective folly.* Berrett-Koehler Publishers, p. 190.

of collectives, we choose the appearance of unity or agreement to maintain the illusion of group cohesion rather than confronting the divergence or difference in the group. We prefer to uphold the illusion that we are the same than to risk being different. When difference feels threatening, you know you're falling into that version of collective folly.

All collectives, no matter how good the aim or how wonderful the people are, are subject to that. I have found in my experience with consulting, in particular, that the more mission-driven or spiritual the aim of a group, the greater the potential for collective folly to happen (and to be harder to undo if it does) because people are more focused on the group's goals than on what is actually happening in practice. In collectives where there is pressure to be and do the right thing, it is tempting to adopt the persona of goodness, rather than evaluating whether we are actually doing good or not. If we believe that we're good people, do we actually track that we're doing good? Or do we just wear the identity of "good?" I also see this with excessive politeness or conflict avoidance in some teams I work with. When I hear "we never have conflict," that is always a red flag for me.

To reiterate: Every collective has the potential to achieve collective wisdom, but it also has the capacity to spiral into collective folly. The difference often lies in how well we attend to the container of the group—the shared space that holds the collective together. Even when a leader or facilitator is aware of what's happening, divisions within the group and the tendency to replicate the very dynamics we're trying to combat can still emerge. This happens because, despite our best intentions, we're all socialized in similar ways within a single culture. Unfortunately, this is a common pitfall, and it's why many collectives struggle to sustain themselves. If we're constantly forming groups only to see them dissolve, it takes ten times as much energy to keep rebuilding rather than forming, sustaining, and learning how to "dance" together over time.

So what do we have to do to find a healthy dance between wisdom and folly? We bring our diversity to the table, and we find the common ground.

The Common Ground

My favorite stand-up comedian is Hannah Gadsby. I have essentially memorized all of their shows because they are my go-to when I'm feeling down. One of the brilliant things they do at the beginning of every show is they take the time to create a common ground. They inform the audience about what they will be presenting and help them develop a shared sense of the context and background before the actual show begins. This is most exemplified in their 2020 show called *Douglas* (you should watch all of their shows, but that one is a good example of what I'm talking about). Somehow, they accomplish this while also being hilarious.

When we hear "let's find a common ground," we usually think of compromise or finding a mutual place where we can agree, or at least agree to disagree. However, what I mean by common ground here is slightly different. **The common ground refers to our collective reality—what we all understand to be true.**

The Common Ground

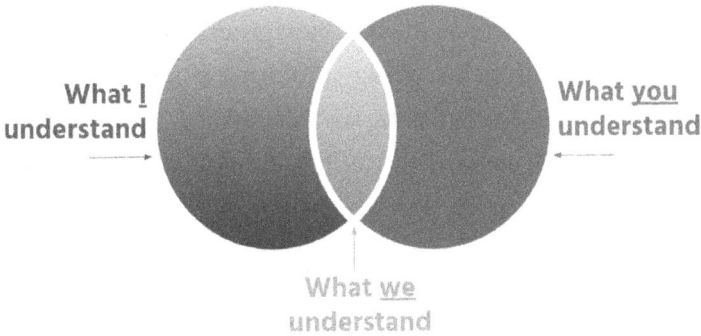

What **I** understand

What **you** understand

What **we** understand

In a collective, it's common for certain individuals to possess knowledge or information that's relevant to the group, while others remain unaware. When this happens, that knowledge doesn't become part of the collective's common ground. Without transparency from leadership, the information they hold doesn't contribute to the group's shared understanding, and as a result, the collective can't move forward in unison. Imagine being new to a group or witnessing people whispering or sharing an inside joke you're not privy to—how does that feel? It's isolating, right? It creates a sense of not belonging. Conversely, if you're the one sharing the inside joke, it feels intimate and affirming, like you're strengthening a bond by referencing shared experiences. But what does this do to the collective as a whole? The reality is, when there's no common ground, fragmentation occurs, and true cohesion becomes impossible.

So we actually have to tend to the common ground, even when it's uncomfortable. This means sharing information openly, even if it risks upsetting people or feels uncertain. Ted Rau, one of the founders of Sociocracy for All and author of *Collective Power*, emphasizes this point. His work is particularly valuable for those in distributed governance models. Rau reminds us that we live in an imaginary, human-made world of mutually agreed-upon statements. In other words, the common ground is essential because it's built on mutually acknowledged information, which forms the foundation for decision-making and shared agency. *Let me repeat that: the common ground is crucial because mutually acknowledged information is the basis for decision-making and shared agency.* If the group doesn't share the same information, we can't make the best collective decisions.

Another insight from Rau is that inconsistencies in the common ground are deeply unsettling. When there's lying, gaslighting, or contradictions within the group, they're particularly troubling because they violate the common ground. These actions disrupt the shared understanding that holds the collective together, making it harder to maintain trust and cohesion. Therefore, maintaining a stable and transparent common ground is not just important—it's vital for the collective's success. And for each member of the collective to contribute to the common ground, we must be able to access our personal power.

Personal Power Access

When I teach about collective power, I often use an exercise called Collective Counting. The goal is simple: to count to 20 collectively without anyone interrupting anyone else. You have to rely on intuition, and each person must be really attuned to the group for it to work. Often the first few tries result invariably with interruptions. Then I ask everyone to pause and to root into their personal power. Almost always, there is a shift, and the very next try (or soon after), the group can reach the goal. Is this purely coincidental? Or is there something to it?

One of the key questions we're trying to address within collectives is: Are we co-creating a container that allows us to heal, be heard, tap into our personal power, and manifest something greater than the sum of our parts? Or are we unintentionally replicating the very systems we're trying to change? I see this happen far too often in collectives—people unknowingly recreate the dynamics they're seeking to transform.

This is why it's crucial to remember that when we talk about systemic power and the importance of collective power in changing those systems, we must first be rooted in our own personal power. Only then can we take active responsibility for our role within the collective and bring our full selves to the group. This is what allows us to show up in ways that make the collective wisdom manifest. So, it's essential to keep this in mind: personal power is the foundation for collective power, and both are necessary for creating sustainable, transformative change.

Learning to Dance with Collective Power

Being in a collective is like a dance. Think of a starling murmuration: it's not as if starlings form a cohesive whole and then stay that way forever. The murmuration is dynamic; sometimes the birds drift apart, but they always come back together. Similarly, there's no fixed point where a collective reaches wisdom and can then relax. Instead, there's a constant back-and-forth between collective wisdom and collective folly. To stay in this dance, we need a mindset shift—away from the individualistic mindset that dominates many cultures, especially in the West, and increasingly globally. This mindset is often ego-centered, dualistic (right vs. wrong, us vs. them), and rooted in fear and scarcity. When this individualistic approach infiltrates a collective, it can wreak havoc.

Instead, we need to learn how to engage in collective thinking, which involves holding complexity, embracing difference and diversity, and fostering generative conflict. This means being able to hold opposing ideas and perspectives in tension, moving toward a more strength-based approach to collaboration.

As Jacob Needleman, the American philosopher, once said, "We obviously cannot confront this tangled world alone. It takes no great insight to realize that we have no choice but to think together, ponder together in groups and communities. The question is how to do this, how to come together and think and hear each other in order to touch or be touched by the intelligence we need."

This is the call toward collective wisdom—the greater-than-the-sum-of-its-parts dynamic that emerges when we come together in meaningful ways. We must learn how to exist in collectives in ways that are nourishing, sustainable, and capable of driving systemic change. This requires a commitment to collective thinking, a willingness to root into your personal power and hold complexity, and the courage to embrace the dance of collective wisdom and folly.

Reflection Questions:

1. Have you been part of a collective that felt empowering and aligned with your values? What was your role in that collective, and how did it impact your sense of personal power? Conversely, have you been part of a collective that felt disempowering? What lessons did you take away from that experience?

2. Have you ever experienced a lack of Common Ground in a collective? What happens when there's a lack of transparency or shared information in a collective?

3. How do you see the relationship between personal power and the success of a collective?

4. How can groups stay attuned to the dance of wisdom and folly and avoid falling into patterns of folly? What practices or habits can help maintain collective wisdom?

5. How do you see collective power evolving, especially in the face of global challenges like climate change, social inequality, and political polarization? What role do you think collectives will play in shaping the future?

11

Universal Power

"*The most beautiful thing we can experience is the mysterious. It is the source of all true art and science.*" - Albert Einstein

"*The universe is under no obligation to make sense to you.*" - Neil Degrasse Tyson

Universal Power - *the effect or influence from a vast force beyond cognitive understanding that connects and encompasses all that exists.*

On my morning walks, I often listen to a podcast called The Living Myth with Michael Meade. He uses myth and ancient ideas to highlight what is often missing in our modern lives. In one of the episodes he recounted an ancient story that I thought was relevant to my attempt to talk about universal power. I've captured a version of the story here:

Jalaluddin Rumi, a highly respected scholar and teacher in 13th-century Persia, was known for his deep understanding of Islamic teachings. He often shared his wisdom by reading from his father's books, treasured texts filled with religious knowledge. One day, while reading aloud by a town fountain, a crowd gathered to listen.
Suddenly, a mysterious figure named Shams of Tabriz appeared.

Shams was a wandering mystic, a man who lived a life detached from conventional society. Shams was listening to Rumi and, in a dramatic and surprising move, Shams walked up to Rumi, snatched the book from his hands, and threw it into the fountain! This was shocking, not just because it was disrespectful, but also because in those days books were incredibly rare and precious – often painstakingly hand-copied, representing years of work and accumulated knowledge. Both Rumi and the crowd gasped.

Rumi, initially stunned, was deeply affected by Shams's actions. This seemingly destructive act marked the beginning of a profound and transformative friendship, and influenced Rumi's poetry that is so popular today.

I had become frustrated with this chapter and with the words that eluded me. After hearing this story I realized that I was trying to put into words what can't really be put into words. Shams understood that to connect with the eternal or universal, you can't get it from books—it has to be experienced directly. And yet here I am trying to write about it.

While Shams' and Rumi's aim was spiritual in nature, my inquiry is related to power. And the road to understanding power led me right to the place where all the things we can't yet fully grasp merge (like the divine, quantum physics, consciousness, highly complex systems, and unconditional love). I will not attempt to explain the unexplainable, but I do want to do a little exploration that will hopefully lead us to how universal power influences us (and all the other types of power).

Whenever I talk about universal power, no one asks questions as if they don't know what I'm talking about. They may challenge me and say that it is idealistic or too "woo-woo," or call it by different names, but I've never had anyone not know what I was generally referring to. We have an innate knowing of it if we allow ourselves to be in relationship with something larger than ourselves and systems. How do you think of "the Something Larger"? How do you acknowledge and nurture your relationship with that Something Larger? The influence from that Something Larger is what we call universal power. Whether you call it God, Collective Consciousness, Life, or All that Exists, there is a sense that something is present that is larger than us, but it is so vast and complex that it is beyond our cognitive grasp. Some of us are more comfortable with that than others. Tyson Yunkaporta said:

> "In a world where spirit has been colonised by cults, it is tempting to take refuge in reason, to the exclusion of all other knowledge. We do this because we need something to tether us to reality, but ironically the only things that do this well are superstitions and myths, because they inspire the supra-rational understandings needed to navigate complexity. We need right story more than ever as the world becomes less complex and more complicated, as it becomes increasingly difficult to know what is true, or whether truth even exists at all. The idea that no such thing as truth is true, but it's only half-true. There's no such thing as one truth. For every right story there are a hundred other right stories that contradict it, and we need to be comfortable with that."[1]

I'd like to propose one version of "right story" about universal power. These are presumptions about universal power just to give us a place from which to explore. One is that universal power, as

---

1. Yunkaporta, T. (2023). Right story, wrong story: Adventures in Indigenous thinking. Text Publishing, p. 268.

I have been discussing, is a mystery. It is the unknown and it is meant to be that way. It lives in the questions, the curiosity, the longing—not the answers. When we allow the unknown to be actively present, universal power is also present.

The next idea proposed here is that universal power is the power that connects all that is in existence—it is universal, as in pertaining to everyone and everything without exception. It is the glue between us, the entanglement of particles, the thread of connection. I like to think of it like qi, which is a fundamental concept in traditional Chinese medicine (TCM) and various schools of Chinese philosophy. Qi is considered a fundamental force permeating the universe and all living things. It's the animating principle, the force that gives life and structure to everything. It's not something separate from matter but rather intrinsic to it.

This leads me to the understanding that Universal Power is the power that encompasses and manifests through all the other types of power. As RUPI Facilitator, Maya Shaw Gale, says, it acts as a "through power" rather than an "add-on" type of power because it is in everything that exists. And when there is an intentional awareness and connection with universal power, the other types of power tend to show up differently.

An example of this is an experience I had recently when mystery and a connection to something larger than ourselves was not only allowed but served as a focal point for a group. Last summer we had our first Power & Equity Challenge in-person retreat. There were close to twenty of us, some more or less familiar with our work, but, for a variety of reasons felt called to take 7 days out of their lives to attend. I sent out an invitation prior to the retreat to the participants inviting them to reflect on what the "something larger" is for them and to find a symbol, an object of some kind, that represented it. Some people jokingly asked if they were inadvertently joining a cult. I wasn't surprised by the comment as I also had to confront the discomfort of exploring the spiritual in a secular context by offering the prompt. But there was something telling me that it was essential for the group that this be a focal point. I had even explored that discomfort with the other facilitators, secretly hoping for a reason to not venture too far into the metaphysical. Fortunately, none of the facilitators blinked an eye at my request. They all agreed that it was important to bring in universal power in a personal way.

So, on the first day of the retreat, we created a circle of seats and in the center of the room we placed a circular cloth in the middle. We invited everyone to place their sacred object on the cloth. Each person was able to say however much or little about the object they wanted with a prompt around what it represented for them. Every person brought a very different kind of object—from natural elements like a stone or sand, to personal objects like photos or drawings.

What I find amazing is that the symbols didn't have to be the same for us to have a similar idea of what we were referring to, of what we were orienting to. By making our personal connection to universal power the first thing we did as a group and the focal point of our physical space, we invited a different energy into the room. From my view, this was an intentional request for the "Something Larger" to help us hold the space—for universal power to have a doorway to enter. It was also an invitation for me as a facilitator to bring my personal power and role power to rest in something larger than myself. It was both a surrender *and* a fuller acceptance of my role power. For the group it was a container that was larger and more personal than anything we could have constructed and maintained as facilitators.

The outcome of inviting space for universal power to have its influence was bigger than I can fully explain. For myself, I felt more capable of holding the considerable responsibility of facilitating a diverse group of people who were directly confronting the challenges of status and systemic power. In that space, universal power was like the glue between my personal power and my role power. It gave it flexibility and strength. It is the stuff that allows us, as Dr. Barstow says, "to stay in our heart while standing in our strength"—not a skill or our personal power alone. It felt like the presence of universal power allowed us to stretch beyond our egos into our higher selves.

Ultimately, universal power serves as the foundation of our inherent belongingness—it is the stuff we are rooted in. We've talked about the importance of rooted personal power—universal power provides the soil into which those roots spread, get nourished, and thrive. It is also a container infinitely bigger than all the systems in the world combined. Whenever I feel overwhelmed by systems or the pain of the world, I try to remember this. For a long time, I had a picture of the solar system as my computer's wallpaper. Nerdy, yes. But it reminded me that I am a speck on a speck in an ever-expanding universe more infinite than I can even imagine. It invited the perspective that there is something much, much larger than anything happening on earth.

This is the importance of including universal power in the conversation about social power dynamics. It is easy to get caught in the heaviness and destruction that power can bring. It is easy to feel powerless in the face of big systems and damaging policies. It is easy to forget how small systems are in the span of the universe.

The Whole of the Configurative and Emergent

I have mentioned in both the systemic and collective power chapters about the complementary forces of the configurative and the emergent. Some types of power lend themselves toward one or the other, but universal power represents their convergence - the dynamic whole. You can think of universal power as the influence that promotes the healthy balance of the configurative and the emergent. As we have already discussed, the interplay between emergence and configuration is a dynamic between two forces, much like yin and yang. Too much focus on configuration (order) can stifle creativity and innovation, while too much focus on emergence (chaos) can lead to instability. A healthy system balances both, allowing for both creativity and stability.

So when we need help promoting the healthy flow of these two dynamic forces, calling on universal power is key—in ourselves, in our relationships, in collectives and systems. It will give us the fortitude to sustain access to our personal power and create the change we want to see in our lives and in our world.

I'd like to end with an excerpt from one of my favorite episodes of Michael Meade's podcast which I feel points as directly as one can to universal power. It is called *The Sacred Fifth* from the Living Myth Podcast:

Back at the beginning, they say, the twin culture heroes of the Navajo found a little reed and began to follow its axis and it led them all the way to the house of heaven. On this path of exploration, they undergo many trials and they endure much confusion and hardships. But they return with the sacred healing device. The device they received while in the house of heaven, involved a technique from making sand paintings. Each time they would make a sand painting, they would place the sacred corn plant at the center, depicting it as a giant plant, through the center of which the ancestors had crawled through the four worlds that eventually led them to this world, the Fifth World.

Each of the first four worlds had its own color. But the Fifth World was the only one where all the colors and all the species came together. In the Fifth World, everything is present but not complete. And humans participate in the ongoing making of the world. The incompleteness of the world can lead to many levels of confusion and chaos, but also many kinds of sickness and illness. Implicit in the myth is the understanding that whatever the current conflict, or confusion, or illness might be, the causes of it exist on more than simply the physical plane. Whether the situation involves an ailing person or a sick society, healing requires reorientation to the center and the invisible axis of the world. In other words, the root problem is that the person or the society has wandered too far away from the branches and roots of the sacred plant, which is the center and the source of life. . .

When the Navajo people name the current iteration of life on the earth as the Fifth World, they are tapping into a deep sense of both mythology and cosmology. The fifth is the quintessence in Latin, the quinta essentia, or the fifth essence, that holds all the other essences of life together. When people say the four directions, there is something missing, not something accidental, but something essential, and that is the fifth direction, which also can be called here, the place without which all four other directions disappear. In terms of sacred technology, whenever we are fully present in a place, it becomes the center, not just the center of our interest, but the center of the cosmos. So the fifth is here, the center where we are now. And as the central place of being, it was also known as this Sacred Fifth or the Secret Fifth.

The fifth, as the quintessential place of essence and being, was under-stood by most traditional cultures. The ancient Irish also had myths about the Secret Fifth, that could be the source of healing and renewal for both individuals and an entire culture. Finding a connection to the Sacred Fifth was a necessary solution whenever people became conflicted, and the world seemed to be falling into chaos and despair. . .

So when the problems of life become huge and overwhelming, when *the tasks seem impossible, and the conflicts become intractable, when the whole thing seems hopeless, and people feel increasingly helpless, then the time has come again to seek for the missing center. For when we are in touch with this mythical, mystical center, everything becomes possible again. And the wonder and the beauty and the essence of the world can return again to our attention.*

Reflection Questions:

- What does the "Something Larger" look/feel/sound like to you?

- What areas of your life feel stuck or chaotic? In which areas of your life would it feel supportive to call on universal power to help balance these forces?

- Are there practices (e.g., meditation, prayer, sex, time in nature, ritual, active listening, creative expression) that could help you build relationship with the "Something Larger" or tap into universal power to promote the healthy flow of configuration and emergence?

- What practices could support the presence of universal power in your relationships, collectives, and systems?

-*Part Two*-

Becoming
Power-Conscious

12

Power Consciousness

"Nearly all men can stand adversity, but if you want to test a man's character, give him power." - Abraham Lincoln

"Awareness requires a rupture with the world we take for granted; then old categories of experience are called into question and revised." - Shoshana Zuboff

"The most fundamental aggression to ourselves, the most fundamental harm we can do to ourselves, is to remain ignorant by not having the courage and the respect to look at ourselves honestly and gently." - Pema Chödrön

Power-Consciousness: *an awareness and understanding of how power operates within relationships and systems and how it shapes individuals' and groups' experiences and opportunities.*

Power is not an easy thing to confront. And, while cognitively understanding the types of power and transforming our language of it is an important step in the wayfinding process, it's certainly not the whole journey. This section of the book is all about the process of becoming power-conscious so that we have the awareness of what shapes power for good—and what could lead us away from or toward right-relationship. Part Two looks at the complexities of systemic power and the power differential, the shadows of power, and the Phases of Power-Consciousness.

But before we get into all of those very rich topics, I'd like to give a little background on how the term "power-conscious" came about. After delving into numerous diversity, equity, inclusion, and belonging methods and approaches, my colleague, Regina Smith, and I found that we were struggling to get at both a broader and more nuanced picture of power. We often found ourselves focusing on just one or two types of power, and there wasn't a precise word for focusing on the types of power collectively. We aimed to fill this void by introducing the concept of **Power-Consciousness**, a crucial state of awareness that encompasses all forms of power influencing equity and health in relationships and groups. I've found that if we just focus on one type or dimension of power, we may miss some of the nuances of the intersections of the six different types of power—to the detriment of our own understanding and our relationships.

At its core, power-consciousness is about transformation—at all levels (personal, interpersonal, collective and systemic). It challenges us to rethink our assumptions about power, to question the status quo, and to envision new ways of relating to one another. By developing power-consciousness, we not only become more aware of social power dynamics, but also more capable of shaping them in ways that promote the kinds of experiences, relationships, and structures we wish to see in the world. This transformative potential is what makes power-consciousness such a vital part of the wayfinding journey. It empowers us to navigate the complexities of power with clarity, compassion, and purpose.

If you imagine relationship as a boat that carries people together, communication would be one of the oars—it helps us to move together, to call out obstacles, to decide which way to turn. But alone, it's not enough. Without a second oar—power-consciousness—the boat either drifts in circles, takes longer to get where we want to go, or one person ends up doing most of the work. Power-consciousness is what lets us row in sync, not just with each other, but aware of the currents beneath us: who has more strength today, whose hands are blistered from past journeys, whose voice gets drowned out by the wind.

Many relationships become unhealthy or harmful, not for lack of talking, but for lack of this deeper awareness. We mistake harmony for equity—assuming that if no one is shouting, the balance must be fair. But power doesn't disappear when we ignore it. Instead, it goes underground, shaping interactions in ways we don't notice until the boat starts leaking. But when both people learn the importance of the second oar, something shifts. You start to notice ways the relationship is steering off course or the stories we've been taught to tell ourselves about others. This awareness doesn't ruin the ride; it makes the journey to right-relationship possible.

In order to develop power-consciousness, we need to become aware of all the devastating and delightful ways power gets shaped. We have to take a hard look at ourselves and of systems—to continually reflect on our interactions and question our assumptions. This requires humility and a willingness to be uncomfortable. The paradox is that power-consciousness *deepens* intimacy even as it highlights difference. When two people can say, "I know my trauma makes me withdraw, and that leaves you lonely," or "I see how my privilege lets me overlook your needs," the relationship stops being a performance of equality and becomes a living negotiation of care. Trust grows not in spite of these acknowledgments, but *because* of them.

And, of course, the more help we have from Universal Power, the more capable we are of stretching beyond our egos into our higher self—which is when we have the clearest power-consciousness. It moves beyond our cognitive understanding and we start to feel our way through the complexities of power dynamics. This, as we will see, is the key to wayfinding to right-relationship.

Finally, power-consciousness teaches discernment. Not every boat is worth boarding. Some people will insist the second oar is unnecessary—that "love" or "professionalism" or "family" means ignoring historical contexts, difference, and identity. But right-relationship belongs to those willing to see the whole river: the currents that divide us, the bridges we've burned, and the possibility of moving—together—toward something new. The choice is ours: Will we paddle in circles, or learn to row with both oars in hand?

I'm going to invite you to feel, sense, and intuit as well as think about the concepts in this second section of the book, which is meant to challenge you—to give you an opportunity to stretch a little more around power. At times I will ask you to suspend judgment and other times to be judgmental and examine for yourself what your beliefs are. These are cognitive exercises meant to invite you into new ways of thinking. Doing the exercises and answering the reflection questions could be even more powerful in a group—to bounce ideas and be challenged in new ways. Power-consciousness, after all, is best developed in relationship!

13

The Intersections of Power

"Power, like energy, must be regarded as continually passing from any one of its forms into any other, and it should be the business of social science to seek the laws of such transformations. - Bertrand Russell

"Intersectionality is a lens through which you can see where power comes and collides, where it interlocks and intersects." - Kimberlé Crenshaw

"You think that because you understand "one" that you must therefore understand "two" because one and one make two. But you forget that you must also understand "and." - Sufi story

As I have learned about being in relationship over the years, I have made many mistakes. One of my most repeated mistakes was not understanding that there is more to a relationship than just two individuals, or even the sum of two individuals. There is the relationship, or connection, itself that needs tending. The same is true for the connection between different types of power. The Sufi quote above beautifully encapsulates the essence of intersectionality and the conversation about the intersections of power. The magic—and the challenge—is in understanding the "and," the relationship between those things. We can't just look at personal power or systemic power on their own and think we've got the whole picture. We need to look at how these forms of power interact, overlap, and intersect with each other.

Intersectionality, a term coined by legal scholar Kimberlé Crenshaw in the late 1980s, has become a vital framework for understanding how multiple forms of oppression and privilege intersect in people's lives. At its core, intersectionality examines how race, gender, class, sexuality, ability, and other identities overlap and interact exponentially, shaping individuals' experiences in complex and often invisible ways. Importantly, as Crenshaw notes in the quote above, intersectionality is not just about status-based identities—it's also about power. How power operates at different levels, how it is distributed, and how it intersects with our identities is crucial to understanding the full picture of social power dynamics.

In this chapter, we'll explore how the types of power are inextricably connected. Even though I have separated the types of power into different chapters in Part One of the book, you cannot separate them in reality. We might understand what personal power is—our ability to influence our own lives—and we might grasp systemic power—the large structures that shape society. But to really see how power works, we have to dig into the "and"—like how personal power is shaped by systemic power, or how collective power can challenge systemic inequalities. It's the same with intersectionality. We can't just look at race or gender separately and think we understand someone's experience. It's the intersection of these identities—the "and"—that creates unique experiences of privilege or oppression that go beyond a single identity alone, or even just the addition of the two. A Black woman's experience, for instance, isn't just about race plus gender; it's about how those identities interact in ways that can't be understood by looking at them individually. Just because we understand "one" doesn't mean we understand "two," and just because we understand one form of power or one identity doesn't mean we get the full picture. Power is relational—it's about how things connect and influence each other. This is what intersectionality is all about: uncovering how multiple systems of power and oppression intersect to shape our lives.

Although it may be an oversimplification, I like to think of the types of power as nested, with systemic power serving as a container (and universal power, the even wider "container").

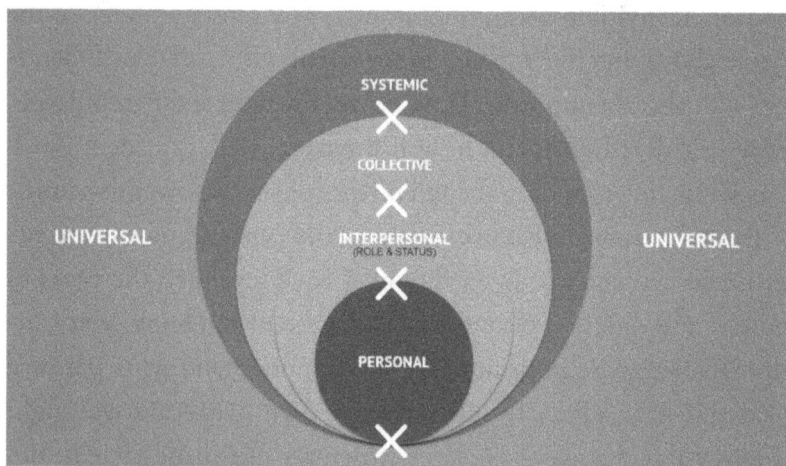

As we discussed in the Types of Power chapter, containers shape their contents. In this case, each type of power influences the others—especially at the points of intersection. In this section, I'll focus on four intersection points: Universal-Personal, Personal-Interpersonal, Interpersonal-Collective, and Collective-Systemic. I like to think of these intersections as the places where the greatest influence is exerted. Each intersection point flows in both directions, so it's not limited to just one direction of influence. This is an important point, as it means we can change how power manifests in our lives, relationships, and systems.

Also at play at the intersections of power are the forces of emergence and configuration. Emergence brings spontaneity, creativity, and change, while configuration provides structure, stability, and order. These two forces are like the yin and yang of power dynamics: they're complementary, interdependent, and constantly shaping one another. When we look at the intersections of power, we can see how these forces play out in the relationships between universal, personal, interpersonal, collective, and systemic power. Each of the following sections will explore the four intersection points, how their intersectionality shows up in the world, and how the dynamics of emergence and configuration appear in each of them.

Universal Power–Personal Power

Universal power is the field in which all power dynamics exist. This intersection point between universal and personal power is unique in that the direction of influence is limited by our relationship with it. Universal power, as defined earlier, is the vast, often intangible force that connects all that exists—the force that binds the universe together. Universal power has a profound influence on how we experience and express personal power, which is each individual's ability to have an effect or influence in their own life and the lives of others. The presence of universal power makes up the primary difference between rooted and socialized forms of personal power. Universal power can serve as a source of inspiration and grounding for personal power (which is why I call it rooted personal power). When we tap into the sense that we are part of something larger—whether that's the natural world, God, the cosmos, or a sense of interconnectedness—it can deepen our sense of purpose and resilience. This connection to universal power can amplify our rooted personal power by supporting our awareness of the much bigger web of existence.

The encouragement we get from Universal Power to think beyond our immediate circumstances and consider the bigger picture can help us use our personal power more thoughtfully and intentionally. When we can "zoom out" and see how things are connected, or get a taste of the vastness we are part of, it can offer an important perspective on our reality—helping us put things into perspective. When I worked at a university in a DEI role, we would welcome incoming students with Joanna Macy's Seventh Generation Practice[1] . It is a powerful exercise rooted in deep ecology and systems thinking, designed to expand our sense of time and responsibility. It invites us to imagine ourselves sitting in a circle with seven generations of ancestors behind us and seven generations of descendants ahead. The indigenous practice of thinking in seven generations is a profound philosophy that emphasizes the interconnectedness of time, people, and the natural world. It reminds us that we are part of a larger story, one that stretches far beyond our individual lifetimes, and that our choices ripple across time, affecting not only ourselves but the collective well-being of all. It is a call to live with long-term vision and intergenerational care, ensuring that we leave a legacy of balance and harmony for future generations. This is what I mean when I talk about the potential of expansion when we connect with universal power.

When universal power and personal power intersect, there is a magic that happens that gives us access to a whole other world of knowing—it might be intuition, universal wisdom, or even extraordinary abilities. In the field of interpersonal neurobiology, Daniel

---

1. https://workthatreconnects.org/resources/seventh-generation /

Siegel has explored how certain meditation practices, particularly those focused on compassion and connecting with the interdependence of all things, can lead to more integrated brain activity. Studies have shown that monks and experienced meditators who engage in compassion meditation—such as loving-kindness (metta) or tonglen—exhibit greater connectivity between different regions of the brain, especially those involved in empathy, emotional regulation, and self-awareness. This increased integration is thought to enhance emotional resilience, improve social functioning, and foster a deeper sense of interconnectedness with others. Siegel's work[2] suggests that these practices that connect us to Something Larger, don't just change how we feel; they literally rewire the brain, promoting a more harmonious balance between its various systems. By cultivating compassion and connecting to universal power, we not only improve our mental health but also create a more integrated and cohesive sense of self.

At the same time, universal power can also remind us of the limits of personal power. While personal power is about our individual ability to influence our environment, universal power highlights that there are forces beyond our control—whether that's the passage of time, the laws of nature, or the unpredictability of life. This recognition can be humbling and help us approach our personal power with a sense of humility—accepting our small yet integral part of the whole.

Personal Power-Interpersonal Power

---

2. Siegel, D. J. (2007). The Mindful Brain: Reflection and Attunement in the Cultivation of Well-Being. W.W. Norton & Company. & Siegel, D. J. (2010). Mindsight: The New Science of Personal Transformation. Bantam Books.

Personal power is the power we carry within ourselves that is ours alone—our confidence, skills, and agency. However, personal power doesn't exist in a vacuum. It is shaped by the other forms of power that surround us, such as the roles we hold, the status we're assigned, and the systems we navigate. Personal power—our individual ability to influence our environment and make decisions—plays a crucial role in how we navigate and engage with the interpersonal types of power (role power and status power), which are externally-sourced forms of power tied to positions and extrinsic valuations. In other words, our personal power is amplified or diminished depending on factors such as our access to resources, social standing, and the support we receive from our families and communities.

The personal and interpersonal power interplay is probably the intersection we are aware of most. And it is a powerful one. Each time we interact with another being, we create a third entity: the relationship. Even if that relationship lasts only a few seconds, it still influences us. In fact, it shifts our intrapersonal experience. Take, for example, a brief exchange with a stranger where a simple smile leads to a warm conversation—this momentary interaction can uplift our mood, remind us of our shared humanity, and alter our internal landscape.

As our internal state shifts, it, in turn, influences the relationship, which reverberates back to affect the other person's internal experience. We are engaged in a perpetual cycle of shaping one another's internal worlds—not merely the shared dynamic but the individuals within it. Let that sink in for a moment.

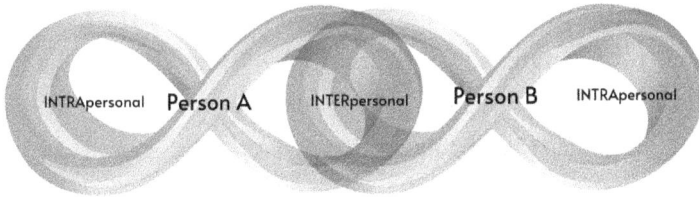

Our internal states can be profoundly contagious. A kind gesture, a thoughtful word, or even a small act of generosity can ripple outward, inspiring others to do the same. This chain of positive energy can extend far beyond the initial exchange, leaving a lasting legacy of goodwill. And of course, the opposite is also true. When we are down-capacity and unable to be kind to ourselves, we tend to show up in ways that are aggressive or unkind—this too has a ripple effect.

We wield significant power in shaping not only our own internal landscapes but also the lives of those we touch. Awareness of this dynamic encourages us to attend to and nurture our internal state—it is essential for finding right-relationship. This intersection of power is highly influential and is present in every interaction with every being, whether a power differential is present or not.

Personal Power and Role Power

While role power is externally defined, how we wield it is deeply influenced by our access (or lack thereof) to our personal power. This realization alone, I think, would help shift a lot of power dynamics in the workplace. There is a form of dehumanization that I find happens in "professional" spaces and it is normalized and promoted because it is considered "professional." But what is considered professional is a norm that can be shifted. When I work with organizations, I often promote a more humanizing professionalism—where we get to be human beings alongside our roles. That means acknowledging we have lives outside of work, that we have feelings, get sick, and need connection and belonging, no matter where we are. And it doesn't mean that we have to process all of our feelings or that our boss becomes our therapist. It just means that we are inviting an awareness that we don't stop being human when we step into our roles. I feel like I shouldn't have to name that, but I have repeatedly seen leaders in organizations expecting their employees to be more, or less than, human. But we are more than just our roles—and when we are allowed to be, we perform at much higher levels (even more so, when we are encouraged to be).

Research by Kark and Shamir (2013)[3] shows that transformational leadership, which recognizes individual employees' personal lives, emotions, and unique contributions, can significantly boost engagement and overall well-being. When leaders acknowledge that their team members are more than just roles or job descriptions, they foster a workplace environment rooted in respect and human connection, which in turn enhances both performance and satisfaction. As Kark and Shamir suggest, by intentionally shifting toward a more humanizing approach—where acknowledging our feelings, outside lives, and need for connection is accepted—we can create more resilient and engaged workplaces.

---

3. Kark, R., & Shamir, B. (2013). The dual effect of transformational leadership on followers' engagement and wellness. *The Leadership Quarterly*, 24(5), 860–872. https://doi.org/10.1016/j.leaqua.2013.07.002

Kramer and Schmalenberg (2011)[4] also conducted a study that supports this perspective. Through their research, they demonstrated that when organizations empower staff with autonomy and respect for their full identities (i.e. access to their personal power), performance improves and patient care is safer. When employees are allowed to be themselves—whether that means bringing their emotions or acknowledging external stresses—they are more motivated, creative, and committed. When leaders promote this kind of human-centered professionalism, employees perform at higher levels, feel more connected, and experience greater fulfillment. In essence, embracing our shared humanity doesn't weaken professionalism; it strengthens it, allowing people to bring their whole selves into their roles and thrive inside and outside the workplace.

Beyond humanization, having access to our personal power transforms how we show up in the other types of power. Being connected to our values, our sense of self, and our full identities (that we choose for ourselves) can have a profound impact on how we show up in power differential relationships. Developing our access to personal power and our relational capabilities can go a long way toward promoting more positive role power differential relationships. For example, a manager who cultivates strong personal power—with self-awareness, good communication skills, and emotional intelligence—can wield their role power in a far more impactful way. They tend to lead with empathy, communicate with clarity, and inspire their team. This kind of leadership fosters a positive, energized workplace where trust and collaboration thrive. Conversely, a manager without connection to their personal power may find it harder to fully step into their role, which can result

---

4. Kramer, S. J., & Schmalenberg, C. (2011). Staff nurse autonomy, control over practice, and patient safety. *Western Journal of Nursing Research*, 33(2), 227-246. https://doi.org/10.1177/0193945910388440

in confusion, miscommunication, or even resentment from team members. When personal power is lacking, it's like trying to steer a ship without a rudder—less effective, more chaotic, and less likely to create the motivating environment teams need to succeed.

Personal power also allows us to challenge or redefine the boundaries of our position. I was teaching in an organization recently, and one of the participants approached me after the training. She was in charge of enforcing a policy, and the limitations of that policy meant that she would have to cause significant harm to an individual. She felt terrible about it, but also trapped because she didn't have the authority to change the policy. I asked her if she could leverage her personal power, along with her role power, to speak with someone who could change that policy. She was able to do so, and they devised a creative solution that would prevent this kind of harm from occurring in the future. When we are coming just from our roles and role power, we tend not to think about the possibilities beyond what systems have created for us. When we introduce personal power, our relational responsibilities become more visible, and our ability to influence our roles and the systems that create them expands. Toni Morrison said, "As you enter positions of trust and power, dream a little before you think." I like to think she is referring to accessing our personal power here. As we enter role power, remember to access your personal power as you engage with others—it will greatly expand your influence and support your reach toward right-relationship in role power differentials.

Personal Power and Status Power

There is a critical intersection between personal and status power—one that is missing in Dominant Culture. Accessing our personal power is a necessary first step before we can become aware of and effectively navigate status power dynamics. Without it, finding right-relationship in status power differentials becomes almost impossible. Most often, when we are up-status, we don't bring into conscious awareness that there is a power differential, much less any responsibilities that might be related to that differential. Accessing our self-awareness and personal power allows us to be more conscious of the fact that where we are in the status power differential is socially constructed—meaning we did not inherently deserve this greater value in society. This will make the difference in how we show up in our status power. Whether we are in down-status power or up-status power, being able to access the power we do have (personal power) is essential for reducing harm and finding our way to right-relationship.

When we become conscious of the extrinsic nature of status power, we can not only come closer to right-relationship, but we can also use that status power in ways that help deconstruct those false differentials. When I was a kid, I would go every day after school to my dad's small engine repair shop in West Texas. One day, I was the only one in our storefront office. Although this was not unusual for me, the customer clearly believed it to be problematic. He was a gruff-looking, older man with a frown on his face. He looked at my 13-year-old, scrawny girl self, looked around the storefront, then grunted. I welcomed him in with genuine confidence, but he said nothing. After a few minutes of uncomfortable silence, he finally asked to speak to a "grown man." I informed him that no one was available at the moment, except for me, and that I'd be happy to help. Another grunt—this time with a flare of sarcastic disbelief. He had a mangled string trimmer head in his hand with the trimmer line tangled. I asked if he needed help with the trimmer head, and he said he would wait until a man could help him. After another twenty minutes of uncomfortable silence, my father walked in from the back, wiping grease from his hands. He noticed the man and me sitting there in rigid silence. My dad asked, "Is everything ok?" The man replied that he had been waiting for almost half an hour. My dad looked at me and asked if I had offered to help. The man said, "I was waiting to speak with you." My dad heard what he needed and then turned to face both me and him and said to the man, "You're in luck! We have the best trimmer head stringer in the county right here." He took the trimmer head, handed it to me, and left. I looked over at the old man whose mouth was slightly gaping, and his forehead was mangled in confusion. Then I got to work untangling and restringing the trimmer head. I gave him some pointers on how to string it so it wouldn't get tangled again. Then I handed back the trimmer head to him and told him to have a good day.

Apart from another experience of being dismissed due to my gender and age (which I had grown accustomed to early in life), I learned a few valuable lessons from this encounter. One is that people can miss out on a potentially beneficial connection because of a generalized belief or stereotype. What that man didn't know (and didn't think to be curious about) was that I had been working in my dad's engine shop since I was 9 years old, every day after school, learning about engines, business, and things like how to string a trimmer properly. This belief prevented him from being curious and accepting the help he needed.

Second, I learned that a simple act can have a profound effect. My dad could have chosen to re-string the trimmer head himself, but he didn't. He used his power to both empower me and challenge a stereotype. This small act contributed to a significant shift for me—from feeling discarded and scorned, to feeling seen and valuable.

Third, how my dad chose to show up in that moment deepened my respect and trust in him. I wanted to be able to show up like that—in a way that honors the dignity in every person. It was only much later that I learned how to understand the nuance and complexity of encounters like these—and just how devastating they can be, depending on the circumstances. Many misuses of power end in much more harm than a social slight. But, no matter the circumstances or those involved, how we show up in relationship matters. And how we show up in relationship is directly tied to our access to personal power.

Autonomy: Boundaries and Consent

One of the most important aspects of the Personal-Interpersonal Intersection is our ability to bring autonomy into role and status power differentials—no matter where we find ourselves in that differential. Autonomy is the capacity to make decisions for ourselves, free from external coercion or undue influence. It's a cornerstone of personal freedom and self-determination, allowing us to shape our lives according to our own values, desires, and beliefs. However, autonomy doesn't exist in a vacuum—it relies heavily on two critical concepts: boundaries and consent. Without these, autonomy becomes fragile, if not impossible to maintain.

Boundaries are the limits we set to protect our physical, emotional, and mental well-being. They define what is acceptable and what is not in our interactions with others. Healthy boundaries are essential for autonomy because they allow us to assert our needs and preferences without feeling overwhelmed or violated. When boundaries are respected, we feel safe and empowered to make choices that align with our true selves. Conversely, when boundaries are ignored or trampled, our sense of autonomy diminishes, leaving us feeling powerless or controlled by others.

Consent is the voluntary agreement to engage in a specific action or relationship. It's a clear and enthusiastic "yes" that is given freely, without pressure or manipulation. Consent is deeply tied to autonomy because it ensures that our decisions are respected and honored. Whether it's in personal relationships, medical decisions, or professional settings, consent is the mechanism that allows us to exercise control over our bodies, time, and resources. Importantly, consent must be informed—meaning we have all the necessary information to make a choice—and it can be withdrawn at any time. Without consent, autonomy is undermined, as decisions are made for us rather than by us.

The interplay between boundaries and consent is what makes autonomy possible. Boundaries help us define what we're comfortable with, while consent ensures that others respect those limits. In power differential relationships, our ability to bring our personal power (which encompasses boundaries and consent) into the relationship is essential for maintaining respect and dignity for one another as human beings. This is essential.

Personal power deeply influences how we engage with role and status power. It allows us to wield our roles with confidence and creativity, challenge status power, and bridge the gap between external authority and internal agency. When rooted in something larger than ourselves, personal power can transform how we show up in interpersonal power dynamics, making our influence more positive, inclusive, and impactful.

Interpersonal Power–Collective Power

When I teach in person, I like to do an exercise where I ask everyone to take a moment to focus on their internal experience—what sensations, emotions, or thoughts might be present for them. Then I ask them to shift their attention to notice the external environment—the energy of the room, the information from their senses. And then I invite them to move around the room and find something that brings them joy. I ask them to notice what happens to their internal experience while experiencing that joy. Now, mindfulness and joy are both worthy things to pursue, but it is not the purpose of the exercise. The purpose comes in what I ask them to do next. I ask them to find a partner and share the thing that brought them joy and what happened to them internally as a result. After a few minutes, I ask them to take a breath and then notice their external environment again. What has shifted? Usually the entire energy of the room! This, I say, is collective power. And it comes from everyone intentionally focusing their attention in similar ways and then sharing it in relationship. Simple. And yet we rarely get to this in collectives.

Similar to systems, collectives can create both role and status power. However, instead of forming from structures as they do in systems, role and status power in collectives tend to form from the bottom up—from the majority within the collective. Essentially, the interpersonal types of power form naturally through social norms and the values of the collective. Which attributes are considered to be valuable typically manifest according to the collective's aim. Role and status power intersect with collective power in complex and dynamic ways.

Role Power and Collective Power

Role power, which is tied to specific positions or titles, can either support or hinder the development of collective power. When individuals in leadership roles (role power) use their authority to facilitate collaboration and shared decision-making, they can amplify collective power. Conversely, if someone in a leadership role uses their role power to dominate or control, it can stifle collective power by discouraging participation and creating division.

Role power can also provide structure and direction to collective efforts. For instance, in a social movement, organizers with clear roles (e.g., strategists, communicators, fundraisers) can help channel the collective power of the group toward achieving specific goals. However, if these roles become too rigid or hierarchical, they can limit the group's flexibility and inclusivity, weakening collective power. The key is to balance role power with a commitment to collaboration and shared leadership, ensuring that everyone feels empowered to contribute.

Status Power and Collective Power

Status power, which is derived from societal hierarchies like race, gender, or class can significantly influence collective power. Individuals with high status power—such as well-known activists, influential leaders, or celebrities—can use their visibility and credibility to amplify collective efforts. For example, a prominent figure lending their voice to a social justice movement can attract media attention, resources, and public support, boosting the collective power of the group. However, this can also create a reliance on individual status power, potentially overshadowing the contributions of others in the group.

On the other hand, individuals with low status power can still contribute to collective power by leveraging their personal power and forming alliances. For instance, marginalized communities often build collective power by uniting around shared experiences and goals, even when they down-status identities. Grassroots movements, like those led by low-income workers or immigrant communities, demonstrate how collective power can emerge from the bottom up, challenging systemic inequalities and creating change despite limited access to status power.

Balancing Individual and Collective Power

One of the key challenges in building collective power is balancing the contributions of individuals with the needs of the group. While role and status power can provide valuable resources and leadership, they must be used in ways that promote inclusivity and shared ownership. For example, leaders with high role or status power can use their influence to create space for marginalized voices, ensuring that collective power is truly representative and equitable. Similarly, collective power can be strengthened by recognizing and valuing the diverse roles and statuses within the group, creating a sense of shared responsibility and mutual respect. In his book, *Awakening Together: The Spiritual Practice of Inclusivity and Community*, Larry Yang said, "The etymology of the word *community* is from the Latin terms cum, meaning 'together' or 'among each other, ' and munus, which indicates giving or a gift or exchange. Integrated into one word, community represents a form of exchange or giving among and between individuals. It suggests the development of a relationship and the act of relating with each other, since in the act of relating, there is an exchange and sharing."[5] Collectives are inherently dynamic—they thrive on interaction and interdependence. The act of relating, as Yang points out, is not passive; it requires engagement, vulnerability, and a willingness to both give

---

5. Yang, L. (2017). *Awakening Together: The Spiritual Practice of Inclusivity and Community*. Wisdom Publications, p. 44.

and receive. This exchange fosters trust, understanding, and a sense of belonging, which are essential for any community to function harmoniously. In this way, a collective is not just a static group of individuals but a living, evolving network of relationships.

When used thoughtfully, role and status power can amplify collective efforts by providing leadership, structure, and visibility. However, if misused, they can reinforce hierarchies and undermine the group's unity and inclusivity. The key to building strong collective power lies in balancing individual contributions with a commitment to collaboration, ensuring that everyone feels empowered to participate and that the group's goals remain the central focus. By navigating the intersections of role, status, and collective power with awareness and intention, we can create movements and organizations that are both effective and equitable.

Collective Power–Systemic Power

Collective power is uniquely positioned to challenge and transform systemic power, which is the entrenched, institutionalized power embedded in laws, policies, and cultural norms. Systemic power is often maintained by institutions and structures that are resistant to change, such as governments, corporations, or cultural norms. Collective power, however, can act as a counterforce by mobilizing large numbers of people to demand accountability and reform. For example, social movements like the Civil Rights Movement, #MeToo, and Black Lives Matter have used collective power to challenge systemic racism, sexism, and other forms of institutionalized oppression. By organizing protests, advocating for policy changes, and shifting public opinion, these movements have forced systemic power structures to adapt and, in some cases, dismantle.

One of the most direct ways collective power influences systemic power is through policy change. When large groups of people come together to advocate for specific reforms, they can pressure institutions to enact new laws or policies. For example, the labor movement of the early 20th century used collective power to demand fair wages, safe working conditions, and workers' rights, leading to systemic changes like the establishment of minimum wage laws and workplace safety regulations. Similarly, environmental movements have used collective power to push for systemic changes like the Paris Agreement and other climate policies.

Collective power is the only kind of power that can effectively challenge and transform systemic power because it operates on a scale large enough to disrupt entrenched institutions and norms. By mobilizing people, shifting cultural narratives, advocating for policy changes, holding institutions accountable, and leveraging economic pressure, collective power can reshape systemic power in ways that promote equity and justice. However, for collective power to be truly transformative, it must be inclusive, intersectional, and rooted in a commitment to shared goals and values

How Systemic Power Shows Up Within Collectives

There are influences by the larger systems that often show up within the collective, which is (surprisingly) not often conscious. I see countless collectives emulating the very conditions they are trying to change in systems. Collectives that promote peace but use aggressive communication, or those that preach tolerance but do not tolerate certain individuals within their group. The truth is that we are all socialized within systems, and we unconsciously manifest systemic tendencies even when we are actively trying to change them. This phenomenon can be understood as a kind of systemic mimicry, where the very structures and behaviors we seek to dismantle inadvertently replicate themselves within our own efforts. It's a paradox that reveals how deeply ingrained systemic conditioning is in our collective psyche.

For example, a collective advocating for equality might unconsciously reproduce hierarchical dynamics within its own leadership, where certain voices are prioritized over others, or where decision-making power is concentrated in the hands of a few. Similarly, a group dedicated to environmental justice might inadvertently perpetuate exploitative labor practices in its own operations, mirroring the same extractive systems it aims to critique. These contradictions often arise not from a lack of intention or commitment, but from the subtle, unconscious ways in which systemic norms shape our behavior and relationships.

This unconscious replication of systemic conditions is particularly challenging because it often goes unnoticed. Even when collectives are explicitly committed to creating alternative, more equitable ways of being, the default patterns of the larger systems—such as dominance, exclusion, or competition—can seep into their internal dynamics. This is partly because we are all products of the systems in which we've been socialized, and breaking free from these ingrained patterns requires not only awareness but also ongoing, intentional practice.

To address this, collectives must engage in a process of reflexivity—a deliberate examination of their own structures, behaviors, and power dynamics. This means creating spaces for honest self-reflection and critique, where members can openly discuss how systemic influences might be showing up within the group. It also requires a commitment to unlearning and relearning—actively challenging the norms and behaviors that have been internalized from larger systems and replacing them with more inclusive, equitable practices.

Ultimately, the work of transforming systems is not just about external change but also about internal transformation. Collectives must be willing to confront the ways in which they themselves are shaped by the very systems they seek to change. This is a humbling and often uncomfortable process, but it is essential for creating movements and organizations that truly embody the values they advocate for. By becoming more conscious of these systemic influences, collectives can move closer to their ideals, breaking the cycle of systemic mimicry and paving the way for more authentic and transformative change.

Ultimately, collective power and systemic power are balancing forces—each playing a crucial role in shaping the world we live in. Collective power is essential because it provides the feedback systems need to stay healthy and responsive. Systems, after all, aren't static; they're constantly evolving, influenced by the people and groups that interact with them. Without ongoing feedback from collectives, systems can become rigid, unaccountable, or even harmful. This feedback loop is vital to ensure that systems serve the needs of the many, not just the few.

But here's the catch: even when we design systems to encourage feedback, we can still fall into patterns where we become overly identified with the system itself. This can lead to complacency—where we stop questioning the system, stop pushing for change, or even stop forming the collective power needed to hold systems accountable. When this happens, our ability to influence the system diminishes, and in turn, our personal power can erode. This erosion can occur for a variety of reasons—maybe we feel disempowered by the system's complexity, or perhaps we've been conditioned to accept the status quo. Whatever the cause, the result is the same: we lose the capacity to effectively challenge or reshape the systems that shape our lives.

As we move toward collaboration and begin to deconstruct rigid power structures, it's clear that we have a lot of work to do. Holding ourselves and our systems accountable requires integrity, vigilance, and a commitment to collective action. It's not enough to simply critique systems from the sidelines; we must actively engage in the process of change. This means forming collectives that are inclusive, equitable, and focused on the greater good. It also means being willing to challenge the systems we're part of, even when it's uncomfortable or inconvenient.

Through collective action, we have the power to create systemic change that benefits everyone, not just those who already hold power. This isn't just about dismantling oppressive structures; it's about building new ones that are more just, more responsive, and more aligned with our shared values. It's a challenging task, but one that's essential if we want to create a world where power is distributed more equitably and where everyone has the opportunity to thrive.

In the end, the balance between collective power and systemic power is a dynamic, ongoing process. It requires us to stay engaged, to keep questioning, and to never stop striving for a better way of being together. It's not always easy, but it's worth it—because the systems we shape today will determine the world we live in tomorrow.

14

Systemic Power Lenses

"You can see some things through the lens of the human eye, other things through the lens of a microscope, others through the lens of a telescope, and still others through the lens of systems theory. Everything seen through each kind of lens is actually there. Each way of seeing allows our knowledge of the wondrous world in which we live to become a little more complete." - Donella H. Meadows

"Story and standpoint matter, and you need many of them to understand how a system works." - Tyson Yunkaporta

I served in a "DEI" (diversity, equity, inclusion) role at a university for about four years. Like many folks in similar roles, I was frequently frustrated. We are typically given vast expectations for transforming cultures with very little resources and a lot of obstacles. And, as a white person, I encountered only a fraction of the obstacles my colleagues of color have faced in similar roles. As a result of these mostly unnecessary obstacles, many DEI efforts resort to shifting a rule here or resolving a difficulty there. However, those fixes are bandaids to a much bigger wound underneath. That wound is systemic, and to heal it and address it effectively, we have to employ systems thinking.

Systems thinking is particularly useful for addressing complex problems involving multiple stakeholders and interdependent factors. It encourages looking beyond immediate symptoms to understand underlying causes. When we think systemically, we seek to understand how the parts of a system are connected.

As I studied systemic power, I came to understand that there are different types of systems, each impacting how the other types of power manifest. It was like the *story* of power differed in each of these types. I started to uncover and define these stories about power so we can examine their purpose and their effect on us. While there are more systems than I can possibly count, let alone study, I can easily see that particular patterns emerge within the social systems I have been a part of or have been able to observe.

I discovered three fundamental aspects of social systems: their shape, their paradigm, and the way those influence our reality. As I listened to and read various stories and perspectives about power, I started to group the systemic paradigms into four different categories:

Types of Systemic Power Paradigms

- Domination Power Paradigms (power-over)

- Commodified Power Paradigms (power-of)

- Inclusive Power Paradigms (power-to)

- Interdependent Power Paradigms (power-with)

Each of these paradigms creates a different shape for how power operates in systems which I call **Systemic Lenses**. I chose the word "lenses" because I want to emphasize how these shapes/paradigms influence how we perceive the world. Shawn Ginwright said, "A lens defines what we see even before we see it." Through the ongoing process of socialization that begins when we are born, we are shaped by the beliefs, values, and ideas around us. These paradigms that we are steeped in are largely invisible, but they guide virtually everything we think and do. As Ginwright says, what we see and how we perceive the world is pre-defined by the systems we are embedded in. They are so ingrained in our thinking that we don't realize they originated elsewhere or that we are contributing to their continued existence.

As we have discussed, part of the issue of being embedded in something larger is that we often cannot see "the something larger." This is what gives systems so much power. It is hidden in plain sight, but only because we suffer from a narrow perspective. If we were to venture to take a few (or many) steps back, we may start to see the shape of things that have guided us without our full awareness. It is like our ability to zoom in and out of satellite images. As we begin looking around us (zoomed in), we can see the familiar details, but as we zoom out, things become increasingly unrecognizable. We can't see the shape or topography of the land we live on unless we get a view from the sky, and we can't see the shape of the Earth unless we see it from space. And we can't see the shape of our solar system unless we see it from the galaxy. There is almost always a perspective further out we can go from the largest perspective we have—always a place to stretch to. So this is my invitation: to stretch with me so we can zoom out to see the shape of things.

As you read about the lenses, you will likely want to make some more valuable than others or more "right" than others. This is inevitable because we're all steeped in systems and have beliefs about what is right or wrong. However, I encourage you to suspend your tendency toward the binary and challenge yourself to see these as different lenses that, by the nature of their structure or shape, create particular outcomes and consequences.

The four systemic lenses are: the Authority Lens, the Achievement Lens, the Pluralistic Lens, and the Interdependent Lens. If you'd like to experience these lenses through a guided meditation, you might get additional information from your own exploration of them. You will find the written version in Appendix A and there is a QR code you can scan for the audio.

Four Systemic Lenses

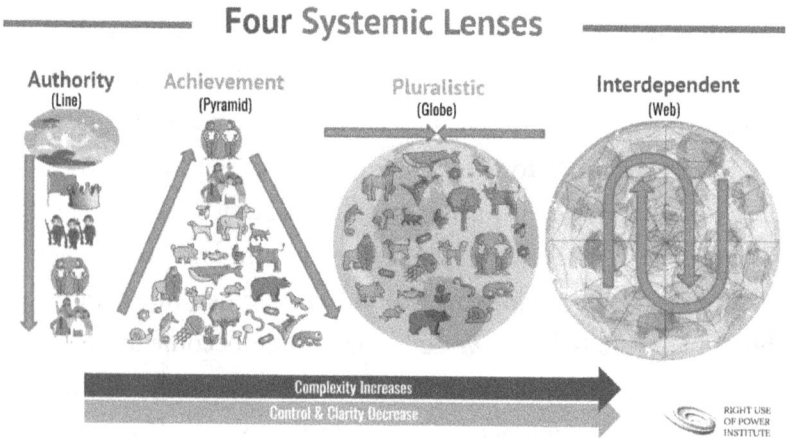

Authority Lens

Paradigm: Domination (power-over)
  Shape & Direction: Line (unilinear)
  *Inter*personal: Structured Power Differentials
  *Intra*personal: Loyalty, Suppression
  Collective Potential: Hegemony
  Governance:
    • Rigid Hierarchy

- High Control

- Punitive

- Passive Accountability

Authority
(Line)

The first systemic lens we will explore is the Authority Lens, represented by a single line that starts at the top and extends downward. The Authority Lens is created in line with the belief that there are certain entities endowed with greater ability/faculty and, therefore, need to take care of the others in the system. This is the basis of most systemic paradigms in the Authority Lens.

This is a linear system where hierarchy is most clearly seen. A higher authority at the top determines the roles and rules of those at the bottom.

That higher authority could be God, a religious institution, a government, a Board of Directors, a dictator, royalty, C-Suite Executives, etc. The whole system is understood and expressed through rigid, stable hierarchies, so that everyone knows their place and what role they play. There is simplicity, constancy, and clarity throughout the system—and, no matter where you are in the system, it is fairly fixed.

Authority Systems are most commonly seen when there is a need to respond with high specialization and immediacy (e.g., emergency medicine and military operations), coordinate complex efforts with consistent standards (e.g., multinational corporations), or exercise high control (e.g., jails and prisons). They involve clear lines of authority, role clarity, specialization, standardization, efficient execution of orders, and effective coordination. In the

Authority Lens, there are very clear definitions of things, including what is "right" and "wrong" or "good" and "bad." This makes things like rules or laws very easy to write down and to ensure compliance to a standard of what is considered "right" or "good." This linear, systemic shape aims for a mechanistic flow: pull this specialized lever, and this standardized result will occur.

Most everyone in the system is assigned a purpose, and sometimes even relationships are assigned (e.g., in arranged marriages). You are generally told who to be, how to act, and with whom you can and can't be in relationships (and how those relationships look). Everything is already prescribed for you. Just follow the rules, stay in line, and the machine will work properly. This requires very little conscious awareness or need to navigate relationships outside of giving and receiving directives, orders, or instructions.

Domination Power Paradigm - "Power-over"

If we take the history of the understanding of power over time and examine the dominant lens or shape of power, we start to see what I call the Domination Paradigm of Power. This paradigm is foundational to the Authority Lens. It involves a "power-over" approach that is ultimately about maintaining a well-controlled environment. The mentality of control, whether external or internal, directly stems from the Domination Power Paradigm. Let's take a look at how this particular paradigm shapes the other types of power.

Interpersonal Power (Role & Status)

In the Domination Paradigm, most relationships are shaped in some way by a power differential—whether it is status or role power.

The rules of engagement in a relationship are predetermined by roles and status. Very rarely in this kind of system are interpersonal power differentials not emphasized in relationships.

A power-over approach is common in interpersonal types of power. As we will explore in the power differentials section, when we have access to role power, we tend to engage in power-over practices because it is the historical norm—it is what we have seen modeled the most. Some neurobiological underpinnings create a tendency toward power-over participation within power differentials, though this may reflect how our brains have evolved within these systemic norms.

To achieve high control, obedience is valued, and punishment is typically the consequence of not conforming. Because the line is the shape this system takes, getting "out of line" is fundamentally contrary to its operation. Stepping outside prescribed roles or behaviors is often met with a quick intervention, such as punishment, to maintain order and control. This creates an environment where loyalty to the system is prioritized over individual expression or dissent.

Collective Power

In this lens, collective power manifests as hegemony in the Authority Lens. Hegemony refers to the dominance or leadership of one group over others, often maintained through cultural, ideological, or societal means rather than direct force. For example, large multinational corporations, such as Amazon and Google, wield significant power over market trends and consumer behavior, often dictating terms to smaller businesses and shaping economic practices globally. Alternatively, we could examine the dominance of certain countries in international organizations, such as the United

States' influence in the United Nations or NATO, which often shapes global policies and political agendas, sometimes sidelining the interests of smaller nations. In other words, the "power-over" framework is at play in collective power through this lens, alongside other types of power.

Personal Power

This "power-over" frame even plays out intrapersonally for us. With the pressure to conform, personal power gets shaped into loyalty (to the system). Individuals develop their identities and understandings of themselves and others through the socialization of the system. Since resistance is typically met with quick intervention by the system and/or pressure to conform by others, very few are willing to rebel.

Internalizing the "power-over" paradigm can lead to personal power that manifests as high achievement, discipline, and willpower. The ultimate measuring stick is how well a person uses their power to fit into, maintain, and develop the system.

Achievement Lens

Paradigm: Commodified (power-of)
  Shape: Pyramid (bi-directional)
  *Inter*personal Dynamics: Transactional, Competitive
  *Intra*personal Dynamics: Autonomy, Individualism
  Collective Potential: Meritocracy
  Governance:
  - Semi-Flexible Hierarchy

  - Some Control

- Carrots & Sticks

- Passive Responsibility & Accountability

Achievement
(Pyramid)

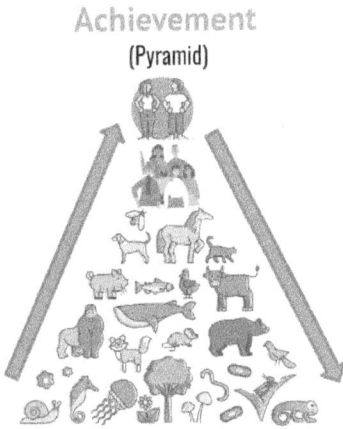

The Achievement Lens, represented by the pyramid, shows up very clearly in modernity. It has a semi-flexible hierarchy: there's still a clear top and bottom, but there's some bidirectional movement up and down the pyramid. There are more moving parts than the Authority Lens, but there's still a clear systemic value of movement toward the top. The Original Paradigm of this lens is the belief or worldview that success is attainable for anyone through hard work and determination.

The concept of earning and working your way to the top is the socialized focus for individuals in this system: if you want success, get to the top and stay there. The "top" is usually defined as the accumulation of assets considered valuable for that system. Of course, the top of the pyramid only has so much room; it is the smallest part of the pyramid. This naturally cultivates both a sense of scarcity and of competition. Capitalism is the archetypal expression of the Achievement Lens. It creates the conditions for significant economic growth, is dynamic, and offers consumers a diverse range of goods and services. Capitalism is based on and promotes several fundamental concepts, including ownership, profit, individualism, and, of course, achievement.

Commodified Power Paradigm - "Power-of"

In the Achievement Lens, the concept of ownership is central. For example, at the core of capitalism is the principle of private property, which allows individuals and businesses to own, use, and transfer property. This includes tangible assets such as land and buildings, as well as intangible assets such as intellectual property. Because whatever is "owned" leads to profit, people in this system are incentivized to own as much as possible.

Following this paradigm, power is thought of as something you can own—or at least some people can. It is considered to be an intangible *thing* that you get, have, or can lose. This is what I refer to as the **Commodified Power Paradigm.** It is the idea that there is a limited amount of power that can be possessed by those who have earned it or deserve it. The concepts of "earning" or "hard work" are central to the system's function. Stories like "The early bird gets the worm," "Pull yourself up by your bootstraps," or "Time is money" reflect the core of this paradigm.

I use the term "power-of" to represent this paradigm, emphasizing the ownership of power. I also think it is appropriate that "power-of" also refers to exponential power in mathematics. An exponent multiplies itself, much as capitalist systems exhibit unregulated growth.

Interpersonal Power (Role & Status)

Role and status power are interpreted as power that is earned in this Systemic Lens. Based on the organizing paradigm, people believe that they must have a position or social capital because they have done something to earn it or are otherwise deserving of the distinction and privileges that accompany it. This leads to interpersonal relationships that are comparative and competitive. Without comparison, one doesn't know where they stand in the pyramid and what needs to be done to compete and win the position or status.

Another hallmark of interpersonal relationships in the Achievement Lens is that they are, to some extent, transactional in nature: we engage in a relationship in order to get something from it. I will give you this if you give me that. Again, everything is centered around what can be possessed—even relationships.

Collective Power

In the Commodified Power Paradigm, collective power manifests primarily in two ways, and both typically move from the ground up. It can look like individuals working together to create innovative solutions and progress, like startups with a vision that develop new technologies promising big change and big profits. Or, because there are very few with the most resources in this system (the top of the pyramid), collective power can manifest as grassroots movements originating from the bottom and seeking to effect change by influencing those at the top. This can look like unions working together to advocate for fair wages and working conditions with the owners of an organization.

Personal Power

The "hero's journey" is the quintessential example of how personal power is socialized within this systemic paradigm. The emphasis is on autonomy, originality, and individuality. Since competition is the primary activity of the Achievement lens, a lot of attention is devoted to being the best. The best can be defined in many ways, depending on the circumstances, but it's usually about winning. The Guinness Book of World Records is a great example—you don't have to have done anything important for humanity, you need to have done the "est" of something: the greatest, longest, shortest, fastest, lightest, weirdest, etc.

Pluralistic Lens

Paradigm: Inclusive (power-to)
  Shape: Globe (multi-directional)
  Interpersonal Dynamics: Relational, Collaboration
  Intrapersonal Dynamics: Empowerment
  Collective Potential: Equality
  Governance:

- Flexible Hierarchy

- High Support

- Compromise

- Active Responsibility, Passive Accountability

Pluralistic
(Globe)

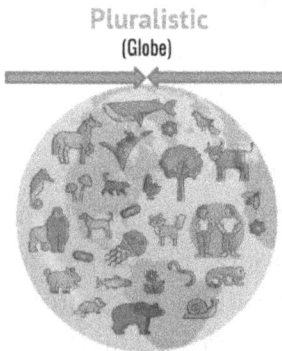

The Pluralistic Lens, represented by the globe, is characterized by multiplicity and diversity. It is through this lens that the complicated starts to meet the complex. Multiple value systems, cultures, and groups co-exist within the same system, giving this lens a multi-directional shape. Multiple social groups, defined by various factors such as values, ideologies, and practices, exist and interact within the system. These groups retain their distinct identities and cultural expressions.

Although there is diversity present and there is movement toward equality and the "common good," there is also conflict and chaos in trying to find what is "right" and determine what equality actually looks like. It is a dynamic and complex system that requires ongoing effort to maintain its balance and to ensure that all groups have a fair opportunity to participate in shaping the system.

While acknowledging diversity, some shared values and norms usually exist that underpin the functioning of the pluralistic system. These shared values might include respect for the rule of law, tolerance, and freedom of expression. Groups may compete for influence and resources, but also cooperate on issues where common interests exist. This dynamic interplay between competition and cooperation shapes the system's evolution.

In terms of structures, you see more distributed governance models and democratic processes in pluralistic systems. There is an emphasis on consensus, coalition-building and strong social mechanisms for managing cultural differences. The strength of a sustainable pluralistic system lies in its mechanisms for managing conflict, ensuring participation, and protecting the rights of all groups.

Inclusive Power Paradigm – Power-To

In contrast to "power-over," which is often associated with dominance and control, and "power-of," which emphasizes ownership, "power-to" highlights the potential for individual and collective action to create social change. Focusing on building capacity and enabling individuals and groups to achieve their goals, it highlights the potential inherent in individuals and groups to effect meaningful change in their lives and communities.

A central characteristic is the focus on strengthening individual and collective capabilities. This involves providing resources and support for enhancing personal and collective power. Rather than focusing on deficits or weaknesses, a power-to approach emphasizes the strengths and assets within individuals and communities. It builds upon existing capabilities to enhance potential and achieve goals.

In the "power-to" approach, individuals and groups are empowered to make their own choices, pursue their own goals, and take ownership of their actions. The focus is on internal or intrinsic motivation and self-directed action, rather than external or extrinsic control or influence. It actively works to address power imbalances and promote social justice.

Interpersonal Power (Role & Status)

In this system, the emphasis is on equality and relationships. Instead of viewing things from a single, dominant perspective, a pluralistic lens encourages considering a wide range of viewpoints, recognizing their validity, and understanding how they interact and shape social realities. Diverse ideologies are not only tolerated in this lens but also actively valued and respected.

The presence of diverse perspectives necessitates regular communication and dialogue. In interpersonal relationships, each person must learn to articulate their views effectively, listen to others, and find common ground to build consensus and achieve shared objectives. Decisions reached through collaboration are often viewed as more legitimate and representative than decisions imposed by a single dominant group.

Collective Power

Collective Power has a strong presence in a pluralistic system. Collectives bring together diverse skills, knowledge, and experiences. The diversity of expertise allows for effective strategy development, problem-solving, and implementation. In the Pluralistic Lens, collective power strives for equality. However, like pluralism, equality often proves to be elusive and challenging to achieve and maintain. Because power is dispersed across multiple groups with diverse interests in a pluralistic system, collaboration becomes necessary to achieve collective goals. No single group has the power to dictate outcomes; therefore, negotiation and compromise are essential tools for reaching agreements and advancing shared concerns.

Personal Power

Individual empowerment is a hallmark of a pluralistic system. In this kind of system, individuals are more likely to have the freedom to express their views, pursue their interests, and live according to their values without undue interference from a dominant group or ideology. Individuals can develop and exercise their "power-to" approach independently, although from this lens it's understood that collaborative efforts often amplify the impact. With the encouragement and support from collectives, the active development of personal power tends to be more evident in this system.

Interdependent Lens

Paradigm: Interdependent (power-with)
  Shape: Web (all directions)
  Interpersonal Dynamics: Reciprocal

Intrapersonal Dynamics: Belonging
Collective Potential: Mutuality
Governance:

- Sociocracy/Holacracy

- High Support and High Consequence

- Collaboration

- Active Responsibility, Active Accountability

Interdependent
(Web)

The interdependent system is the most complex of all the lenses outlined here. It's where the arrows intertwine, revealing the web of life and the interrelatedness of all individuals or components within the system. Interdependent systems are characterized more by emergence and relationships than structures. This can create a sense of chaos, with unpredictable, complex behavior arising from interactions and relationships among the system's interdependent components. It can also make understanding and managing the system more difficult, as the whole may behave in ways that are counterintuitive.

Interdependent systems are often more adaptable to environmental changes, as reliance on diverse components enables flexibility and resilience. Different parts of the system can provide support or compensation when faced with challenges. With more fluid structures, components and relationships can shift and flex more easily as needed in the moment.

Because there are fewer structures, rules and standards aren't as prevalent, which can lead to confusing operations, especially in systems with many members or parts. No static right or wrong exists, which can lead to more work as individuals continually need to come up with solutions that work for the system or themselves. This approach works well for smaller systems, but as the system grows larger, the challenge increases.

An ecosystem is a good example of an interdependent system. Ecosystems are complex networks of living organisms, including plants, animals, and microorganisms, that interact with each other and their physical environment (such as soil, water, and climate) within a specific area. Every component of the system relies on every other through their symbiotic relationship. These interactions involve the flow of energy and nutrients, supporting the diversity of life and maintaining ecological balance. Ecosystems can vary in size, from a pond to a forest or an ocean.

Interdependent Power Paradigm (Power-With)

The power-with paradigm reflects fundamental mutuality. Unlike the "power-to" paradigm, there aren't various groups trying to equalize dynamics or empower others. Instead, there is an inherent realization that all are connected and therefore interdependent. With this lens, belonging is an innate and ongoing experience for everyone in the system. It does not make sense to question one's or anyone else's belonging, because everyone sees and experiences the interdependent nature of everything in the system. In other words, there is a shared identity with *everything*, not just certain groups.

The Interdependent Power Paradigm emphasizes the need to view the system as a whole rather than as isolated parts. It is the *relationships* among all individuals or components that are prioritized. Naturally arising from this paradigm is a sense of shared responsibility and reciprocity—where all parties contribute to and benefit from the relationships within the system. A "power-with" paradigm emphasizes collaboration, shared decision-making, and collective action among individuals or groups.

Interpersonal Power (Role & Status)

Because relationships are the priority, the interpersonal types of power are especially important. However, in interdependent systems, roles are less structured, and status power is more often determined by the exigencies of the moment rather than by a static definition of value. Relationships are defined by reciprocity—the mutual exchange of benefits, actions, or support between individuals. Members or components often have overlapping or shared objectives, fostering collaboration and cooperation to achieve common outcomes. Each component or person in the system relies on others to function effectively, underscoring the need for each to take active responsibility.

From an interdependent lens, the inherent complexity necessitates ongoing communication to identify emergent relationships among parts of the system and the optimal arrangement of those relationships for a particular scenario or situation.

Collective Power

Collective Power in interdependent systems is expressed through mutuality. Collectives form and disperse as different needs come and go. There isn't always a need to establish an organization around it—if it serves, then it continues to function; if it doesn't, it falls away. There are as many different kinds of collectives in an Interdependent System as there are different species in the universe. They are heavily context-dependent and always factor in their surrounding environment in their formation and existence. Any interdependent system requires diversity to survive and thrive; therefore, this is often a priority in collectives that employ a power-with approach.

Personal Power

In an interdependent system, belonging is innate. In this case, one doesn't have to prove one's worth, which creates fewer obstacles to accessing personal power. Personal power comes from an expression of one's belonging in the system. If you think of a baby who doesn't understand the concept of belonging, there is just direct experience. When they are hungry or uncomfortable, they use what they have available to them to get their needs met. This is an influence that is not tied to comparative or competitive needs. While there is a more primal personal power in this paradigm, it is not necessarily selfish because it is accompanied by an awareness of others and their health and well-being, which is tied to our own. Through this paradigm, it matters to me that you be well because I can only be well if you are well—so I use my influence to make sure my own and others' needs are met.

After going through the lenses, did you want to make some right and some wrong? Did you resonate more with one than others? Did some feel more familiar, and others were maybe hard to imagine? I have presented these lenses to many different groups, and it is noticeable how diverse the reactions are to each lens. While I recommended suspending judgment while going through the lenses as a cognitive exercise, I do not mean to imply that I am unbiased (as you will see in the following chapters). Because, of course, we all are.

The reality is that we were all socialized through a particular lens — or lenses —and we don't necessarily realize that we see the world through any lens at all. We just see what we see and call it reality. But we are all looking through at least one systemic lens that shapes how we see the world. The question is: can we become aware of that lens and *how* we are shaped by it? And how others have also been shaped by other lens(es)? When we can't see that we have all been socialized in different ways, we tend to get into a competition around "rightness" and lose the ability to find right-relationship. Competition is unnecessary for challenging the way systems shape power. Instead, it is by being in relationship and attempting to understand the natural consequences of the lenses we are shaped by that can help us shift away from harmful impacts.

15

The Health of Systems

"It is no measure of health to be well adjusted to a profoundly sick society." – Jiddu Krishnamurti

Now that we have looked at different shapes of systems and how they might influence us and the types of power, I want to explore what makes a system healthy or unhealthy. Certainly, each lens shapes stories, structures, and behaviors in particular ways, with consequences for the components and the relationship between them in that system. Different shapes will naturally have different outcomes. But there are circumstances in every system that potentially create *unhealthy* social systems. I'd like to call attention to three of them here. But before I do I feel it necessary to name my bias.

While I have tried to remain relatively neutral (perhaps unsuccessfully) for the purposes of presenting the overall understanding of power, for the remaining chapters, I'd like to make the case for partcipating in power in ways that bring us closer together or that highlight ways where our relationships need tending or boundaries. I am intentionally going to focus on the development of the Interdependent Paradigm of Power (power-with). This is not to deny the other paradigms of power and their place, but to say that power-with is a powerful antidote to many of the misuses and abuses of power we see and experience in the world.

Regardless of my bias, these factors could be considered in any systemic structure. Any of them could serve to highlight where systemic health could be threatened:

1. When the health of components/individuals or the relationships between the components/individuals are ignored, neglected, or abused

2. When the purpose and the priority of the system aren't aligned

3. When systems let configurative and emergent qualities get out of balance

When individual or relational health and power are ignored, neglected or abused

When a social system prioritizes its own power over the health of individuals and their relationships, it creates an unhealthy system, regardless of its purpose or structure. So the first measure of health in a social system is the degree of access to personal power for everyone in the system (not just some people). This is ultimately because it influences our capacity for right-relationship. If finding right-relationship with oneself or others is inhibited by the stories and structures of the system, the system tends toward being unhealthy or imbalanced.

If systems construct role or status power to promote the personal power and health of each individual, there will likely be more overall health and capacity within the system. However, if certain components or individuals are kept small or unhealthy, the entire system suffers. Of course, health isn't like an on-off switch—it's not a binary. So let's think of it more like a continuum. The more people in the system that have access to their personal power, the healthier the people, the relationships, and the system.

I'd like to share an example of how this happens. I have the frustrating predicament of having a chronic disease in a country that profits from my illness. Not only do I have to navigate a privatized healthcare system, spend at least a quarter of my salary on health insurance, health care, as well as medication and other treatments, but I also have to deal with medical doctors who typically don't like to deal with patients who have developed their personal power. On more than one occasion, I have been labeled a "problem patient" (which has literally been written in my medical file). Why would I be labeled that way? I am active in my care, I like to understand my diagnosis and treatment plan in detail (Why this medication? Why now? What does it do? What are the risks? What is the research around it? What are the alternatives?) and I like to be treated like an intelligent person, not like an annoying child who asks too many questions. Fortunately, I finally found a doctor (after going through 7 or 8 specialists) who treats me with respect and takes the time to answer my questions, often without me even having to ask them.

Why did it take me going through so many doctors to find one that would use their role power in a way that helped me to connect to my own sense of agency with my health? First, as a reminder, systemic power creates role power and status power (Systemic power creates what's considered to be valuable which becomes status power. And systemic power also creates roles that fulfill the purpose of the system). It is essential to recognize that how role power and status power are structured by the system will have a direct impact on how people present themselves in those roles and in that status.

So, in the example of a healthcare system that prioritizes profit and a privatized health insurance's authority, the doctor is bound by the structures of that system, which influences the way they show up with the down-power patient. In other words, doctors are not rewarded by this particular system for spending a lot of time with a patient (time is money) or for considering the patient's agency in their own care (the authority of the doctor and the health insurance is prioritized). So doctors are less likely to take the time to explain their diagnosis and treatment plan with a patient in such a system.

As we have discussed, the way a person shows up in role and status power can have a huge influence on the people down-power from them. In a study on agency and medication adherence, Nafradi, Nakamoto, and Schulz (2017) found that patients who were most compliant in taking their medication as prescribed by their doctor were those who had both an internal locus of control (personal agency) and had trust in their doctor. Nafradi, Nakamoto, and Schulz (2017) came to this conclusion:

"To sum up, patient empowerment can promote medication adherence, but it requires a co-constructed sense of control in the doctor-patient dyad. . . . As finding this equilibrium might be challenging, it requires building a strong collaborative doctor-patient relationship and continuous negotiation during the medical encounter."[1]

In other words, if patients do not have access to their own agency, they are not as likely to care for their health, nor follow the care of their doctor, as someone who is supported by that doctor in accessing their personal power. So why do some systems restrict or ignore the power of individuals? This leads us to the next parameter of health in a social system.

---

1. Náfrádi L, Nakamoto K, Schulz PJ. Is patient empowerment the key to promote adherence? A systematic review of the relationship between self-efficacy, health locus of control and medication adherence. PLoS One. 2017 Oct 17;12(10):e0186458. doi: 10.1371/journal.pone.0186458. PMID: 29040335; PMCID: PMC5645121, p. 11-23.

When the purpose and the priority of the system aren't aligned

As we saw in the different systemic lenses, some systems (like the U.S. Healthcare System) are set up in such a way that systemic power emphasizes things other than the health of the individuals in the system (which is ironic given that it is a *healthcare* system). In the example we have been using, this particular healthcare system might have a stated mission or purpose to serve the health of individuals, but its underlying priority is actually shareholder profit and the authority of privatized health insurance. Thus, the focus of the system shifts from its stated purpose to profit and authority. In a sense, the system's energy is split, which ultimately leads to an unhealthy system.

To return to our question, limiting the power of individuals could be an unfortunate byproduct of competing priorities (doctors limiting consultation time to increase profits could lead to less agency for the patient). Or it could be an intentional strategy of the competing priority (if patients stay sick or don't have time to get all of their questions answered, they have to book another appointment, which would increase profits). Either way, the result is the same: the individual's health and access to personal power suffer. But because this supports the underlying or hidden priority (profit), there is a sacrifice to the stated purpose or mission (supporting the health of people in the system).

Often, this misalignment comes from competing systemic lenses within the system itself. You might have some people in the system who are operating from a Pluralistic lens, highlighting relationships and health for all, and then you might have others operating with an Achievement lens, prioritizing profits, personal benefit, and company growth. Whoever has more power in the system tends to get to determine which direction the system goes.

When systems let configurative and emergent qualities get out of balance

The last major component of unhealthy systems is when the configuration aspect of systems becomes imbalanced or configurative forces take over the emergent qualities. As the two dynamic forces in social power dynamics, configurative and emergent qualities need to be present for balance to exist. When one of them is overly suppressed, then the health of the system is threatened.

When systems fail to account for emergent properties, they become rigid and brittle—like a tree that refuses to bend in the wind, only to snap under pressure. Emergence is the lifeblood of adaptation; it's how societies innovate, how marginalized groups organize, how new cultural norms take root. But when institutions and structures prioritize control over responsiveness, they create conditions ripe for dysfunction. Imagine a school system that designs curricula based solely on standardized tests (configuration), while ignoring the organic ways students actually learn through collaboration and curiosity (emergence). Over time, this imbalance stifles creativity, fuels disengagement, and ultimately produces graduates ill-equipped for a world that demands adaptability. The system, by refusing to incorporate emergent realities, becomes unhealthy—not just ineffective, but actively harmful.

Healthier systems—whether ecosystems, economies, or relationships—thrive by holding configuration and emergence in tension. Think of a forest managed with controlled burns: the intentional structure (configuration) prevents wildfires by making space for regenerative chaos (emergence). Similarly, democracies function best when constitutions (configuration) can be amended through public demand (emergence). The imbalance happens when one force dominates: too much configuration creates stagnation; too much emergence creates volatility. But when systems honor both, they become capable of growing stronger through disruption. The task isn't to "solve" the tension between these forces, but to design systems that let them converse, collide, and co-create.

16

The Power Differential

"Any society that ranks people based on race or gender or any other arbitrary characteristic teaches that trust should be allocated not by personal merit but by how closely one conforms to social norms—and so trust becomes little more than the reification of existing social structures and mythologies." - Prentis Hemphill

One of my favorite studies[1] by Dacher Keltner and his colleagues was a simple yet revealing experiment involving cookies. In this study, Keltner and his team divided participants into groups of three, randomly assigning one person to be the "leader" or the person with up-role power. The groups were given a task to complete, and afterward, they were offered a plate of cookies as a reward. The findings were striking: the leader (up-role power) person consistently took more cookies, often leaving fewer for the others. Not only did they take more, but they were also more likely to eat messily, showing less consideration for others. This behavior, Keltner argued, was a manifestation of the "power paradox"—the idea that power can corrupt, making individuals less empathetic and more self-centered.

---

1. Keltner, D., Gruenfeld, D. H., & Anderson, C. (2003). Power, approach, and inhibition. *Psychological Review*, 110(2), 265-284.

We have all witnessed, and many of us have participated in, the self-serving ways that people engage in power dynamics. The most potent expressions of power happen in relationships where there is a difference in one or more types of power. As we introduced in the Types of Power chapter, we call this the **power differential**. Beyond understanding how to access and navigate personal power, one of the most complex and impactful aspects of power-consciousness lies in recognizing and addressing power differentials in relationships. These imbalances, whether subtle or overt, shape us profoundly—from the earliest moments of our lives. Yet, many of us remain unaware of how we actively participate in these dynamics or even that a power differential exists at all. This lack of awareness can perpetuate inequities and influence our interactions in ways that deeply affect our emotional, psychological, and social development. With power differentials comes an imbalance of power between the parties, greatly increasing the risk of harm in relationships. Understanding when power differentials are present, how they play out, and what our responsibilities and vulnerabilities are within them can help us navigate those imbalances, regardless of where we find ourselves in the power dynamic.

There are two different categories of power differentials[2] in interpersonal relationships: differences in personal power and differences in interpersonal power. The first are differences in the extent to which we can access our personal power in a given moment, as well as differences in our overall degree of personal power development. And then there are the differences in the access we have to role and status power (interpersonal types of power).

---

2. There are also differences in power and influence between collectives, between systems and between groups and individuals. While we touched on this a little in The Intersections of Power chapter, the detail of these are beyond the scope of this book.

Becoming more power-conscious in each of these areas will help us to shape social power dynamics with more skill and wisdom. Let's look at the specific considerations for each type of differential.

Personal Power Differentials

In the disability movement, there is a metaphor called "The Spoon Theory." It was created by Christine Miserandino in 2003 to explain the daily experience of living with chronic illness or disability. In the metaphor, "spoons" represent units of energy that people have to spend on daily tasks. While healthy individuals may have an abundance of energy (spoons) and can easily perform multiple tasks without much thought, people with chronic illnesses or disabilities have a limited number of spoons each day. For someone with a chronic condition, even simple tasks like getting out of bed, showering, or cooking a meal can consume a significant number of spoons. Once the spoons are used up, the person may have no energy left for other activities, leading to fatigue, pain, or the need to rest.

The Spoon Theory has become a powerful tool for raising awareness about the challenges faced by people with chronic illnesses or disabilities. It helps others understand that what might seem like a simple task can be incredibly taxing for someone with limited energy. By using the spoon metaphor, people with chronic conditions can communicate their experiences and navigate the power differential more effectively.

While spoon theory is inherently linked to status power, the concept of being at different levels of capacity is a such a helpful way to communicate about our personal power as well. At the Right Use of Power Institute, we use the terms "up-capacity" and "down-capacity" to describe where we're at on a given day or moment. There are countless reasons why our capacity might shift—maybe we get sick, didn't sleep well, just had a fight with a partner, haven't eaten enough, or are feeling emotionally off-balance. These factors can all impact the personal power we have to draw from in the moment.

But it's not just about our internal state—our capacity can also fluctuate depending on who we're interacting with, the context of the situation, who else is around, and what other power dynamics might be at play. For example, you might feel more "up-capacity" in a supportive environment with people who uplift you, but "down-capacity" in a tense or hierarchical setting where power imbalances are more pronounced. I just facilitated a process on racial microaggressions and the people of color in the room mentioned that the toll of consistently being in spaces dominated by white people is taxing in and of itself. They have to consider if it's safe to show up in certain ways, assess whether they need to code-switch, and be more careful in general about what they say and do. This is a lot of extra decision-making and stress that white people in the room never have to navigate in the same way. This extra expenditure of energy can reduce the ability to direct energy toward other needs, which ultimately impacts personal power.

Whenever there's a difference in personal power between two people—whether it's in the moment or related to our long-term development—a personal power differential exists. Unlike role or status differences, which are often created and shaped by external systems, personal power differences are fluid and depend on our intentional development of personal power. The development of personal power often hinges on a combination of internal and external factors. Internally, self-awareness and a tendency toward growth—those who reflect on their strengths, weaknesses, and values—are more likely to take intentional steps toward building their rooted personal power. External influences, such as upbringing, social environment, how society values our identities, and cultural norms, also shape one's sense of personal power. For instance, when we have supportive relationships and constructive feedback, it might be easier to develop our connection to personal power, while harsh criticism, lack of encouragement, abuse, or oppressive environments stifle it. However, those who are born with a lot of down-status identities, who don't have as much access to role and status power, only have access to one type of power: personal power. For this reason, you will see many people with down-status identities and down-role power who have intentionally and deeply developed their personal power.

One of the most important growth periods of my life was being a single mother for 7 years. I was raising a toddler, finishing a doctorate, and working full-time. I was pushed and stretched in ways that I never considered, and grew in ways I never thought possible. I realized when we are handed everything and experience no hardships, there is nothing to sharpen ourselves against. I see countless people who were born with white skin, a lot of money, and/or male gender who were handed status power and role power early and consistently. With so much access to status and role power, there isn't a strong need to develop rooted personal power – and in such cases, people can begin to conflate their own sense of "power" with the role and status power that is being conferred to them from the broader systems in which they operate. Unfortunately, this can cause them to miss out on developing rooted personal power that supports resilience and groundedness. There are so many misuses of power precisely because people lean on role and status power for their sense of self and agency in the world. We might live in a much different world if we focused a little more on developing our rooted personal power.

Of course, we are all handed a different set of circumstances when we are born, and we all have access to different opportunities, resources, or environments. Ultimately, the interplay between self-perception, external support, and life circumstances determines whether someone cultivates their personal power or remains constrained by internal or external barriers. The challenge comes when we find ourselves in relationship with someone with very different capabilities, self-development, or levels of awareness. These differences alone can make finding right-relationship complex, as they often lead to misunderstandings, mismatched expectations, or even harm. For example, one person may be highly self-motivated and proactive, while another may struggle with self-doubt or lack the tools to assert themselves, for any number of reasons. This divergence can create friction, especially if one person feels overshadowed or the other feels unsupported. However, these differences can also be an opportunity for growth if both people approach the relationship with empathy, patience, and a willingness to learn from each other. We don't need to try to achieve perfect equality in personal power, which is impossible; rather, we can choose to create a dynamic where both people feel valued and empowered to grow in their own way.

With personal power differentials, we often won't be aware of the differences until we start interacting. I have been able to greatly lessen the impact of that power differential when I can name when I am feeling down-capacity and when I check in with whomever I'm relating with about their capacity. This allows me to navigate the power differential and bring balance to the relationship. Brené Brown often uses the idea of percentages to talk about how much energy or capacity we have in relationships, especially in co-parenting. She explains that in any given moment, one person might only have 40% to give, while the other has 60%, and that's normal. The key is to recognize that these levels shift depending on stress, energy, or life circumstances, and to support each other when one person is running low. It's not about always being at 100%—it's about teamwork, understanding, and being there for each other even when things aren't perfect. Brown's message is about letting go of the pressure to always be fully capable (which is not realisitic) and focusing on showing up as best we can, even when we're not at our best. It's not about always being at full capacity—it's about being aware of where we are and making intentional choices based on that awareness. It is also about communicating with one another about our capacity so we can better navigate differences and support one another in our access to personal power.

Interpersonal Power Differentials

The power differentials that exist in interpersonal relationships are perhaps the most widely recognized and discussed. These differences come from role and status power, which, as we have discussed in previous chapters, are constructed and shaped by systems and the power paradigms of the people in the differential relationship. In other words, role and status power differentials are externally constructed—by societal norms, cultural expectations, and institutional structures—but they are interpersonally performed. We enact these differences according to the rules and parameters these systems prescribe, often without even realizing it. The ways we are socialized to navigate these power dynamics are so deeply ingrained that we frequently perform them unconsciously.

The impact of these power differentials on our brains, bodies, and relationships is significant. Similar to the cookie study mentioned above, numerous studies show how a role or status power differential changes us. In one article, they even talk about the effects of interpersonal power differentials as "functional brain damage.[3]" This is due to the impact these relationships have on our ability to have perspective[4] and empathize,[5] our level of generosity[6], our tendency to follow rules[7] or social norms[8] or be accountable[9] for our actions, the standards[10] we hold for ourselves versus others,

3. Useem, J. (2017, May). Power causes brain damage. The Atlantic. Retrieved from https://www.theatlantic.com/magazine/archive/2017/07/power-causes-brain -damage/528711/

4. Galinsky, A. D., Magee, J. C., Inesi, M. E., & Gruenfeld, D. H. (2006). Power and perspectives not taken. Psychological Science, 17(12), 1068-1074. & Harris, L. T., & Fiske, S. T. (2009). Social neuroscience evidence for dehumanized perception. *European Review of Social Psychology*, 20(1), 192-231.

5. Van Kleef, G. A., Oveis, C., Van der Löwe, I., LuoKogan, A., Goetz, J., & Keltner, D. (2008). Power, distress, and compassion: Turning a blind eye to the suffering of others. Psychological Science, 19(12), 1315-1322.

6. Piff, P. K., Kraus, M. W., Côté, S., Cheng, B. H., & Keltner, D. (2010). Having less, giving more: The influence of social class on prosocial behavior. Journal of Personality and Social Psychology, 99(5), 771-784.

7. Piff, P. K., Stancato, D. M., Côté, S., Mendoza-Denton, R., & Keltner, D. (2012). Higher social class predicts increased unethical behavior. Proceedings of the National Academy of Sciences, 109(11), 4086-4091.

8. Keltner, D., & Robinson, R. J. (1997). Defending the status quo: Power and bias in social conflict. Personality and Social Psychology Bulletin, 23(10), 1066-1077.

9. van Kleef, G. A., Oveis, C., van der Löwe, I., LuoKogan, A., Goetz, J., & Keltner, D. (2008). Power, distress, and compassion: Turning a blind eye to the suffering of others. Psychological Science, 19(12), 1315-1322.

10. Lammers, J., Stapel, D. A., & Galinsky, A. D. (2010). Power increases hypocrisy: Moralizing in reasoning, immorality in behavior. Psychological Science, 21(5), 737-744.

how we make decisions[11] , how stress[12] impacts our bodies, and even how we engage in humor[13] . The research is clear: power differentials shape our behavior in profound ways, often without us being fully aware of it.

Given this, it's crucial that we become more aware of how power differentials affect us, regardless of where we stand in the hierarchy. We need to make more intentional choices about how we behave in these relationships. After all, we all move back and forth between up power and down power in our daily lives, to varying degrees. For example, I might wake up as a human being, then step into the role of mother as I help my kids get ready for school, teach a class as a professor, visit the doctor as a patient, and return to my office as a therapist or coach. Each of these roles involves different power dynamics, and being aware of these shifts—noting how responsibilities and vulnerabilities change—is essential for navigating them effectively.

What many people don't realize is that they often get stuck in one mindset—either "I am powerful" or "I am powerless"—and carry that perspective into every relationship. This fixed mindset overlooks the nuance and complexity of power dynamics, which are rarely black-and-white. The existence of power differentials,

---

11. Lammers, J., & Galinsky, A. D. (2010). The power to be immoral: Power increases the likelihood of engaging in unethical behavior. *Social Psychological and Personality Science*, 1(1), 15-19. & Fast, N. J., Gruenfeld, D. H., Sivanathan, N., & Galinsky, A. D. (2009). Illusory control: A generative force behind power's far-reaching effects. *Psychological Science*, 20(4), 502-508.

12. Sherman, G. D., Lee, J. J., Cuddy, A. J., Renshon, J., Oveis, C., Gross, J. J., & Lerner, J. S. (2012). Leadership is associated with lower levels of stress. Proceedings of the National Academy of Sciences, 109(44), 17903-17907.

13. Keltner, D., Young, R. C., Heerey, E. A., Oemig, C., & Monarch, N. D. (1998). Teasing in hierarchical and intimate relations. Journal of Personality and Social Psychology, 75(5), 1231-1247.

while often uncomfortable, serves multiple functions in society. It's precisely because of these differentials that we need to think deeply about ethics and how we use power. There are so many ways people in down-power positions can be harmed, and unfortunately, most, if not all of us, have experienced harm in a power-differential relationship at some point. This is a universal experience, and it's one of the reasons why many of us fear, ignore, or even avoid power altogether. We don't want to harm others, so we either underuse our power or shy away from it entirely.

As we explore the shadows and complexities that often arise in power differentials in the following chapters, it's important to emphasize just how much these dynamics impact our day-to-day lives. Whether we're aware of it or not, power differentials shape our interactions, our decisions, and our sense of self[14].

Key Features of any Power Differential

No matter whether we are encountering a differential in role, status, or personal power, or a combination of power differentials, there are key features to keep in mind as we navigate the complexity of power differentials. As a reminder, we use the words "up-power" and "down-power" to label positions in any interpersonal power differential. We constructed this language to give us the ability to discuss power in relationships. Being able to talk about the

---

14. If you're interested in diving deeper into this topic, I recommend *Right Use of Power: The Heart of Ethics* by Dr. Cedar Barstow if you're in the helping professions, or *Power: A User's Guide* by Julie Diamond if you're in a corporate or business setting. Both books do an excellent job of exploring personal and role power and how to navigate these dynamics in professional relationships. Understanding these nuances is key to using power ethically and effectively, no matter where we find ourselves in the power spectrum.

differences in power between us is essential for navigating toward right-relationship. Let's build out the language of power differentials a bit more so we can have a richer discussion.

The key differences between up-power and down-power have to do with the impact those positions have on each individual and on the relationship itself. When one person has more influence, decision-making ability, access to resources, greater social capital, more mental, emotional, or physical capacity, etc., an imbalance is created in the relationship. How each person thinks about and treats that imbalance ultimately determines the health of that relationship. Here are some factors that influence any power differential:

1. Each person's power paradigm.

Each person in a power differential relationship has a belief about how power works in general. We typically learn how power works through the systems that shape us. As we outlined the different power paradigms in the Systemic Lenses chapter, each person might lean more towards one than the others. Whether those paradigms align or differ, beliefs about how power works greatly influence how each person shows up in the relationship and how they respond to the power differential. If the paradigms are similar, the relationship will likely be easier and more harmonious. And if they differ, the relationship will likely suffer or fail without conscious communication about it. So if a boss (up-role power) operates largely from the Domination Power Paradigm (power-over) and their employee (down-role power) operates from an Interdependent Power Paradigm (power-with), there will likely be some confusion, frustration, and conflict. The boss will expect the employee to comply without question, and the employee will expect the boss to be collaborative. The boss will likely view the employee as disrespectful, and the employee might view the boss as oppressive.

The context of the system in which the relationship operates can also have a substantial influence here. If the system in which the boss and employee work operates under an Authority lens, the boss will feel justified in their paradigm, and the employee will feel pressure to acquiesce. The alignment or misalignment of these paradigms has a significant impact on the health of power-differential relationships.

2. Access to Personal Power

In both positions of the power differential, the degree of access each person has to their personal power will determine the health of the relationship. It is the ultimate measuring stick for relational health in a power differential. When we bring our personal power into our up or down power positions, it allows our humanity to be present and acknowledges that we are each more than our role or status power positions. Without this, there is a much greater potential for harm in the relationship.

The presence of personal power in the relationship means there is some capacity for self-reflection, empathy, boundaries, courage, and resilience. These are all necessary ingredients for tending to the needs of the relationship. It makes us capable of giving and receiving feedback and of engaging in generative conflict. It allows us to tolerate differences and to be curious. And, most importantly, the presence of personal power within the power differential allows us to hold ourselves accountable, take responsibility for our actions, and assert our needs and boundaries. This balance of accountability and agency is crucial for maintaining a healthy dynamic. The bottom line is that personal power on both sides of the power differential is essential for right-relationship.

3. Trust Building

There are many reasons we may not trust or hold the other person in a power differential in high regard. Because trust doesn't inherently accompany either position in a power differential, it has to be continuously earned. The concept of moving at the speed of trust, popularized by Stephen M.R. Covey in his book *The Speed of Trust: The One Thing That Changes Everything*, highlights the critical role of trust in the health and effectiveness of relationships, teams, and organizations. Covey argues that when trust is high, processes move faster, decisions are made more efficiently, and collaboration flows more smoothly. Conversely, when trust is low, everything slows down—communication becomes strained, progress is hindered, and relationships can become dysfunctional. While Covey focuses primarily on work environments and outcomes, I think of moving at the speed of trust as something more related to the health of a power-differential relationship.

In both positions of a power differential, trust is a dynamic process that requires ongoing attention and effort. In down-power, it's about using discernment, protecting ourselves, and remaining open to building trust when it's safe to do so. In up-power, it's about using our influence in ways that foster trust and respect, rather than reinforcing the power differential in harmful ways. When you are in up-power, your focus will give you insight into which direction you are going. Do you focus on your authority, or the health of the relationship? Are you aware of the down-power person's experience in the relationship because you foster an environment of open feedback and communication? Or do you assume and dismiss the down-power experience because you are so focused on fulfilling the obligations of your role?

Ultimately, moving at the speed of trust in a power-differential relationship means recognizing that trust is the foundation of healthy, equitable, and productive interactions. It is about balancing vulnerability and responsibility. By prioritizing trust, both parties can create a healthier, more equitable dynamic that allows for smoother collaboration, greater mutual respect, and more meaningful outcomes. Trust isn't a given—it's a continuous process that requires effort, transparency, and accountability from all sides. And trust building cannot begin until we learn to accept and acknowledge the responsibilities and vulnerabilities inherent in the power differential.

4. Acceptance and/or Acknowledgment of Responsibilities and Vulnerabilities

When someone enters a power-differential relationship, each person has a felt sense of their power position. In role power, each person accepting their position enters an implicit agreement regarding the vulnerabilities and responsibilities of that position within the power differential. If they do not accept their position, there is no chance that those responsibilities will be fulfilled or that those vulnerabilities will be acknowledged and addressed. The health of role power differentials depends fundamentally on both parties accepting their positions.

However, in status power, it is the acknowledgment of the power differential (not the acceptance of it) that is the critical element. When we find ourselves in a status power differential, it can be disturbing for different reasons, depending on our position in the differential relationship. When we are down-status, the complexities and injustice of the power differential are obvious and painful.

We are vulnerable in down-status because of the way systems have shaped structures to our disadvantage, because of the way others have been socialized to ignore, dismiss, or exclude us.

And when we are up-status, we rarely recognize the potential for harm that comes from that up-status—especially when we aren't conscious of the differential at all. And when we do recognize it, we usually get caught up either in the discomfort of our up-status or in taking advantage of our position to boost our ego, line our pockets, or gain social capital. When the up-status ignores (willfully or otherwise) their up-status position, the responsibilities are dropped, and the vulnerability of the down-status person increases. Because of this dynamic in power differentials, the key to navigating them well lies in our considering the presence of both vulnerabilities and responsibilities for each person involved.

The Power Differential

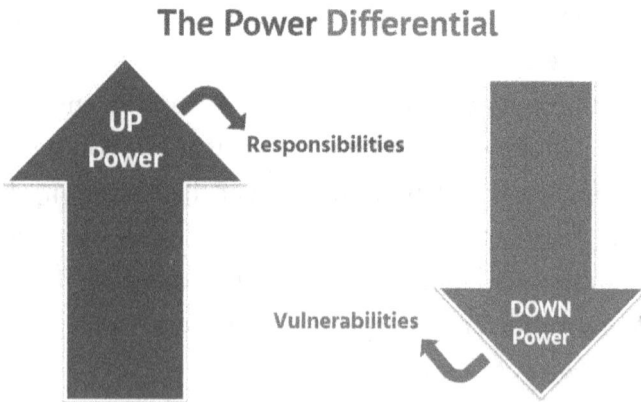

17

The Interdependence of Responsibilities & Vulnerabilities

"Between stimulus and response there is a space. In that space is our power to choose our response. In our response lies our growth and our freedom." - Viktor Frankl

"Vulnerability is the birthplace of connection and the path to the feeling of worthiness." - Marshall Rosenberg

In the sun-drenched city of Syracuse, on the island of Sicily, there once ruled a man named Dionysius. He was a tyrant in every sense of the word - powerful, wealthy, and feared by all. His palace gleamed with gold and precious stones, and his word was law throughout the land.

Among his court was a man named Damocles, a sycophant who never missed an opportunity to flatter the great Dionysius. "Oh, what a fortunate man you are!" Damocles would exclaim. "Such power, such riches, such splendor! Surely, you must be the happiest man alive!"

Day after day, Damocles sang the praises of Dionysius's enviable life. Finally, the tyrant's patience wore thin. With a sly smile, he turned to Damocles and said, "Since you think my life is so wonderful, perhaps you'd like to try it for yourself?"

Damocles's eyes lit up. "Oh yes, my lord! Nothing would please me more!"

"Very well," said Dionysius. "Tomorrow, you shall be king for a day."

The next morning, Damocles was led to the palace in royal robes. He was seated on a golden couch, surrounded by the finest delicacies and most beautiful servants. Damocles could scarcely believe his luck. He reached for a goblet of wine, ready to toast his good fortune.

But as he raised his eyes, he froze. There, suspended directly above his head, hung a massive, razor-sharp sword. It was held in place by nothing more than a single strand of horsehair.

Suddenly, the food lost its taste. The wine turned sour in his mouth. Every moment was filled with terror as Damocles sat, rigid with fear, expecting the sword to fall at any instant.

Unable to enjoy any of the luxuries surrounding him, Damocles begged Dionysius to let him step down. He had learned a powerful lesson: with great power comes great anxiety, and the price of luxury is constant peril.

From that day forward, the "Sword of Damocles" became a powerful symbol, reminding us that those who appear to have it all often carry a heavy crown. It serves as a warning about the hidden perils of power and the ever-present dangers that come with great responsibility.[1]

When I first read this story, I couldn't help but roll my eyes a little. Am I supposed to feel sorry for tyrants who "have it all?" But upon further reflection, I realized that this story points to even more complexity present in the power differential. No matter how much we may want to feel invincible when we are in up-power, or how much we want to dehumanize the other person when we're in down-power, the reality is that we are all still human, no matter where we find ourselves in the power differential. In being human,

---

1. This is an ancient Greek parable that was first recorded by the Roman philosopher Cicero in his 45 B.C. work, *Tusculan Disputations*, and was re-generated by Deep Seek AI for the purposes of this book.

ultimately, we are all fundamentally vulnerable. The poet, David Whyte, said, "Vulnerability is not a weakness, a passing indisposition, or something we can arrange to do without. Vulnerability... is the underlying, ever-present, and abiding undercurrent of our natural state." Being vulnerable is a starting place as living beings, and then systems build in differences that create power differentials, and those power differentials create a great deal more vulnerability precisely because there *is* a power differential. So why would we intentionally create *more* vulnerability? My proposal is that in attempting to escape the vulnerability of being human, the power differential was intentionally created. The creators of up-power wanted to separate themselves from the chaos and messiness of being human. However, in attempting to escape the vulnerability of being human or the down-power position, I'm sure neither Dionysius nor Damocles anticipated the level of vulnerability they would experience in the *up*-power position.

In running away from or ignoring vulnerability, we actually make the power differential—and the experience of being human—much more challenging. What if instead of Damocles taking the place of the king, the king took Damocles' place? That would have had a much more impressive impact on the city of Syracuse. Unfortunately, in most societies, we have moved in the direction of avoidance and separation. Since many of us are in cultures where power differentials prevail and those power differentials create greater vulnerability, what is needed is greater *responsibility* to create balance and reduce harm.

You might have heard the phrase, "With great power comes great responsibility." While this phrase was popularized by the comic book *Spiderman* in 1962, it has been said in many forms, across societies, for thousands of years. Despite the prominence of the phrase, its meaning has been lost along the way. How this phrase is interpreted and implemented (if at all) varies greatly depending on how we understand vulnerability, power, and responsibility. Similar to vulnerability, one of the tragedies of our time is that we have become so afraid of, or weighed down by, responsibility that we tend to either avoid it or engage with it in ways that lead to greater disconnection from others. This is unfortunate, as the point of responsibility is to *strengthen* our relationships—not to make them a nuisance. Responsibility is the most important element in any relationship, especially when there is a power differential.

In the intricate dance of human connection, few dynamics are as pivotal—or as overlooked—as the interplay between responsibility and vulnerability. We've spent a good amount of time digging into what power means, but responsibility and vulnerability are just as layered—and just as often avoided. These two forces, when understood and balanced, can transform the way we relate to one another, especially in relationships where power is unevenly distributed. Because I believe that the dynamic of responsibility and vulnerability is one of the most important keys to finding right-relationship, I want to spend some time offering slightly different definitions or adding nuance to the concepts of responsibility and vulnerability. Let's start with responsibility, then move to vulnerability, and finally look more closely at the dynamic between the two.

Responsibility

In many cultures, responsibility is often framed as a duty or obligation—something we have to do, whether it's chores, work, or caring for others. In the United States, we even use the words duty, obligation, or accountability interchangeably with the word responsibility. However, the differences between these concepts are important and ultimately influence how we engage with our responsibilities. I want to get clear on what we mean when we talk about responsibility in the context of a relationship.

Duty typically refers to a moral or ethical commitment, something you feel bound to do because of your role, values, or principles. It's often tied to a sense of honor or loyalty, like a soldier's duty to their country or a parent's duty to care for their child. The challenge in thinking of responsibility as a duty in the context of power differentials is that we tend to narrow our view to fulfilling the role or principles we have, and it can leave out the other person or the relationship itself. And, of course, abiding by the ethics and fulfilling the agreed role are also important, but this distinction often gets lost in translation. If we get caught up in focusing on the duties and the ethics, checking the boxes and making sure we are a "good person following the rules," we can easily lose touch with the needs of the moment and the other unique human being with whom we are in relationship.

Similar to duty, **obligation** involves being bound by external factors—like laws, contracts, or social expectations. It's something you *have* to do, whether you want to or not, such as paying taxes or abiding by the laws enforced by a system. When we are obligated to do something, there is a heaviness there. It is psychologically overwhelming when it is tied to performance or when there is an enforceable or evaluative component. And it originates from outside of ourselves, rather than an internal motivation. Add to that the fear of failure (which is common in cultures that emphasize perfectionism or harshly judge mistakes), and responsibility as an obligation or duty can quickly become something to dread.

So, where does this leave us in our definition of responsibility? Viktor E. Frankl, the Austrian psychiatrist and Holocaust survivor, spoke of responsibility as "response-ability" — our ability to respond. This is a powerful reframing that shifts the focus from obligation or burden to an active, intentional capacity to respond. At its core, "response-ability" is about choosing how we respond to situations, people, and challenges in ways that align with our values and the well-being of the relationship. It's not just about reacting passively, following the rules, or saying the right thing, but about engaging thoughtfully and intentionally. When we think of responsibility as "response-ability," we're emphasizing agency and choice. It's about recognizing that we have the power to shape our interactions and outcomes through how we respond. This is one of the ways we can bring our personal power into our power-differential relationships.

This reframing also highlights the relational aspect of responsibility. In any interaction, our "response-ability" isn't just about us—it's about how our response impacts the relationship as a whole. It's the ability to respond in ways that acknowledge the power differential and the inherent vulnerabilities it creates—in ways that nurture trust, respect, and connection. So, to be more specific, when we talk about responsibility in the context of power differentials, we aren't referring just to role or positional responsibilities; we are focusing on the **relational responsibility**. This means we are attending to the other person as a human being as well as attending to the relationship itself. It is the commitment to actively care for and nurture the well-being of a relationship, recognizing that the health and success of the connection depend on the actions, intentions, and accountability of all parties involved. In practice, relational responsibility means being attentive to others' needs and feelings, communicating openly and honestly, and taking ownership of one's role in the relationship's dynamics—whether in moments of harmony or conflict. It's about understanding that relationships are co-created and that each person has a role to play in maintaining and strengthening the health of the relationship.

Responsibility versus Accountability

Another aspect of responsibility I want to highlight has to do with time—and, from my view this is really the distinction between responsibility and accountability. Responsibility is our willingness and ability to respond in the present or our commitment to respond in the future. In addition to the description of "response" noted above, by responding I mean attending and attuning to the relationship, tracking for impact, acknowledging the vulnerabilities, and being an active participant in the relationship, rather than a passive bystander. In contrast, **accountability** refers to our ability to account for what happened in the past (even if the past was just a minute ago)—it's about answering for the outcomes of our responsibilities. It's the part where you own up to what you've done, whether it's a success or a failure, and are willing to face the consequences (or accept the compliments).

While duty and obligation often come from outside pressures, responsibility and accountability are more internal, driven by a sense of personal commitment and integrity. Together, these concepts form a spectrum of how we engage with the world, from the external demands we meet to the internal standards we hold ourselves to. Our focus (internal or external) will determine how we drive or influence the relationship. And where we are in the power differential will determine how heavy that influence is on the other person. If you'd like to read more about responsibility, I've included a model called "The Window of Responsibility" in the Appendix of the book.

The 150% Principle

At its core, responsibility in an interpersonal relationship means that each person has the opportunity to engage thoughtfully and ethically with their various types of power. Dr. Barstow created the "150% Principle," which illustrates this through a power differential. When we are in any relationship, we are 100% responsible for accessing our personal power, when we have capacity to do so. An exception exists in abusive or oppressive relationships where accessing our personal power becomes virtually impossible without support. So when we are down-power in relatively healthy power differentials, we are 100% responsible for showing up with our personal power as fully as our capacity allows. Responsibility for the down-power person involves bringing their personal power into the relationship, engaging discernment, creating boundaries, and offering feedback.

But when we are in up-power we have *an additional 50% responsibility* for the health of the relationship. As the party with greater ability to influence or cause an effect, the person with more up-power has even greater responsibility to behave with care and intention. This isn't just about avoiding harm; it's about actively creating conditions where the down-power person can thrive. This means we create structures and build awareness to ensure the health of the relationship, monitor our impact on the down-power person, and create opportunities for down-power to more easily access their personal power. So in up-power, we are 100% responsible for bringing our personal power into our up-power position, and we have an additional 50% relational responsibility, for a total of 150%.

For both sides in a power-differential, responsibility is about listening deeply, making decisions with care, and being accountable for the impact of one's actions. Responsibility, in this sense, is a form of stewardship—a commitment to engage in power dynamics in ways that uplift rather than diminish.

Vulnerability

Vulnerability, on the other hand, involves a risk of harm and the possibility of being unseen or misunderstood. For a person in down-power, there isn't much choice in the experience of vulnerability. We are vulnerable to how the up-power person chooses to participate in the power differential. The up-power person could choose to use their greater influence or access to benefit everyone in the relationship, or they may decide to use it to benefit only themselves. The outcomes of up-power using their access and influence to only benefit themselves can range from exclusion or dismissal to physical or psychological harm to the down-power person. The stakes are high for the down-power person and, beyond personal power, they have very little ability to control those outcomes. This makes us fundamentally vulnerable when we are in down-power.

However, for the up-power person, vulnerability is a choice *in relationship with the down-power person.* We can choose to admit mistakes, to seek feedback, and to acknowledge our own limitations. Unfortunately, vulnerability isn't often chosen by the up-power person, leaving the down-power person even more vulnerable (since they are the only one who is vulnerable *because* of the relationship). But if the up-power person is able and willing to recognize and navigate vulnerability well within a power differential, it can be a powerful tool for building trust, fostering connection, and creating healthier relationships.

While it must be approached with discernment, intention, and awareness of the power dynamics, both the up-power and down-power person have a role to play in ensuring that vulnerability is approached constructively and respectfully. By setting boundaries, practicing empathy, and focusing on shared goals, vulnerability can help bridge the power gap and create a more equitable and supportive dynamic. The key is to ensure vulnerability serves as a tool for connection and growth rather than a source of harm.

Types of Vulnerability

In relationships with power differentials, vulnerability becomes a complex, multifaceted experience with multiple types of vulnerability at play. When one person holds more power — whether through social status or structural authority — the other person may find themselves in a position where their needs, emotions, and autonomy are at risk. Understanding the different types of vulnerability in these relationships is essential to fostering healthier dynamics in which both individuals feel respected and empowered. By exploring these vulnerabilities, we can begin to address the underlying power imbalances and work toward relationships that prioritize mutual support and equity.

Emotional vulnerability in relationships with power differentials often stems from the down-power person's reliance on the up-power individual for validation, approval, or emotional support. This dynamic can leave the down-power person feeling exposed or at risk of being hurt, particularly when they perceive that their emotional well-being is tied to the up-power person's responses. A study by Park and Raile (2010) found that employees often feel a heightened sense of risk when discussing personal matters with supervisors, particularly when they perceive the supervisor as unsympathetic or judgmental. This emotional vulnerability can lead to decreased job satisfaction and increased stress, as employees struggle to balance their personal needs with professional expectations.

In status power differentials, emotional vulnerability can be even more intense because of the frequency with which those who are down-status encounter microaggressions. These are reinforced by systemic, cultural, and historic structures and beliefs that make the emotional vulnerability constant. Smith et al. $(2021)^2$ found that Black employees in predominantly white workplaces often feel emotionally vulnerable when discussing racial issues with white colleagues or supervisors, anticipating dismissive or defensive responses. This can lead to emotional exhaustion and a sense of isolation, as they suppress their true feelings to avoid conflict or retribution. Similarly, in personal relationships, people of color may feel emotionally vulnerable when addressing racial biases or insensitive comments from white friends or partners, fearing that raising these issues could strain the relationship or lead to invalidation.

Psychological vulnerability is also common in power differentials. This occurs when the down-power person over-identifies with their down-power, to the exclusion of their personal power. When we internalize the power dynamic, it can lead to feelings of inadequacy, self-doubt, or diminished self-worth. Over time, this psychological vulnerability can erode the down-power person's confidence and autonomy, making it harder for them to advocate for themselves or seek change. consequences, which can further

---

2. Smith, W. A., Mustaffa, J. B., Jones, C. M., Curry, T. J., & Allen, W. R. (2021). "You make me feel so uncomfortable": The emotional labor of navigating racial microaggressions in the workplace. Journal of Diversity in Higher Education, 14(3), 321-335.

entrench the power imbalance.[3] A study by Stephens et al. (2014)[4] explores how socioeconomic status differences can exacerbate psychological vulnerability. They found that students from lower-income families often experience feelings of inadequacy at school when interacting with peers or teachers from higher socioeconomic backgrounds. This can manifest as imposter syndrome, where students doubt their abilities and feel they don't belong in academic environments dominated by wealthier peers. This dynamic not only affects individual students but also perpetuates broader inequalities in education, as those from lower socioeconomic backgrounds are less likely to thrive in environments where they feel psychologically vulnerable.

In personal relationships, psychological vulnerability can also emerge when there is a significant socioeconomic status difference. For instance, in romantic partnerships where one partner has significantly more financial resources or social capital, the less affluent partner may feel a sense of inadequacy or dependency. This can lead to a loss of autonomy, as they may feel they have less say in decision-making or that their contributions to the relationship are undervalued.[5] Over time, this can create a dynamic where the less affluent partner feels they must conform to the expectations of the more affluent partner, further reinforcing the power imbalance.

Another form is **relational vulnerability**, which arises when

---

3. Van Kleef, G. A., Oveis, C., van der Löwe, I., LuoKogan, A., Goetz, J., & Keltner, D. (2008). Power, distress, and compassion: Turning a blind eye to the suffering of others. Psychological Science, 19(12), 1315-1322.

4. Stephens, N. M., Markus, H. R., & Phillips, L. T. (2014). Social class culture cycles: How three gateway contexts shape selves and fuel inequality. Annual Review of Psychology, 65, 611-634.

5. Ridgeway, C. L. (2019). Status: Why is it everywhere? Why does it matter? Russell Sage Foundation.

the down-power person depends on the relationship for stability, resources, or identity. This dependence can create a dynamic where the down-power person feels unable to assert their needs or set boundaries, leaving them susceptible to exploitation, neglect, or manipulation. In caregiver-dependent relationships, for example, the dependent person—whether a child, elderly individual, or someone with a disability—may feel unable to challenge the caregiver's decisions, even when those decisions are not in their best interest. This vulnerability is often compounded by the caregiver's control over essential resources like food, shelter, or medical care, which can make the dependent person feel they have no choice but to comply, even if they are unhappy or mistreated[6].

Finally, **structural vulnerability** refers to the systemic inequalities that reinforce power imbalances, making it difficult for those in down-power to escape or challenge the dynamics of the relationship. This type of vulnerability is deeply rooted in systems and expressed by status power—societal norms, institutional policies, and cultural practices that privilege certain groups while marginalizing others. Unlike individual or relational vulnerabilities, which can often be addressed through personal or interpersonal interventions, structural vulnerability requires broader systemic changes to dismantle the barriers that perpetuate inequality.

One example of structural vulnerability can be seen in the workplace, where systemic gender inequalities often place women, trans and gender expansive people at a disadvantage. A study by Correll et al. (2007)[7] found that women are frequently penalized

---

6. Nussbaum, M. C. (2000). Women and human development: The capabilities approach. Cambridge University Press.

7. Correll, S. J., Benard, S., & Paik, I. (2007). Getting a job: Is there a motherhood penalty? American Journal of Sociology, 112(5), 1297-1338.

for behaviors that are rewarded in men, such as assertiveness or ambition. This double standard creates a structural barrier that makes it difficult for women to advance in their careers, as they are often perceived as either too aggressive or not assertive enough. Additionally, institutional policies like lack of paid parental leave or flexible work arrangements disproportionately affect women, who are more likely to take on caregiving responsibilities. These structural barriers not only limit women's career opportunities but also reinforce the power imbalance between men and women in the workplace, making it harder for women to challenge or escape these dynamics.

Addressing structural vulnerability necessitates systemic changes that challenge the norms and policies that perpetuate inequality. This includes advocating for policy reforms, such as equitable workplace practices, criminal justice reform, and economic policies that reduce income inequality. It also involves creating spaces where marginalized voices are heard and valued, and where systemic barriers are actively dismantled.

The Benefits and Risks of Vulnerability

In relationships with power differentials, both the up-power and down-power individuals can show up in vulnerability in healthy ways, though the benefits and risks differ for each position. When we are in up-power, embracing vulnerability might mean acknowledging our limitations, seeking feedback, or admitting when we've made a mistake. This can humanize us, deepen connection, and make us more approachable to those in down-power. For example, a manager who openly admits they don't have all the answers can create a more collaborative environment where employees feel safe to contribute ideas. The benefit here is that it fosters trust and mutual respect, which can lead to more open communication and better teamwork. However, the risk for the up-power person is that showing vulnerability might be perceived as a weakness, potentially undermine their authority, or end up being more harmful than helpful. The up-power person needs to balance vulnerability with appropriate boundaries, ensuring that they aren't over-sharing or centering themselves.

When we are in down-power, while we are inherently vulnerable through the power-differential, we can also show our human vulnerability when the up-power person has built trust and demonstrated their ability to handle our vulnerability with care. We have to make calculated risks when we are in down-power to explore the possibility of introducing more vulnerability into the power differential. It takes an incredible amount of courage, discernment, and intentionally developed boundaries to do this in a sustainable way.

When both sides engage in healthy vulnerability, it can transform the power dynamic into one of mutual respect and collaboration. With 150% responsibility, the up-power person, must have the willingness and ability to create structures and opportunities where the down-power person feels more comfortable expressing themselves without fear of negative consequences. When done well, vulnerability can be a powerful tool for creating healthier, more balanced relationships where both parties feel seen, heard, and valued. But this simply cannot be done at all without the presence of clear responsibility and accountability.

Balancing Forces

Responsibility and vulnerability are two sides of the same coin—they are balancing forces. When we're able to accept—or at least acknowledge—these responsibilities and vulnerabilities, we take a significant step toward creating a healthier, more balanced dynamic. In cases where we cannot eliminate the power differential, we must work to uncover the vulnerabilities and accept the responsibilities within. Seeing them more clearly allows us to work toward a more equitable and respectful connection—to come closer to right-relationship.

When we are vulnerable, it can help to look for what we can be responsible for, and when we already hold a lot of responsibility, it is important to tend to the vulnerabilities. There was a famous study[8] conducted by Ellen Langer and Judith Rodin in 1976 exploring how having a sense of responsibility and control over a small aspect of life could impact the well-being of elderly people. In the experiment, nursing home residents were divided into two groups: one group was given a plant and told they were responsible for its care, while the other group was also given a plant but told the staff would take care of it. The researchers wanted to see how this small shift in responsibility would affect the residents' health and longevity.

The results were quite remarkable. The group that cared for their plants showed significant improvements in overall well-being, including increased happiness, engagement, and activity levels. Even more striking, this group had a lower mortality rate compared to the group that wasn't responsible for their plants. The study suggested that having even a small sense of control and responsibility over their environment had a profound positive effect on the residents' health and quality of life. If we find an overabundance

---

8. Langer, E. J., & Rodin, J. (1976). The effects of choice and enhanced personal responsibility for the aged: A field experiment in an institutional setting. Journal of Personality and Social Psychology, 34(2), 191-198. https://doi.org/10.1037/0022-3 514.34.2.191

of vulnerability, it is essential for us to pause and consider which responsibilities are missing. And if the responsibilities are heavily assigned or expressed through control, it's important to consider the vulnerabilities. One can provide an antidote for the other.

Ultimately, the goal is to foster relationships where both people feel supported and respected, even when power differentials exist. This doesn't mean pretending that power imbalances don't matter—it means addressing them with honesty and care, so that both parties can engage in the relationship from a place of mutual understanding. When we do this, we create the conditions for healthier, more meaningful connections, where both people can thrive despite the complexities of power.

When Up-Power Ignores Vulnerabilities & Responsibilities

We established earlier that in power differential relationships, while both sides experience vulnerability and have some responsibility, the up-power person is ultimately responsible for the health of the relationship. This is simply because when an up-power person feels vulnerable, the down-power person is at greater risk for harm. We will explore this more in the Shadow of Power chapter, but when we are under stress and feeling pressured, we tend to ignore the impact we have on others. When we ignore the impact, we could be causing all kinds of harm without even realizing it. And then those down-power from us may react in ways that make us feel we need to be more controlling, when really we need to be more understanding.

If the up-power person doesn't step into their role of being more vulnerable or fully embrace their responsibilities, the down-power person often ends up picking up the slack. This is called emotional labor. This is a common phenomenon in power differential relationships where the more vulnerable person is forced to take the responsibilities that the up-power person has either failed to recognize or hold or both. It is the extra effort the down-power person puts into managing the relationship, compensating for the up-power person's shortcomings, or even smoothing over conflicts arising from the imbalance. Emotional labor is both exhausting and unfair. Over time, it leads to burnout, resentment, and a breakdown in trust. The down-power person may feel like they're constantly compensating for the up-power person's lack of engagement or accountability, which can erode their sense of self-worth and agency.

When we are in up-power we have to bring mindfulness and intention to how our decisions, actions—or lack of action—affect the other person. Otherwise, we can easily slip into becoming dismissive, oppressive, or exploitative. Responsibility in this context is about creating a space where the down-power person feels safe, respected, and valued. It is about making it easier, not harder, for the down-power person to access their personal power. We will explore in the next chapter another expression of up-power vulnerability and one of the biggest obstacles to right-relationship in power differentials: up-power fragility.

18

Up-Power Fragility

"We don't lack motivation to be fair or objective. We're just defensive at the insinuation that we're not. Surveys show that most Americans value equality and fairness in principle. But the common reaction to being told that we have to correct for biases is defensiveness. That's why most proposed solutions to prejudice don't work." - Geoffrey Cohen

There are a lot of uncomfortable feelings around the word "fragility." Many people find this and other words used (especially in spaces that promote diversity and equity) uncomfortable or even problematic. During the course of writing this book, the National Science Foundation, a part of the U.S. Federal government, created a list of words that will trigger further review if found in any grant applications. Those words you can find in the list on the next page. Try talking about any diversity or equity efforts without using the words "equitable," "implicit bias," "race," or even "women." This list was prompted by an executive order signed by Donald Trump on the very same day that he was inaugurated as President of the United Statues in 2025. It was entitled "Ending Radical and Wasteful Government DEI Programs and Preferencing."[1]

---

1. https://www.whitehouse.gov/presidential-actions/2025/01/ending-radical-and-was
   teful-government-dei-programs-and-preferencing /

- activism
- activists
- advocacy
- advocate
- barrier
- barriers
- biased
- bias
- BIPOC
- Black and Latinx
- community diversity
- community equity
- cultural differences
- cultural heritage
- culturally responsive
- disabilities
- discrimination
- discriminatory

- backgrounds
- groups
- diversified
- diversify
- enhancing
- equal opportunity
- equality
- equitable
- ethnicity
- excluded
- female
- fostering
- gender
- hate speech
- Hispanic minority
- historically
- implicit bias
- inclusion

- inclusive
- increase
- indigenous
  community
- inequalities
- inequities
- institutional
- LGBTQ
- marginalize
- minorities
- multicultural
- polarization
- political
- prejudice
- privileges
- promoting
- race
- racial

- justice
- sense of
  belonging
- sexual
  preferences
- social justice
- sociocultural
- socioeconomic
- status
- stereotypes
- systemic
- trauma
- underappreciated
- underrepresented
- underserved
- victim
- women

Urgent reactions like this Executive Order, and the discomfort that happens for those with up-power being confronted with the harm that they cause with their up-power, are demonstrations of fragility. Even the discomfort with the word "fragility" is an expression of it. Robin DiAngelo first introduced the concept of "white fragility" which she describes as a state in which even a minimal amount of racial stress becomes intolerable for white people, triggering a range of defensive reactions. I am really appreciative of this concept and DiAngelo's development of it—and I'd like to widen the concept of fragility a bit. The reality is that we all experience it - some more than others. It is not just related to race. It is a phenomenon that happens across power differentials. I use the term "up-power fragility." It is **a phenomenon that happens when someone who has more access to role or status power (up-power) feels entitled to the benefits of that power but willfully ignores the relational responsibilities of that power, and then reacts defensively and often aggressively toward the person down-power from them who has pointed out that** they have misused or abused their power in some way—or even when the down-power person simply names the power differential.

In other words, up-power fragility is what inevitably happens when an up-power person is confronted with a down-power person's vulnerabilities without stepping fully into their own up-power responsibilities. As we have discussed, the problem with ignoring your up-power (whether it is status or role) is not only that the responsibilities are not taken along with that power, it also leaves the down-power person in a double bind: either they take on the responsibilities that you do not accept (which is a form of uncompensated labor) or suffer the consequences and impacts of your not taking responsibility.

Another consequence of your disowning or downplaying your up-power responsibilities is that it can leave you feeling powerless (especially if you haven't developed your rooted personal power). If you are reliant upon systems to grant you power vis-à-vis role or status, and you enjoy the honors and benefits of that power but refuse the responsibilities, then you are not owning all of the power you have access to. This results in a pendulum swing from an internal sense of "powerful" to "powerless." Powerful when you are enjoying the benefits, and powerless when you are confronted with the responsibilities that you are not owning.

A sense of powerlessness often accompanies up-power fragility. Powerlessness is a form of "felt power" that can lead to many misuses of power. As Dr. Dacher Keltner suggests:

> "People resort to coercive force when their power is actually slipping. In our professional lives, people who endorse Machiavellian strategies to social life—lying, manipulating, and stepping on others to rise in the

ranks—actually report experiencing less power and influence than the average person. In our personal lives, romantic partners are more likely to treat their beloved in coercive ways—through bullying, physical abuse, and emotional threats—when they are feeling *less* powerful. Parents are vulnerable to abusing their children when they feel relatively *powerless* vis-à-vis a willful child. In schools, bullies are continually engaging in domineering and deceptive actions, but they typically rank near the bottom of their class in status, respect, and influence in their peers' eyes. Today coercive force is a more likely path to powerlessness than to gains in power."[2]

The "kick the dog" metaphor is often used to describe a chain reaction of displaced aggression, where someone who feels powerless in one situation takes out their anger on someone (or something) weaker or more vulnerable. The metaphor comes from the idea of a person who's been scolded by their boss and, unable to retaliate directly, goes home and kicks their dog as a way to vent their frustration. This behavior is often rooted in a cycle of fear and control—and it results from power-over environments and Domination power paradigms. There is always someone above you putting pressure on those below. An up-power person may feel threatened by their own inadequacies or fears of losing their position, so they exert dominance over others to mask their vulnerability. But this only perpetuates the cycle: the more they try to control others, the more they reinforce their own sense of isolation and insecurity.

---

2. Keltner, D. (2016). The power paradox: How we gain and lose influence. Penguin Press, p. 21.

Like the hungry ghost, they're trapped in a cycle of craving and dissatisfaction, lashing out in ways that ultimately deepen their suffering and harm those around them. Keltner said, "Powerlessness amplifies the individual's sensitivity to threat; it hyperactivates the stress response and the hormone cortisol; and it damages the brain. These effects compromise our ability to reason, to reflect, to engage in the world, and to feel good and hopeful about the future. Powerlessness, I believe, is the greatest threat outside of climate change facing our society today."[3]

The sense of powerlessness we experience when we abandon our relational responsibilities, supported by an over-identification with systems (or over-reliance on role and status power) leads us to a convergence of most of the shadows of power—and then it gets expressed as fragility and experienced physiologically as a survival threat. When we are in survival mode, we start to experience emotion dysregulation and have less access to our brain's executive functions. Cohen conducted several experiments on belonging, and he found that survival threats surfaced often. In one study, he brought white and Black adults together for conversations about race (status power), and here is what he found:

> "...white adults display a physiological threat response when they're engaged in conversations with Black people, especially about racially charged issues, such as police profiling. The threat can be so intense that they show decrements in performance on cognitive control tasks even after these conversations are over. . . The threatening nature of these conversations can be

---

3. Keltner, D. (2016). The power paradox: How we gain and lose influence. Penguin Press, p. 10.

particularly strong among white people who say they are committed to racial equity. . .An unfortunate outcome of the stereotype threat that many white people feel is that many of them avoid such conversations, especially across racial lines—and when they do participate in them, they tend to focus more on protecting their views of themselves than on learning."[4]

I want to emphasize the part that reveals those who say they are committed to racial equity experience a stronger feeling of threat in these conversations. It's not just those who engage in power-over approaches that fall victim to fragility. Once again, we see that when we have the label of some version of "good," like "woke" or "anti-racist," there is actually a greater likelihood for fragility to arise—and it can surface even when there is just a conversation about the topic. The fear that is experienced by up-power people who want to be fair and use their power well in conversations about inequity is palpable. But it is ultimately about our ego and how we want to be perceived. It's also extremely disruptive to having productive conversations that could help move the needle on how power gets expressed.

So what do we do about this? We will talk about this in depth in the Phases of Power-Consciousness and their Strategies. But first, we need to learn the signs of fragility so that we can recognize when we might be experiencing it. There is a list I've created which is not an exhaustive one, but gives you an idea for what it looks like when fragility arrives. How does fragility show up for you?

---

4. Cohen,y G. L. (2022). *Belonging: The Science of Creating Connection and Bridging Divides.* W. W. Norton & Compan, p. 184.

Signs of Up-Power Fragility

- Emotional dysregulation (nervous system overload or survival response: fight, flight, freeze, fawn)

- Not having the time (or never having the capacity)

- Speaking rather than listening

- Bringing in other types of microaggressions (paritcularly the ones *you* are vulnerable to)

- Thinking that microaggressions are only something other people do

- Denial, wilful ignorance, or shutting down

- Gaslighting

- Crying

- Joking

- Leaving

- Being defensive or shifting blame to others or to circumstances

- Justification or over-analyzing

- Over-agreement or over-apologizing

- Minimizing/exaggerating

- Centering your own response, intentions, feelings or experience

- Using the switchback - attack the one who gives feedback

- Thinking you don't have any biases

- Being unwilling to receive feedback

- Inability to tolerate discomfort

- Not taking responsibility for your up-status or up-role

- Avoiding conversations about responsibilities and vulner-abilites

- Taking it personally—making it about your identity rather than your behavior

- Confusion - repeating that you don't understand

Next, we need to understand the difference between fragility and vulnerability. These are two concepts that often overlap but carry distinct meanings. While both involve a sense of susceptibility or openness to risk of harm, they differ in how they manifest and the implications they have for individuals and communities. Fragility refers to a state of being easily damaged, broken, or destabilized, particularly in response to challenges to one's beliefs, identity, or worldview. It stems from a lack of resilience in facing difficult conversations, owning responsibilities in a power differential, or acknowledging systemic inequities. Fragility often involves a re-sistance to change or growth, as the individual or group clings to a familiar, albeit flawed, understanding of themselves or the world.

Vulnerability, on the other hand, is more about openness and exposure, but it doesn't necessarily imply a lack of resilience. It is a willingness to be in authentic connection with another person—even when the potential of harm exists between you. I appreciate the concept of vulnerability as "woundableness," as explored in *Lesbian Ethics* by Sarah Lucia Hoagland. In many conventional ethical systems, vulnerability is viewed as a weakness, something to be avoided or overcome. The ideal is often invulnerability—being self-sufficient, emotionally guarded, and impervious to harm. Woundableness, however, flips this idea on its head. Instead of seeing vulnerability as a flaw, it embraces it as a strength, recognizing that being open to harm is a fundamental part of being human. This openness, rather than something to be ashamed of, becomes the basis for genuine, ethical relationships.

Vulnerability can be a conscious choice, as in the case of woundableness, where individuals willingly expose themselves to emotional risk in order to build deeper connections or engage in ethical relationships. Vulnerability doesn't always lead to defensiveness; instead, it can foster empathy, understanding, and growth. It's a form of courage, a commitment to ethical engagement even when it's risky. In this way, woundableness transforms vulnerability from something to be feared into a powerful tool for building trust, solidarity, and ethical communities. While fragility often shuts down dialogue, vulnerability can open it up, creating space for honest communication and mutual support. Vulnerability acknowledges that we are all susceptible to harm, but it doesn't see this susceptibility as a weakness—it's simply part of being human.

Another key difference lies in how fragility vs vulnerability handle discomfort. Fragility tends to avoid or resist discomfort at all costs, often leading to a retreat into familiar, unchallenged patterns of thought or behavior. Vulnerability, by contrast, leans into discomfort, recognizing that growth and connection often come from facing difficult truths or emotions. For example, someone who is fragile might react with anger or denial when their privilege is pointed out, while someone who embraces vulnerability might feel uncomfortable but remain open to learning and self-reflection.

Fragility is about defensiveness, resistance, and a lack of resilience, often tied to privilege and comfort. Vulnerability, on the other hand, is about openness, courage, and the willingness to face discomfort in order to grow or connect. While fragility can shut down important conversations, vulnerability or woundableness can create the space for meaningful dialogue and transformation. A simple way to think about the differences are:

- Fragility is reactive

- Vulnerability is receptive

- Woundableness is responsive

Another thing to take note of when we are in up-power is that when we draw from our rooted personal power, we tend toward vulnerability and woundableness—responding from a place of shared humanity. And when we fail to access our rooted personal power, or when we are caught up in socialized personal power (that is based in ego), we tend toward fragility—reacting from a place of threat.

The truth is, we are all susceptible to reacting from fragility. None of us comes from our rooted personal power 100% of the time—unless we have reached enlightenment and there is no sense of separate self at all. Feeling vulnerable can serve as a prompt to root into our personal power—whatever amount we have access to in the moment. Transformation of fragility into vulnerability is available at any moment if we are regulated and willing (and if external factors are not preventing us from accessing our rooted personal power). We can choose to receive with discernment rather than react—but it takes practice! This is the process of developing power-consciousness, and the journey has distinct phases (which we will explore in the Phases of Power-Consciousness). Just remember: we will all misuse our power, no matter how well-intentioned or developed we are. The sooner we can accept this and learn about our shadows, cognitive strategies, and tendency toward fragility, the better prepared we can be to mitigate their effects.

19

Shadows of Power

"*Injustice anywhere is a threat to justice everywhere. We are caught in an inescapable network of mutuality, tied in a single garment of destiny. Whatever affects one directly, affects all indirectly.*" - Dr. Martin Luther King, Jr.

"*But more so than we like to admit, we can all be authoritarians in our day-to-day lives, assuming that 'our way' is the 'right way' and that those who disagree must be converted, vilified, or banished.*" - Geoffrey Cohen

"*Power is tolerable only on condition that it masks a substantial part of itself. Its success is proportional to its ability to hide its own mechanisms.*" - Michel Foucault

More and more, as I teach about power, I realize how many times I answer questions about interpersonal challenges in a power differential with, "You need to make that explicit." While easier said than done, making visible the invisible is the foundational work of shifting power dynamics. Michel Foucault's quote above points to the subtle and often hidden nature of power-over dynamics, suggesting that the efficacy of domination relies heavily on its ability to remain partially concealed. In other words, dominant ways of engaging up-power operate most efficiently when they don't fully reveal their mechanisms or intentions. Essentially, power-over approaches thrive not by flaunting their presence but by embedding themselves so deeply in systems and structures that they become almost invisible, making it harder to challenge or dismantle.

The truth is, we cannot change power dynamics if we cannot talk about them. If they aren't on the table and power remains the elephant in the room, it will continue to take up all the space, and no one will say a word about it. This is part of the reason why power can feel so oppressive and unchangeable. When I talk about the shadows of power, I'm referring to the aspects of power that make it less visible and lead to its misuse and abuse. So let's make some of the invisible more visible by exploring the shadow of power, which arises no matter the power paradigm we come from. First, we will look at the over-reliance on role and status power and the insatiable drive for more power before examining the opposite: the reactions and over-compensations when we avoid up-power. Next, we will take a look at the dynamics of what I call Guru Culture and Cancel Culture—two sides of the same coin. Then, we will explore the shadow that appears when we fail to take care of ourselves. Finally, we'll look a little deeper at some of the neurobiological consequences of power that can lead us to use less of our brain *and* to become over-reliant on our role and status power (not a great combination!).

Over-Reliance on Role & Status Power

When someone is born with a lot of *status* power (financial wealth, light skin, cisgender male, etc.), they often get access to *role* power earlier and more frequently than those who are born into less status power. While this gives those up-status individuals more systemically created power, they are disadvantaged in a very crucial area that actually shapes how they use their role and status power. When you are given power that systems have created (especially at an early age), you tend to believe that power *only* comes from systems. Therefore, you are less likely to develop your personal power. Because why invest time in cultivating a different type of power when others are given so easily to you? Or as Lizzo says, in my favorite critique of the patriarchy, "Why men great 'til they gotta be great?"

I want to first point to the belief that power only comes from systems. From this belief sprouts an over-reliance on role and status power for your sense of agency in the world. High-status people with a lot of role power tend to cling to that status and role power as if their lives depended on it. A few people on the current world stage immediately come to mind for me. Can you think of any people like this in your life?

When we lean on role and status power for our sense of self and become overly identified with the systems that confer these types of power, we actually generate a great internal poverty. The internal emptiness from the lack of personal power development is filled with fear, scarcity, and insecurity. And then we act on our role and status power (using our privilege, access to resources, etc.) from this place of lack, covered over by the performance of confidence that rests solely on our grasp of status and role power. You probably witness daily (or at the very least imagine) the number of misuses and abuses of power that follow from this sad state. Becoming overly identified with systems also creates significant personal fragility when those systems are criticized or attacked. We end up investing all our time, energy, resources, and life force into building and maintaining systems—all so we can continue to hold on to our precious role and status power to fill the inner void.

There is a concept in Buddhism called "the hungry ghosts" (known as preta in Sanskrit) which represents beings consumed by insatiable desires and unfulfilled cravings. These spirits are often depicted with thin, emaciated bodies and enormous, gaping mouths, symbolizing their endless hunger and inability to find satisfaction. Hungry ghosts are said to inhabit a realm of suffering, constantly searching for nourishment but unable to consume it—food turns to ash or fire in their mouths, and water becomes undrinkable. This image often arises for me when I see some people on the world stage who are constantly seeking and trying to maintain power, and it's usually the "power-over" or "power-of" kind of power they seek. Just as hungry ghosts are driven by an unquenchable thirst and hunger, individuals who crave power often operate from a place of lack, scarcity, or fear. They may feel that they never have enough—enough control, enough recognition, enough security—and so they continually seek more, believing that acquiring power will finally prevent their experience of vulnerability.

At the beginning of the book, we discussed treating power as an object rather than a dynamic, and the scarcity that arises from that line of thinking. This is the shadow that is always lurking behind power-as-a-noun. When it is objectified, it becomes another thing to possess. And when someone has all the other resources at their disposal, power is the final treasure. But like the hungry ghosts, this pursuit is often futile; the more power they gain, the more they feel the need to accumulate power, trapped in a cycle of craving that can never be fully satisfied.

Reflection Questions:

1. How do you relate to power in your own life? Are there

areas where you feel you rely too much on role or status power? If so, how can you focus on developing your personal power instead?

2. Can you think of people in your life or in the public eye who seem to rely heavily on their role or status power for their sense of self? How does this reliance manifest in their behavior or decision-making?

3. Have you ever witnessed or experienced the "internal poverty" that comes from leaning too much on role and status power? How does this lack of personal power show up in people's actions or attitudes?

4. What lessons can we take from the Buddhist concept of the hungry ghost when it comes to understanding and addressing our own desires for power and recognition?

Reactions & Over-Compensations: Avoiding Up-Power

One of the biggest shadows I see in my coaching and consulting work, particularly with people in the helping professions and spiritual groups, is people who have committed to doing good but ignore the additional power they have access to beyond their personal power. We may ignore our role and status power for a variety of reasons. Maybe we are uncomfortable with the power differential because it's unjust, we don't want to cause harm, or we think power only works in a power-over way. Or perhaps we don't believe we are worthy of that additional access to power, or we don't want the additional responsibilities that come with the up-power position.

It makes sense that we would want to avoid power when so many of us have been on the receiving end of misuses and abuses of power. For most of us, we have only experienced power in very hierarchical and "power-over" ways. So when we find ourselves in up-power, we may react to the discomfort of it by trying to collapse the hierarchy (i.e. ignore the power differential). For example, we may want to ignore the *relative* reality that power differentials have been constructed and exist, and instead emphasize the reality of the *absolute*—that we are all equal as human beings having a human experience. When we recognize the relative reality that we are *not* all equal, we acknowledge that systems have very clearly given some more access to certain kinds of power than others. Insisting that "we're all equal" ignores the pervasive power dynamics created by systems. In role power, this can look like a newly appointed manager who doesn't feel ready to lead, a parent who wants to be considered a friend by their kids, or a therapist who believes that the client's power is the same as theirs (or even thinks the client has more power than them).

The problem here does not lie in wanting to acknowledge the down-power person's humanity—this is certainly something we should be doing if we want to engage in power-with ways of being in a power differential. The absolute still exists. It is when we do not acknowledge that the relative *also* exists that we get into trouble. When the role power differential is ignored, so too are the responsibilities and vulnerabilities. If we are not holding the responsibilities in up-power - who is? Either the down-power person (who has even more emotional labor to do in an already vulnerable position) or no one. And as we have already discussed, when the responsibilities are not being held well or at all, the vulnerability and risk of harm in the relationship dramatically increases.

In terms of status power, we can look to the denial of a power differential in how some people reacted to the social movement #BlackLivesMatter (BLM), which began in 2013 in the United States. In 2012, George Zimmerman fatally shot unarmed Black teenager Trayvon Martin and was later acquitted of the murder. The BLM movement became even more widespread after the deaths of multiple other Black people at the hands of police, including Michael Brown in Ferguson, Missouri (2014), Eric Garner in New York City (2014), Breonna Taylor in Louisville (2020), George Floyd in Minneapolis (2020), and multiple others. The BLM movement was meant to highlight the unjust deaths of Black people, not only throughout history, but also specifically in modern times at the hands of police. In response, many people responded with an alternative slogan: #AllLivesMatter (ALM). This was a reflexive response that consciously or unconsciously served to deflect away from the specific call for attention being made by BLM. Some people advocating for ALM explicitly stated that they believed it was a more inclusive viewpoint (because it recognized everyone's lives as valuable, not just a subset of people). Here, BLM highlights the relative reality (the context of the power differential and the abuses that occur there), while ALM highlights the *absolute* reality (the independent reality that every human life matters). Unfortunately (as many of us when we're in up-power do), ALM completely missed the point of the BLM movement. Of course all lives matter, but who is being disproportionately harmed and killed by police? By focusing on the absolute to the exclusion of the relative, we actually end up causing more harm. ALM is an erasure response and an example of the way many white people respond when they are uncomfortable facing the reality and history of black lives being disrespected, disregarded, and destroyed. They ignored the relative reality in favor of the more comfortable absolute perspective. In other words, they attempted to collapse the hierarchy —not in any real way, but in their minds —so they could continue to believe that the power differential doesn't exist and that the abuse of that differential isn't happening.

This erasure response is similar to when people say "I don't see color" or other phrases that keep us from having an experience of cognitive dissonance. **Cognitive dissonance** is something we experience when what we are presented with in reality is different from our understanding of the way the world works or different from our understanding of ourselves. Unfortunately, the lack of awareness or denial of role or status power actually results in misuses of power that are even more insidious than those that are overt or intentional. The misuse of power is in abandoning the up-power responsibilities. Remember the bystander effect we mentioned in the Responsibility chapter? Our up-power makes us more likely to stand by while violence happens around us, and cognitive strategies like these only reinforce it. Ultimately, denying the power differential, is not only a dismissal of our responsibilities, it is also a form of gaslighting that can normalize the misuse of power. And since you are denying your up-power you never have to be accountable for those misuses. Isn't that convenient for our egos? Cognitive errors make up a big part of the power shadow as they prevent us from seeing ourselves in a negative light—but they also prevent us from growing and finding right-relationship. We'll take a look at more of our cognitive errors in the next chapter. For now, take a moment to reflect on the ways that you avoid your own up-power.

Reflection Questions:

1. In what areas of your life do you hold up-power (role or

status)? Are there times when you've ignored or down-played this power? Why do you think you did so?

2. Think about a situation where you've tried to "collapse the hierarchy" by emphasizing equality while ignoring power differentials. What was the outcome? Did it lead to unintended harm or imbalance?

3. How do you balance the absolute truth (that we are all equal as human beings) with the relative reality (that power differentials exist)? Are there times when you've focused on one at the expense of the other?

4. How do you ensure that you're amplifying the voices of those in down-power positions, rather than speaking over them or ignoring their experiences?

5. What would it look like for you to fully embrace your up-power position, including its responsibilities and po-tential vulnerabilities? How might this shift impact your relationships and the systems you're part of?

Guru & Cancel Culture

I've watched several documentaries about cults because I'm fasci-nated by the power dynamics. How is it that these "spiritual leaders" can recruit hundreds or thousands of people who are convinced to do and endure horrific things—all in the name of some form of spirituality? It's astonishing how a convincing leader who claims access to universal wisdom or divine insight can create such a harmful environment. These gurus often draw people in with their charisma, making them feel seen, special, and understood. They tap into a deep human need for belonging and purpose, offering answers to life's big questions—answers many people are desperately seeking. In a world that can feel chaotic and uncertain, the promise of clarity, community, and enlightenment is incredibly appealing. Over time, followers begin to see the leader not just as a guide, but as the only source of truth and salvation.

While cults have existed in many corners of the world across time, what is more pervasive is **Guru Culture**. This is a cultural norm in which people focus more on a person than on the teaching or service they provide. This can happen with any kind of teacher, up-role, or up-status person. There is something that happens to our perspective when the teacher or leader takes their seat in up-power. The up-power is often accompanied by the potential for idealization and even idolization. When the focus is on the up-power person (the guru) rather than the teachings, the people down-power from them (the followers) can begin to project their own ideals onto the guru, treating them as infallible or beyond criticism. We essentially put them on a pedestal. This can lead to a situation where the up-power person's word is taken as absolute truth, even when it might be flawed or self-serving. Over time, followers may become more concerned with pleasing or emulating the guru than with their own development, safety, or access to rooted personal power.

Another issue with guru culture is the potential for dependency. When followers place too much emphasis on the up-power person, they may neglect their own inner wisdom and intuition. They could even abandon their personal power altogether (as is the case in many cults). Instead of cultivating self-reliance and inner strength, they constantly look to an up-power person for answers, validation, and direction. While a good teacher, parent, or leader can offer valuable insights and support, the ultimate goal of up-power should be to encourage the down-power person to locate and develop their personal power and find their own path.

On the other side of the coin is **Cancel Culture.** After someone in down-power has idealized the up-power person (the guru), and the up-power person inevitably proves to be human by making some kind of mistake or misusing or abusing their up-power, down-power people are enraged by what feels like betrayal. How dare they not be human! And then we cancel them. Cancel culture refers to the practice of withdrawing support for or publicly calling out an up-status or up-role person who is perceived to have done something offensive, harmful, or morally wrong. This often happens on social media, where public shaming, boycotts, or calls for accountability can quickly gain traction. The idea is to hold people accountable for their actions, especially when those actions perpetuate harm, discrimination, or injustice. But often what happens in canceling is a dramatic devaluation of the up-power person, which can reduce the possibility of real responsibility, growth, or repair from that person[1].

Both sides of the coin—idealization and devaluation—are forms of dehumanization. We refuse to acknowledge their humanity on either side. As human beings, we are prone to mistakes (which is how we learn), and power influences us no matter how intentional or wise we may be. This is not to say that accountability is not important. As we have already established, responsibility is critical

---

1. I want to name that this is tricky, because the act of canceling has been a powerful tool for marginalized voices to demand accountability. And I agree that demanding accountability is necessary—and as a promoter of restorative and transformative justice, I believe there are other ways to achieve true accountability while staying in relationship or consciously ending relationship. I recommend adrienne maree brown's book, *We Will Not Cancel Us* for further reflection.

to the healthy functioning of power dynamics. However, when we come from a place of fear and react rather than respond, we are not helping to make a healthier world.

In her book, *Emergent Strategy*, adrienne maree brown said: "I have talked with other leaders who got bumped into rock star status as young organizers, and almost all of us share a few core experiences: People stopped seeing us. We became a place to project longings and critiques. We lost touch with the fact that it's ok to make mistakes. Then we made the biggest mistakes of our lives. And we learned the hard way that rock star status is a cyclical thing. It becomes its own work, maintaining and promoting the rock star in the organization. The work of promoting and protecting one's personality is as different from the work of organizing as holding one's breath in is from an exhale."[2]

The Guru/Cancel coin ultimately creates a culture that paralyzes, dehumanizes, and separates us from our personal power. This dynamic promotes fear and makes it very hard for us to be actively responsible. Take a moment to reflect on the ways that you tend to dehumanize those in up-power (by either making them a "guru" or by canceling them). And when you are in up-power, asking yourself: are you encouraging the idealization because it feels good?; and are you taking active responsibility when you make mistakes or misuse your power?

Reflection Questions:

1. Can you think of a situation where you or someone you know focused more on the person delivering the teachings

---

2. brown, a. m. (2017). Emergent Strategy: Shaping Change, Changing Worlds. AK Press, p. 99.

rather than the teachings themselves? What were the consequences of this focus?

2. When you're in a down-power position, how do you ensure that you're humanizing those in up-power, rather than idealizing or devaluing them?

3. When you are in an up-power position, how do you encourage those in down-power positions to develop their own personal power and find their own path?

4. How do you typically react when someone up-power from you makes a mistake or misuses their power?

5. How do you distinguish between holding someone accountable for their actions and dehumanizing them? What are ways accountability can be achieved without "canceling" them?

6. How does social media amplify the dynamics of idealization and devaluation? What can be done to mitigate the negative effects of these platforms on power dynamics?

Lack of Self Care

I remember very clearly when I was a single mom, how challenging it was to have time for myself. I was working full-time, trying to finish my doctoral dissertation, and raising my daughter, who was a toddler at the time. Then COVID hit. To say I was overwhelmed is an understatement. I thought I was handling things ok and balancing, though far from perfectly, each of the spinning plates. I remember rushing around and ranting about something frustrating, when my daughter, in her infinite 3 year old wisdom, said, "Mama—stop. You take a nap." I couldn't help but smile. I told her she was right, so I sat down with her to read a book, and then we took a nap together. The spinning plate that had fallen without my notice was my own self-care.

Perhaps Dr. Barstow's most famous saying is, "Self-care is an ethical imperative." When we fail to set good boundaries or neglect our own well-being, not only are we risking our health and long-term sustainability, we are also more likely to behave in ways that are reactive rather than responsive. This is particularly true in power-differential relationships, where burnt-out up-power folks can create a toxic environment for others. A leader or parent who is overworked and emotionally drained might be more likely to make decisions based on their own stress or frustration, rather than considering the impact on their team or family.

When we aren't attending to our needs and making sure they're met in healthy ways, we run the risk of meeting them in ways that can harm others or damage our relationships. Because there are so many dimensions of self-care, this is easier said than done! Financial health and relationships are two areas where harm often happens. For example, if you aren't getting your relational needs met (sexual, friendship, companionship, etc.), it can be tempting to accept an inappropriate relationship with a very eager down-power person who has idealized you. This is a very slippery slope, where the vulnerabilities of the down-power person and your up-power responsibilities can be easily ignored.

This points to the necessity of a strong support system of folks who are either up-power from us or at least with people where there is no similar power differential. Otherwise, we may end up burdening those who are down-power who are already more

vulnerable. I'm sure in the moment, my rushing around and ranting was an unsettling experience for my three-year-old, and it
shouldn't have been up to her to remind me to slow down. It can
feel isolating in up-power, so finding good support is a critical part
of self-care. Turning to down-power folks for advice or validation
might seem harmless at first, but it can quickly blur the lines and
increase vulnerability. It can put the relationship in jeapordy and
the down-power folks may feel pressured to meet our emotional
needs.

Ultimately, taking care of ourselves isn't just about
personal well-being—it's about creating a healthier,
more ethical environment for everyone. I've included
a self-care reflection co-developed with Dr. Barstow[3]
which you can find at the QR code. I recommend you take a
moment to explore it. We all have areas where are self-care could
improve. Where are yours?

Neurobiological Consequences of Power

As I mentioned in The Power Differential chapter, significant
changes occur in the brain as a result of our experience of power.
One of the things I love about studying and teaching about the
neurobiology of power is that it points to our shared humanity and
the ways in which we are all vulnerable to the changes in our brains
that result from engaging in power in particular ways. No one
is immune to these changes, no matter how well-intentioned or
"good" a person you are. This is, of course, the opposite of what we

---

3. . I also recommend you read Dr. Barstow's wonderful book, *The Right Use of Power:
The Heart of Ethics,* which has more supportive insights on power.

want to believe. We want to understand ourselves as fundamentally different from those who misuse and abuse power. The truth is, we are not *fundamentally* different because we are all vulnerable to the human condition. While we all have the opportunity to make different choices in a given moment about how we participate in the power we have access to, we cannot escape our humanity (the absolute) nor our social contexts (the relative). Our socialization, the pressure from the social groups we're a part of, the way our brains seek reward and avoid pain—all heavily influence how we show up in relationships. We all misuse our power in one way or another, and we are typically not aware of it when we do.

In an experiment[4] conducted by Adam Galinsky, participants were randomly assigned to either an up-power or a down-power role. After this priming, participants were asked to quickly draw the letter "E" on their own foreheads. The key measure was whether they drew the "E" from their own perspective (which would make it look backward to someone else) or from another person's perspective (which would make it legible to someone viewing it from the outside). The results showed that up-power individuals were more likely to draw the "E" from their own perspective, making it illegible to others, while down-power individuals were more likely to draw it from someone else's perspective, making it readable. Being in up-power influences our split-second decisions, often reflecting our bias towards our own perspective. There have been multiple perspective-taking studies involving power, and they consistently show this bias.

---

4. Galinsky, A. D., Magee, J. C., Inesi, M. E., & Gruenfeld, D. H. (2006). Power and perspectives not taken. Psychological Science, 17(12), 1068–1074. https://doi.org/10.1111/j.1467-9280.2006.01824.x

In one of Keltner's key experiments[5], participants were random-ly assigned to roles in a simulated workplace scenario involving a power differential. Up-power participants were given authority over tasks and decisions, while down-power participants were placed in subordinate roles. The researchers then measured the participants' ability to accurately interpret others' emotions and perspectives, often through tasks such as identifying emotions from facial expressions or considering others' viewpoints in hypothet-ical situations. The findings consistently showed that up-power individuals were less accurate in recognizing others' emotions and less likely to take others' perspectives into account compared to down-power individuals. Keltner attributed this to the "power paradox," in which having power can lead to a self-focused mind-set, reducing motivation to attend to others' needs or feelings.

In another experiment[6], participants were asked to engage in a simple task: watching a video of someone else speaking and then mimicking their facial expressions. Once again, participants were primed in a power differential with some in up-power and others in down-power. The results were striking: up-power people were significantly less likely to mirror the other person's emotions. This study revealed that power can reduce empathic accuracy—the ability to understand and share others' feelings. This diminished empathy is one of the key ways power can lead to social discon-nection and even abuse of power.

Another response to the BLM movement was #BlueLivesMatter.

---

5. Keltner, D., Gruenfeld, D. H., & Anderson, C. (2003). Power, approach, and inhibi-tion. Psychological Review, 110(2), 265-284. https://doi.org/10.1037/0033-295X.110.2.265

6. van Kleef, G. A., Oveis, C., Van der Löwe, I., LuoKogan, A., Goetz, J., & Keltner, D. (2008). Power, distress, and compassion: Turning a blind eye to the suffering of others. Psychological Science, 19(12), 1315-1322.

Blue Lives Matter is a movement that emerged in response to the BLM protests, particularly after several high-profile cases of police officers being killed in the line of duty. Having worked with police officers for many years, I've heard countless stories of the dangers and risks for violence there is to officers in their line of work. However, while the intent may be to honor the lives of police officers, this response serves to distract from the fact that two things can be true: that police officers face risks in their line of work, and that Black people are harmed at a statistically higher rate and experiencing significant brutality. #BlueLivesMatter is another example of a reaction by those in up-power, but this time at the intersection of status *and* role power. Police officers and the power differential created by the justice system is one of the most dramatic power differentials in existence, and the more retributive or oppressive the frame, the larger the differential becomes. Police officers face considerable vulnerabilities and responsibilities, but neither negates the other. When we are overwhelmed with our own vulnerabilities it is hard to focus on the vulnerabilities of others. The research clearly shows that when we are in up-power, our capacity for perspective taking and empathy is severely limited. When you combine the two, it is even more challenging. The power differential with the police is at just this intersection.

One of the biggest outcomes of this particular shadow (our ability to empathize or take the perspective of others) is that we are typically unable to see the impact we cause—especially if the impact doesn't match our intention. When we don't like the impact we've caused, we usually focus on our intention instead of really understanding the impact. This is part of power's biggest shadow: the cognitive strategies we use to justify our misuses of power.

20

How We Fool Ourselves

"Sometimes people don't want to hear the truth because they don't want their illusions destroyed." - Friedrich Nietzsche

"It's seldom obvious, and we don't ask questions to put our ideas to the test. Our mind's biases not only cause errors but blind us to those errors. My sense is that it's these cognitive biases, more than any moral failing, that cause much misunderstanding and conflict." - Geoffrey Coehn

"The world as we have created it is a process of our thinking. It cannot be changed without changing our thinking." - Albert Einstein

"The first principle is that you must not fool yourself—and you are the easiest person to fool." - Richard Feynman

Peering over the edge of a cliff, Inigo and Vizzini see the Dread Pirate Roberts climbing their rope. They cut the rope with the hope the Dread Pirate Roberts would fall to his demise. Except Roberts does not fall to his death. He is still there clinging to the side of the cliff. The self-proclaimed genius, Vizzini, says "Inconceivable!" Even though, clearly, they are looking at the reality, which makes it fundamentally *conceivable*. And then comes the famous quote by the brilliant William Goldman in the movie, *The Princess*

Bride. Inigo Montoya says: "You keep using that word. I do not think it means what you think it means." Vizzini keeps repeating the word "inconceivable" throughout the movie until he dies while laughing at the Dread Pirate Roberts—-because Vizzini believes he has outwitted him.[1]

While Vizzini is a movie character, there are many people who believe things are "inconceivable" when they are presented with something outside of their awareness or understanding. They conclude that it must be impossible or wrong or stupid if they haven't already thought of it or just simply haven't been exposed to it. We all fall victim to so many of our own cognitive errors—this is the way we fool ourselves.

In the complex dance of human behavior, power plays a central role—shaping decisions, relationships, and institutions. Yet, power is not wielded in a vacuum; it's deeply influenced by the way we think. This chapter delves into the cognitive errors and mental strategies that often lead to the misuse and abuse of power. From confirmation bias to self-serving justifications, our minds are wired in ways that can distort reality, reinforce bad decisions, and perpetuate harmful dynamics. By exploring these cognitive pitfalls, I'd like to shed light on how even well-intentioned people can fall into the trap of abusing power—and how recognizing these patterns can help us build more accountable, ethical systems. This is not just about understanding the psychology of power; it's about equipping ourselves with the tools to think more clearly, act more responsibly, and come closer to right-relationship.

The Dunning-Kruger Effect:

---

1. Reiner, Rob (Director). (1987). The Princess Bride. 20th Century Fox.

When Confidence Outpaces Competence

Vizzini is the perfect example of the Dunning-Kruger Effect—a psychological phenomenon where people with low ability or knowledge in a particular area overestimate their competence. Throughout the movie, Vizzini confidently hatches elaborate schemes, convinced of his own brilliance, only to have them spectacularly backfire. Whether he's kidnapping Princess Buttercup or challenging the Man in Black to a battle of wits, Vizzini's overconfidence is matched only by his incompetence. His inability to recognize his own limitations leads to a series of hilarious (and ultimately fatal) missteps, making him a classic case of someone who doesn't know enough to realize how much he doesn't know. Let's dive into how Vizzini's overconfidence perfectly illustrates the Dunning-Kruger Effect and what we can learn from his very human mistakes.

The Dunning-Kruger Effect was first identified by psychologists David Dunning and Justin Kruger[2] in 1999. They found that people who perform poorly on tasks often lack the self-awareness to recognize their own incompetence. This happens because the skills needed to perform a task well are the same skills needed to evaluate your performance. If you don't have those skills, you can't accurately assess how bad you are. It's a double whammy: you're bad at the task, and you're bad at knowing you're bad. For

2. . Dunning, D., & Kruger, J. (1999). Unskilled and Unaware of It: How Difficulties in Recognizing One's Own Incompetence Lead to Inflated Self-Assessments. *Journal of Personality and Social Psychology*, 77(6), 1121–1134.

example, in one study[3] , participants who scored in the bottom 25% on a grammar test vastly overestimated their performance, thinking they were above average. Meanwhile, those who scored in the top 25% underestimated their performance, assuming others were just as skilled. This is why experts often underestimate their abilities—they're so aware of the complexity of a subject that they assume others know just as much.

In a power differential this effect is even more dramatic. Up-power people who overestimate their competence may make poor decisions, ignore expert advice, and fail to recognize their own limitations. This can lead to disastrous outcomes, especially in high-stakes environments like politics, business, or healthcare. One reason the Dunning-Kruger Effect is so dangerous in power dynamics is that it creates a feedback loop of incompetence. A leader who overestimates their abilities may surround themselves with yes-men who reinforce their confidence, rather than advisors who challenge their assumptions. This can lead to a culture of groupthink, where dissenting opinions are silenced, and poor decisions go unchallenged. For example, in the lead-up to the 2008 financial crisis, many executives overestimated their understanding of complex financial instruments, leading to catastrophic misjudgments that tanked the global economy. The Dunning-Kruger Effect is a reminder that confidence doesn't always equal competence. In fact, the less we know, the more confident we may feel—a dangerous combination, especially in positions of power.

Collapsing into the Binary: Getting Stuck in the

---

3. . Ehrlinger, J., Johnson, K., Banner, M., Dunning, D., & Kruger, J. (2008). Why the Unskilled Are Unaware: Further Explorations of (Absent) Self-Insight Among the Incompetent. *Organizational Behavior and Human Decision Processes*, 105(1), 98-121.

"Either/Or"

Binary thinking—the habit of seeing things in black-and-white, either/or terms—is a major driver of cognitive errors that skew our understanding and lead to poor decisions. And when there is a power differential, the outcomes of this can be devastating. By boiling down complex issues into two opposing categories, binary thinking pushes us to ignore nuance, overlook alternative perspectives, and make judgments based on incomplete or oversimplified information.

Like many of us, I was raised steeped in the cognitive distortion of binary thinking. I was taught to focus on and learn what was right and what was wrong. On the surface it seemed like a worthy pursuit: I just needed to learn from others what was right and what was wrong and then follow that code. I was taught that focusing on the rules and answers was where we should begin. This made sense to me because everyone around me was focusing on the rules or who was breaking the rules: at school, at church, at home, even while driving.

The problem is that while human beings are complex, rules (usually) are not[4]. The more I focused on rules or the "answers," the more I missed what was happening in the moment. I understood what the rules were but not necessarily the "why" or the "how." I was told in every context to follow what was given to me without question - something I never did very well. It seemed everyone around me was either trying to follow the rules or trying harder to break them. But the focus was always on the rules, rewarding those who followed them and punishing those who didn't.

Then, when I was 21, I moved to India for a year. That's when

---

4. Or the more complex the rule, the more it has to be changed.

knowing what was right and what was wrong wasn't as helpful. It turns out rules are different everywhere you go. And while understanding the rules of the place I am in is important information, there is more to be focused on than just the rules. When I was living in India at that time there were very few traffic signals and, as far as could tell, no traffic laws either - or at least they appeared to be regarded as suggestions. One of the first things I remember was looking at an intersection—and there was a horse standing in the middle of it. No person was riding the horse, nor was there any evidence that anyone nearby was claiming the horse. There were also buses that were leaning to one side because there were people hanging off the sides of them, clinging to the windows. Families of 5 on motorcycles or scooters, pedestrians, rickshaws all were converging on the streets with very few traffic lights. Somehow I managed to learn how to drive a motorcycle and get around on those streets. What I noticed is that virtually everyone around me was fairly conscious of their surroundings - and I witnessed very few accidents. As I thought about that, I realized that people in the United States have gotten so used to being told what to do when in terms of traffic (green light = go, red light = stop) that we've lost the capacity for situational awareness. We've grown accustomed to relying on being told what is the right thing to do instead of being aware of what is the right thing to do in *this* moment or *this* relationship.

It's not that I'm against rules—they have their place—but rules can sometimes shift our focus outward, pushing us toward binary, black-and-white thinking. When we get caught up in determining who's right or wrong, or when we reduce situations to simply good or bad, we lose sight of complexity and nuance. This kind of binary thinking often leads to polarization, where we see people, ideas, or situations as entirely good or entirely bad, leaving no room for middle ground. And once we're in that polarized mindset, it's easy to fall into confirmation bias, where we only seek out information that supports our views and dismiss anything that challenges them. In the process, we lose our situational awareness and the ability to see the bigger picture.

Confirmation Bias: Seeing What We Want to See

I'm re-watching the show *Ted Lasso* and I can't help but notice how many examples of cognitive errors are there—and then the ways that the characters are able to overcome them throughout the show. Initially, the team captain, Roy Kent, dismisses Ted's coaching methods as "American nonsense." Roy is convinced that Ted's upbeat, positive approach won't work in the cutthroat world of English football. He selectively focuses on every misstep—like Ted's unfamiliarity with the offside rule—while ignoring the moments when Ted's methods actually bring the team together. This tendency to cherry-pick information that supports our existing beliefs, while ignoring evidence that contradicts them, is known as confirmation bias. It's the mental shortcut that makes us see what we want to see, rather than what's actually there. Whether it's Roy doubting Ted's coaching or us scrolling through social media for articles that confirm our opinions, confirmation bias shapes how we interpret the world around us. Let's dive into how this cognitive bias works, why it's so hard to shake, and how we can start to see beyond our own blind spots.

Confirmation bias is the tendency to seek out, interpret, and remember information in a way that confirms our preexisting beliefs or assumptions, while ignoring or dismissing evidence that contradicts them. It's like having a mental filter that only lets in what aligns with what we already think, even if it's not accurate.

This happens because it's easier and more comfortable to stick with what we know rather than face the discomfort of changing our minds. For example, if someone believes that a certain political party is always right, they might only pay attention to news that supports that view and ignore anything that challenges it. This bias reinforces our existing mental models, even when they're flawed, and makes it harder to learn and grow. It's closely tied to cognitive dissonance because when we're faced with information that clashes with our beliefs, confirmation bias kicks in to protect us from the discomfort of having to rethink things.

When it comes to power, confirmation bias can be a particularly dangerous force, often leading to the misuse of power in ways that go unnoticed or unchallenged. Confirmation bias can move up-power people to selectively interpret facts or disregard evidence that contradicts their views. This not only skews decision-making but can also create an echo chamber where dissenting voices are silenced or ignored. The combination of power and confirmation bias creates a feedback loop that can be difficult to break. Those in up-power are often surrounded by people who share their views or are hesitant to challenge them, further reinforcing their biases. This can lead to a cycle of poor decision-making, where the same flawed logic is repeated without question.

Confirmation bias ultimately helps us side-step responsibility for our actions—especially when we are in up-power. When we only acknowledge information that supports our narrative, it becomes easier to deflect blame or avoid accountability. We might argue that our decisions are based on "the facts" or "expert opinion," even if those facts are selectively chosen to fit our agenda. When we fail to see multiple perspectives, including those that contradict our own, it allows us to maintain a facade of rationality and legitimacy, even when our actions are deeply flawed. By framing our choices as the only logical or moral option, we can avoid scrutiny and shift the focus away from our own biases or mistakes. In this way, confirmation bias becomes a dangerous tool for self-justification.

Fundamental Attribution Error (FAE): When We Misjudge Others

Picture this: you're driving along, minding your own business, when suddenly someone cuts you off. Your immediate reaction? What a jerk! You assume they're an aggressive, inconsiderate driver—maybe even a terrible person. But what if there's more to the story? Maybe they're rushing to the hospital, or they didn't see you in their blind spot. This tendency to attribute someone's behavior to their personality—rather than considering the situation they're in—is known as the fundamental attribution error. It's the mental shortcut that makes us quick to judge others based on their actions, while giving ourselves the benefit of the doubt. Whether it's a stranger cutting us off in traffic or a coworker snapping at us in a meeting, this bias shapes how we interpret others' behavior—and often not in a fair or accurate way. Let's unpack this cognitive quirk and see how it affects our everyday interactions.

One of the biggest errors that contribute to the self-justification problem is the Fundamental Attribution Error (FAE) which is a psychological tendency where people overemphasize personality traits (like someone being "lazy" or "mean") and underestimate situational factors when explaining someone else's behavior. And we do the reverse when explaining our own behavior. When someone cuts us off in traffic, its because they are rude or inconsiderate. But when we cut someone else off in traffic its because we are late, we didn't see the other car, or there was something in the road. Basically, we're quick to judge others based on who we think they are, rather than considering the circumstances they're in—but we're quick to excuse our own behavior based on our circumstances.

This bias can get especially tricky when power dynamics are involved. Like other cognitive errors, the FAE can make us ignorant of the ways power and privilege shape behavior. In his remarkable book, *The Science of Belonging*, Cohen wrote, "The most undersold discovery in social psychology and, indeed, in social science in general is the sheer complexity of human behavior, which the FAE leads us to simplify. . .Every situation is a unique and complex convergence of many forces."[5] Every power differential, every relationship and every context has it's own set of unique nuances. When we commit the FAE, we are essentially erasing

---

5. Cohen, G. L. (2022). Belonging: The Science of Creating Connection and Bridging Divides. W. W. Norton & Company, p.129.

the complexity so that we can continue to think of ourselves as better than others—so we can maintain our perception of ourselves as "good." As you can imagine, this is one of the driving forces for maintaining the existence of status power.

The FAE reinforces power differentials by letting those in privileged positions off the hook, while blaming those in down-power for their circumstances. For example, someone in poverty might be judged as unmotivated or lacking ambition, while the structural factors—like lack of access to education, healthcare, or job opportunities—are overlooked. Meanwhile, a wealthy person might be praised for their hard work and discipline, even though their success could be heavily influenced by inherited wealth, social connections, or systemic advantages. Any time we label a group or engage in a stereotype, we are committing the FAE. And we all do this—we all engage in stereotypes. Cohen went on to say:

"The prevailing assumption is that if people espouse sexist or racist views, they do so because they are an inveterate sexist or a racist and are unwilling or unable to change their views. Yet while there are people who embrace bigoted views and will resist any attempts to disuade them, many people's ideas have been shaped by the bigotry that pervades our social situations. It is systemic—meaning situation at an institutional or societal scale—infusing even our day-to-day encounters. We commit the FAE when we discount these systemic forces and condemn as hopeless the individuals who hold harmful views. . .By ignoring systemic situational factors, we also let off the hook the people in power who craft our situations."[6]

I see Cohen pointing to the complexity of power dynamics and why it is so critical to understand the different types of power and

---

6. Cohen, G. L. (2022). Belonging: The Science of Creating Connection and Bridging Divides. W. W. Norton & Company, p.114.

how they influence our day-to-day lives. When we ignore systemic power we are actually participating in its maintenance. Similar to binary thinking, the oversimplification that the FAE provides, is an easy out—especially for those in up-power. It allows us to ignore the complexities that lead to human behavior and social power dynamics. But at what cost?

Ultimately, the FAE challenges us to pause and consider the broader context before passing judgment. It's a call to recognize the complexity of human behavior and the ways in which power and privilege shape our lives. By doing so, we can begin to dismantle the oversimplifications that uphold inequality and work toward a more just and nuanced understanding of ourselves and others. The cost of ignoring this complexity is steep—it perpetuates injustice and stifles meaningful change. But by acknowledging the systemic and contextual forces at play, we can take a step closer to right-relationship.

Authority Bias

Has this ever happened to you? You're in a meeting, and your boss proposes a new strategy that feels a little off. Maybe it's ethically questionable, or perhaps it just doesn't align with your values. But instead of speaking up, you stay silent. After all, they're the boss, right? They must know what they're doing. This tendency to defer to authority figures, even when their decisions seem questionable, is known as Authority Bias. It's a deeply ingrained psychological inclination that leads us to overvalue the opinions or directives of those in positions of power, often without questioning their validity. A 2017 study by Fennis and Aarts found that "individuals are more likely to comply with requests from authority figures, even when those requests are unethical or harmful, because they perceive the authority as legitimate and trustworthy" (Fennis & Aarts, 2017). This bias can create a culture of unquestioning obedience, where down-power people follow orders without considering the ethical implications—and it's a perfect fit for the Authority Lens of power.

In power dynamics, Authority Bias can reinforce the up-power's sense of infallibility, making it easier for them to justify unethical or harmful actions. When subordinates are unwilling to challenge authority, leaders may become insulated from criticism, leading to abuses of power. A landmark 2006 study led by Peter Pronovost at Johns Hopkins exposed how authority bias in hospitals—specifically, staff reluctance to challenge senior doctors—directly contributed to patient deaths. The research focused on central line infections in ICUs, a preventable issue killing tens of thousands annually. Nurses and junior doctors often spotted errors (like skipped sterilization steps) but stayed silent to avoid contradicting higher-ranking physicians. This deference to hierarchy had deadly consequences. To combat this, the team introduced a simple checklist for catheter insertions and—critically—empowered nurses to halt the procedure if steps were missed. The results were staggering: infections dropped by 66% in participating hospitals, saving an estimated 1,500 lives in Michigan alone. The real revelation? The checklist wasn't just about remembering steps; it disrupted the "don't question the expert" culture that let small mistakes slide.

There is a cycle that gets perpetuated when Authority Bias is at play. Julie Diamond explains that misuses of power in power differentials often happen in a cycle:

1. The higher your role power, the more people change their behavior toward you. When someone is in a position of authority, others tend to defer to them, agree with them, or even flatter them. This can create a feedback loop where the person in power starts to believe they're always right.

2. The more people change their behavior, the harder it is to see your impact. When everyone around you is nodding along or avoiding conflict, it becomes difficult to gauge the real impact of your decisions. You might not realize that your actions are causing harm or that people are afraid to speak up.

3. The harder it is to see your impact, the easier it is to misuse your power. Without honest feedback or a clear understanding of how your decisions affect others, it's easy to make choices that serve your own interests or reinforce your authority, even if they're unethical or harmful.

This cycle highlights how authority bias and role power can create a dangerous feedback loop, where those in power become increasingly disconnected from the consequences of their actions. The more authority someone has, the more insulated they become, and the easier it is for them to misuse their power without even realizing it.

Authority bias is a powerful force, but it's not inevitable. By recognizing this bias and its role in reinforcing unethical behavior, we can begin to break the cycle. Up-power people can take steps to encourage open dialogue, seek out dissenting opinions, and create a culture where questioning authority is not just allowed, but encouraged. Down-power people can speak up when something feels off, even when it's uncomfortable. As Julie Diamond's cycle shows, misuses of power often happen because those in authority lose sight of their impact. By fostering transparency, accountability, and a willingness to challenge authority, we can create healthier power dynamics—ones that prioritize ethical behavior over blind obedience.

Other Implicit Biases

I had a boss for many years who is a queer black woman. We worked together very closely and we were also close friends. We were both single moms at the time and we took care of each other's kids while the others went to conferences or just needed a break. One time, in the midst of a conflict, she said to me, "Amanda, I just don't trust you." I was floored. I thought, "How can you possibly say that? I've done everything to earn your trust—we work together on deeply personal issues, we help raise each others' kids." I wish I could say I had a deep insight immediately after that thought that shed light, but I didn't. Instead I reacted from up-power fragility and I was deeply confused and hurt. It wasn't until much later in my power-conscious development that I realized what she meant. The trust she was referring to was trusting me as a socialized white woman. She didn't trust my implicit biases that could surface at any moment, likely without my awareness and therefore with little or no responsibility for them.

Biases are mental shortcuts our brains use to make sense of the world quickly. They form through a combination of social conditioning, personal experiences, and evolutionary instincts. From a young age, we absorb societal norms, stereotypes, and cultural messages that shape how we perceive different groups of people. Research shows that biases can form as early as infancy, with babies as young as six months old showing preferences for faces that match their own racial group.[7]

But biases aren't just learned—they're also hardwired into our brains. Evolutionarily, our brains developed to make quick judgments to survive in a complex world. This "fast thinking," as psychologist Daniel Kahneman calls it, helps us make decisions efficiently, but it also leads to errors in judgment. For example, we might unconsciously associate certain traits with specific groups based on limited information, even when those associations are inaccurate or harmful. This is how implicit biases take root.

One of the most insidious aspects of bias is that it often operates outside of our awareness. This is because much of our mental processing happens unconsciously. Studies in neuroscience have shown that our brains make decisions before we're consciously aware of them, and we then rationalize those decisions after the fact.[8] This means that even when we think we're making fair, rational decisions, our unconscious biases might be steering us in a different direction.

Another reason biases remain hidden is self-perception. Most people see themselves as fair-minded and objective, so they're unlikely to recognize their own biases. This is known as the bias blind spot—the tendency to see bias in others but not in ourselves.[9] This is similar to the FAE. We're quick to point out when someone else is being unfair or prejudiced, but we're much less likely to see those same tendencies in ourselves. This makes it incredibly difficult to

7. Xiao, W. S., Fu, G., Quinn, P. C., Qin, J., Tanaka, J. W., Pascalis, O., & Lee, K. (2018). Infant Visual Preference for Own-Race Faces: A Cross-Cultural Study. *Developmental Psychology*, 54(5), 1-12.

8. Soon, C. S., Brass, M., Heinze, H. J., & Haynes, J. D. (2008). Unconscious Determinants of Free Decisions in the Human Brain. *Nature Neuroscience*, 11(5), 543-545.

9. Pronin, E., Lin, D. Y., & Ross, L. (2002). The Bias Blind Spot: Perceptions of Bias in Self Versus Others. *Personality and Social Psychology Bulletin*, 28(3), 369-381.

address biases, because we don't even realize they're there.

In recent years, organizations have invested heavily in bias training programs to combat discrimination and promote diversity. However, a growing body of research suggests that many of these trainings may actually increase bias rather than reduce it. A 2019 meta-analysis by Forscher et al.[10] found that traditional bias trainings often fail to produce long-term changes in behavior and can even lead to reactance—a defensive reaction where people double down on their biases. For example, when people feel like they're being accused of being biased, they may become defensive and resist the message, reinforcing their existing beliefs.

One reason for this is that many bias trainings focus on raising awareness of bias without providing structural change or practical tools for shifting power dynamics—or they don't bring in a context of compassion. Simply telling people they're biased can make them feel attacked or judged, which can trigger defensiveness. A 2020 study by Duguid and Thomas-Hunt[11] found that when bias trainings emphasize the universality of bias—explaining that everyone has biases, not just certain groups—participants are less likely to feel targeted and more open to self-reflection. Helping people with empathy and perspective-taking (remember the brain deficits caused by power?) can also combat our biased tendencies.

Another issue is that bias trainings often rely on one-time interventions, which are unlikely to produce lasting change. Research

---

10. Forscher, P. S., Lai, C. K., Axt, J. R., Ebersole, C. R., Herman, M., & Nosek, B. A. (2019). A Meta-Analysis of Procedures to Change Implicit Measures. *Journal of Personality and Social Psychology, 117*(3), 522-559.

11. Duguid, M. M., & Thomas-Hunt, M. C. (2020). The Paradox of Bias Training: Why Awareness Isn't Enough. *Journal of Experimental Social Psychology, 89*, 1-10.

by Kalev et al. (2018)[12] shows that sustained, ongoing efforts are far more effective than single sessions. For example, organizations that implement structural changes—like diverse hiring committees or accountability measures—see more significant reductions in bias than those that rely solely on training programs. Addressing bias requires more than just changing individual attitudes; it also requires changing the systems and structures that perpetuate bias.

Cohen said, "While we may come to consciously reject many of them, they linger in our minds, distorting our views of individuals we encounter and shaping the way we treat them. What's more, our biases do not have to be overt to inflict great harm, and we do not have to feel disgust, disdain, fear or anger toward others to treat them in biased and harmful ways."[13] The truth is, no matter how much work we do to develop our power-consciousness, we will still have implicit bias. The best we can do is realize this human shortfall and look for it with compassion—and then take responsibility for it as it arises (or as soon as we can after).

All of these cognitive errors are our brains trying to maintain our view of ourselves as "good." But it is not enough to think of ourselves as "good." We have to be aware of our brains' tendency to sidestep the hard stuff. And when we are in up-power, one of the many privileges (and challenges) we have is to make a choice about whether we face up to these cognitive errors and our shadow. Holocaust survivor, author and activist, Elie Wiesel said, "We must take sides. Neutrality helps the oppressor, never the victim. Silence

---

12. Kalev, A., Dobbin, F., & Kelly, E. (2018). Best Practices or Best Guesses? Assessing the Efficacy of Corporate Diversity Policies. *American Sociological Review*, 83(4), 1-27.

13. Cohen, G. L. (2022). Belonging: The Science of Creating Connection and Bridging Divides. W. W. Norton & Company, p.140.

encourages the tormentor, never the tormented." We can step out of neutrality or apathy and choose to intentionally face our shadow and name the cognitive errors when we see them. We can look at our tendency toward confirmation bias and the FAE, and take notice when we are abandoning our up-power responsibilities by labeling ourselves as "good."

Before we move on to exploring the Phases of Power-Consciousness, I encourage you to take a moment to fill out and reflect on the Power Shadow Review by clicking on the QR code. It is a handout originally developed by Dr. Cedar Barstow, who graciously allowed it to be available to the readers of this book. It is such a useful review to increase your awareness of the shadow of power when you are in up-role power, in particular. There are several continuums that reveal different dimensions of typical power shadows. These are called "shadow" because they are obscure and easier for others to see than yourself. This is one good reason for doing this review in a group of peers if that is available for you.

21

The Phases of Power-Consciousness

"The curious paradox is that when I accept myself just as I am, then I can change." - Carl Rogers

"The more you know yourself, the more patience you have for what you see in others." - Erik Erikson

Those of us who facilitate discussions, workshops or groups in areas like power, conflict, equity, belonging, and other areas of social justice often find that one of the more challenging aspects of facilitation is in guiding folks from very different places of readiness, willingness and experience. You have to either be able to define the group or workshop in a way that focuses on people with more experience so they can get something valuable (which ultimately excludes or leaves behind those with less experience). Or you have to offer progressive training starting with those with less experience or exposure and work your way from the basics to a more advanced understanding. Or you invite everyone in and try to attend to all levels of experience and exposure in the room at once. Not an easy task.

Part of how my mind works (if you haven't picked up on this by now) is to look at every part of a thing and go to the smallest detail and then look at the bigger picture so I can better understand how something works. In trying to be a better facilitator, I started to study how people show up in different phases of power-consiousness—and then I designed a visual model of it based on many developmental models[1] that come close to power, but aren't about power directly. I also didn't want it to be a linear model of "development"—which tends to prime people into "being the best" instead of accurately assessing where they are. This, of course, naturally occurs for multiple reasons but mostly because we are human. Especially for those of us steeped in the Achievement Lens, we want to be the best, the highest, and the furthest along. Unfortunately, this does very little to help us learn.

Instead of thinking of power-consciousness as purely developmental, it is important to feel its ebbs and flows. We never "arrive" and we are never done with our growth because a different consciousness is required in every interaction throughout our lives. It is tempting to collapse into checkboxes or rule-following or to engage in comparison and judgment with other people's development. Truly, we are never done in our development of power-consciousness.

So these phases are what we pass through again and again, spiraling to more depth as we go, but never to an achieved state of perfect power-consciousness. This is similar to Dr. Barstow's power spiral. As we teach in Right Use of Power,™ and every relationship

---

1. Bennett, M. J. (n.d.). Developmental model of intercultural sensitivity. Organizing Engagement. Retrieved, from https://organizingengagement.org/models/develop mental-model-of-intercultural-sensitivity/ & The Leader Lab. (n.d.). It's time to give Noel Burch some credit: The four stages of learning. Retrieved, from https://www .theleaderlab.com/blogs/its-time-to-give-noel-burch-some-credit & Van Dyne, L., Ang, S., Ng, K. Y., Rockstuhl, T., Tan, M. L., & Koh, C. (2012). Sub-dimensions of the four-factor model of cultural intelligence: Expanding the conceptualization and measurement of cultural intelligence. *Social and Personality Psychology Compass*, 6(4), 295–313. https://doi.org/10.1111/j.1751-9004.2012.00429.x

in each moment is different, and we cannot possibly hold all of the levels of power-consciousness at once in all of the types and dimensions of power. Accepting this imperfection, I think, is what keeps us on the path of learning.

These are some things to understand about the Phases before I go into detail about the model:

1. It is meant to be a spiral. It is intentionally *not* linear. We don't proceed in life in a line, nor do we do it in circles (even though it may feel that way sometimes!). We advance but not without revisiting the same phases over and over again. Sometimes we can take what seems like one step forward and three steps back. It's just the nature of the work.

2. We could be in any part of the spiral at any time. Just because I am in one phase in this moment, I could be in a different phase in the next. We are not meant to get stuck in a phase and exist there (assuming we value growth).

3. We are in different parts of the spiral with different types of power. Where we are in acceptance and understanding for one type of status power might be completely different from that of another type of status power or any other type of power.

Though it is not linear in its development, power consciousness is developed first through rooted personal power, which, as we previously discussed, helps to mediate all other types of power. Then it is developed through interpersonal relationships with the hard work of generative conflict, closing the gap between intention and impact and the reparation of harm. And, finally, we begin to develop from the level of the collective and are able to take the perspective of systems thinking. And, of course, the primary ingredient for moving from one phase depends, for a large part, on the degree of our connection to Universal Power.

There are four phases in power-consciousness: 1) Denial; 2) Curiosity; 3) Transformation; and 4) Integration. Each phase is characterized by the emotions, behaviors and capacities we demonstrate as we are confronted with power differentials. We spiral through these phases in both role and status power differentials, and it may look different for us whether our experience is that of up-power or down-power in a given moment. It is important to note that these phases apply to everyone, no matter our political leanings, religious views or other belief systems.

If you'd like to experience an embodied guided imagery practice involving the phases, you can scan the QR code. This practice is adapted from an exercise by Regina Smith.

PHASES
OF POWER-CONSCIOUSNESS

DENIAL
Security/Familiarity
Defending
Avoidance/Ignorance
Anger/Numbness
"Unconscious Incompetence"

CURIOSITY
Developing awareness
Willingness
Chaos
Guilt/Shame
"Conscious Incompetence"

COURAGE

1

2

FEAR

COMPASSION

INTEGRATION
Authenticity
Skill
Embodiment
Equanimity/Courage
"Unconscious Competence"

TRANSFORMATION
Clarity/Acceptance
Adaptation
Active Responsibility
Grief
"Conscious Competence"

4

3

ACTION

The Denial Phase

The Denial Phase is characterized first and foremost by security. In this phase, we prioritize what is familiar, comfortable, and convenient—what fits with our existing worldview and understanding of relationships. It is here that power is viewed more like a finite commodity to be sought after and protected. With that commodified understanding of power, we also see the consequences of scarcity that we discussed in previous chapters.

Because security is the primary focus in the Denial Phase, anything that falls outside of what is already known is feared or regarded with suspicion. We engage in what is called "willful ignorance" where we avoid what is new or different in order to remain (what we perceive as) safe. Willful ignorance involves a deliberate choice to avoid acknowledging facts or evidence that contradict one's beliefs, preferences, or interests. This is not simply a lack of knowledge; it's an active decision to remain ignorant despite the availability of knowledge. And we all do this, especially when we are in the experience of up-power.

An aspect of this denial is when we play up our vulnerabilities or center ourselves in the conversation. Unfortunately this leads to a lack of recognition and acknowledgment of inequities or injustices which can lead to their normalization. When something is normalized, it often remains unchallenged and is perceived to be just a part of "reality." This normalization then allows us to excuse our willful ignorance. The Denial Phase is very fond of cognitive strategies like confirmation bias.

This leads us to the primary emotional states of the Denial Phase: either numbness (arising from normalization, avoidance, and apathy) or anger arising from fear (when we are confronted with what we perceive as threatening our worldview). The fear/anger response is quite common and an understandable survival reaction. Typically the more anger there is, the more we have built our identities and realities around our socialized understanding of things. For example, I expect most of us have been socialized, taught and absorbed the binary gender idea: that there is an undisputable (normalized) reality that there only exist two genders and that they are inextricably tied to someone's sex organs at birth. This socialization is so deep in Western culture that our language, colors, clothing, jobs, societal roles, and many other aspects of our identity are directly dependent on there being clear distinctions between two genders. When we are presented with the dissonant reality that there are more than two genders and that they don't always correlate with what we were assigned at birth, our whole understanding of our identities and the identities of those around us comes into question. Not only that, but how our identities are expressed also comes into question. That is a lot of doubt introduced with something that was so basically certain for many people. Not only does it require a shift in the understanding of our reality, but it would also require us to perhaps use different names or pronouns for people, or see clothing or appearance that was previously understood to be assigned to a particular gender, now being worn by other genders.

This is the phase where cognitive dissonance is suppressed. In many cases, we do not have the capacity to go beyond our worldview or understanding of reality, so we actively block new information from coming in, and we shut down or shut out anything or anyone who may offer or represent that new information. This is all in the name of protection. And we will go to great lengths to protect ourselves and our worldview when we are in this phase. We will cut out people from our lives, create inequitable laws, exclude, ridicule and cancel people.

Ultimately, this phase leads us to what Martin M. Broadwell originally called, "Unconscious Incompetence" in the Four Stages of Competence model. In this initial stage, we are unaware of our lack of competence and we are strongly influenced by cognitive errors. Essentially, we don't know what we don't know. Because the denial and protective factors are so strong, we can't even see what we don't know.

The Curiosity Phase

As we come through the denial phase we may start to develop awareness of the tension between what we observe and our beliefs. It may be that they don't quite line up or maybe something happens that directly contradicts a belief we hold or were taught to hold. Perhaps someone we love is impacted by our denial. This is a painful experience. This is actually the phase where cognitive dissonance is most prevalent. We've allowed the dissonant perspective to enter into our minds and it exists in tension with our previously held views or understanding of reality.

Reaching this phase requires a lot of courage to go beyond what is familiar and comfortable. We have to overcome many obstacles, and sometimes, after we've dipped our toes into curiosity, we slide back to the Denial Phase because it becomes too much. The cognitive dissonance creates chaos for us. We not only have to reorient cognitively and emotionally, but sometimes we even have to adjust our lives to accommodate this new reality. This is no small thing! For this reason, it is common for us to go from Denial to Curiosity and back to Denial multiple times before we can really move on.

When we are willing and able to stay in the Curiosity Phase long enough, we start to develop an awareness of the contradicting issue. This is a pivotal moment, as it marks the beginning of our journey towards self-awareness and change. We start to recognize the impact of our denial and willful ignorance, and this realization fuels our motivation to overcome cognitive dissonance. I want to emphasize the willingness aspect of this phase. It is only when we have the courage and willingness to confront and tolerate the cognitive dissonance that we can remain in this phase. This can take time to develop but it is a central aspect of curiosity. It is important to connect with the "why" of your willingness. Why are you willing to be curious? This phase requires a considerable investment of energy - so being able to re-ground in your "why" can help sustain you when your energy dips or if your resolve weakens.

This is what I relate to Broadwell's "Conscious Incompetence" phase, where we become aware of what we don't know. We recognize our incompetence and the gaps in our knowledge, awareness or skills. This can lead us to a willingness to learn and improve. But it can simultaneously bring up guilt or shame. We may become aware of how we have hurt people we love, how much time we spent being so small, or how we have contributed to inequitable conditions. When guilt arises this is a key moment for determining how we will move in the spiral. If the guilt becomes stuck, it often results in shame. With shame, we internalize the hurt and then blame ourselves or others instead of seeing it as a natural outcome of our systemic lens or the ways we were socialized. So when we come to this moment where guilt or shame arises, what we truly need is compassion. Because it is so central to the development of power-consciousness, we'll talk about compassion more in the next chapter. For now, it is important to know that it is compassion that guides us to the next phase: Transformation.

The Transformation Phase

By the time we reach the Transformation Phase we have already done a considerable amount of work. We have cultivated curiosity and have undergone some significant changes in our perspective—we're getting used to the idea that maybe our understanding could use some expansion. With compassion we can make it through the guilt and into a place where we can start to take active responsibility. Our willingness is now starting to turn into acceptance which gives us a kind of clarity. We are no longer actively wrestling with cognitive dissonance as we start to adapt to this new way of understanding the world. We are leaning into humility and allowing ourselves to adapt to this new way of seeing the world.

The process of transformation often requires us to confront the parts of ourselves that we've outgrown—whether it's an old identity, a belief, or a way of being. These "little deaths" can be deeply unsettling, as they force us to confront the unknown. And with death comes grief[2], a natural response to loss. As Francis Weller, a renowned psychotherapist and author of *The Wild Edge of Sorrow*, writes, "Grief is the medicine that allows us to let go of what is no longer needed and to open to what is waiting to be born." Grief, in this sense, is not just a burden to bear but a sacred process that allows us to move through the pain of transformation and emerge on the other side. Weller reminds us that "grief is the price we pay for love," and in the same way, grief is the price we pay for growth. To let go of the familiar, even when it no longer serves us, is to step into the uncertainty of who we might become. This can feel like a loss, but it's also an opportunity—a chance to shed the skin of who we

---

2. Even when that loss is necessary for our growth.

were and step into a more authentic version of ourselves. He goes on to write, "Grief is subversive, undermining the quiet agreement to behave and be in control. It is an act of protest that declares our refusal to live numb and small." When we resist grief—when we try to bypass the pain of letting go—we risk becoming stuck, unable to fully embrace the new version of ourselves that is waiting to emerge. But when we allow grief to flow through us, we create space for renewal. This is the paradox of transformation: we must grieve what we've lost in order to grow into what we're becoming.

When we honor grief as part of transformation, we take responsibility for our own healing. This means acknowledging the pain of letting go, rather than numbing it or pushing it aside. It means sitting with the discomfort of uncertainty, even when it feels easier to cling to the familiar. As we learn to accept, adapt and grieve, we are given the gift of awareness of our responsibilities in whatever dimension of power we are working with. This awareness allows us to be actively responsible—though it may come from a sense of duty when we are in this phase.

Active responsibility also extends to how we engage with others and the world around us. When we have allowed grief to shape us, we become more attuned to the suffering of others. We recognize that grief is a universal experience, and this awareness fosters empathy and compassion. This sense of interconnectedness inspires us to take responsibility for our impact on the world—whether it's in our relationships, our communities, or the larger ecosystem. In essence, the process of transformation and grief cultivates a sense of active responsibility by teaching us to show up fully—for ourselves and for others. It's about embracing the messiness of growth, honoring the losses that shape us, and making conscious choices that reflect our evolving values.

From Broadwell's "Conscious Competence," this phase of learning is a pivotal stage in the transformation process, acting as the bridge between initial awareness and eventual mastery. During this phase, individuals have acquired the necessary awareness to cultivate a new perspective, but it still requires deliberate effort and concentration. This stage is often marked by a heightened sense of focus and intentionality, as we actively apply what they've learned, step by step. For example, a new driver who has learned the rules of the road and can operate a vehicle safely, but still needs to think carefully about each turn, lane change, and traffic signal, is in the conscious competence phase. While they're no longer a beginner, the awareness hasn't yet become second nature. This phase is crucial in transformation because it's where the active responsibility of integrating new perspectives takes place. It's a time of growth, but also of vulnerability, as the individual must remain fully present and engaged, even when the process feels slow or awkward. Conscious competence is where the hard work of transformation happens—where we move from knowing what to do to *actually* doing it, even if it doesn't yet feel effortless. It's a testament to the power of persistence and focus in shaping who we become.

The Integration Phase

This is the phase where all of our hard work starts to pay off. We have taken active steps through the Transformation Phase and have developed the awareness and skills to become attuned to the power dynamics that show up in our lives. We have learned to root into our personal power and loosen our grip on systems and structures that are harmful, which allows us to show up more authentically. Because we aren't as focused on our own transformation, we now have the capacity to be more aware of others and our relationships.

This makes us more capable of guiding others and sharing our perspective and skills.

It is in the Integration Phase where we align our actions with our core values and beliefs, ensuring that our use of power is not just effective, but also true to who we are. This is the phase where the lessons we've learned become deeply embedded in who we are, moving from conscious effort to effortless action. In the context of power-consciousness, integration is about embodying our new-found awareness and skills in a way that aligns with our authentic self, while maintaining a sense of equanimity and courage.

Integration also involves embodiment—the process of internalizing new skills and awareness so deeply that they become part of our physical and emotional presence. This is where power-consciousness moves from being a concept we understand intellectually to something we live. For instance, someone who has worked on managing their emotional reactions during conflicts now embodies a sense of calm and clarity, even in tense situations. This embodiment is closely tied to equanimity, the ability to remain balanced and composed, regardless of external pressures. Equanimity allows us to wield power with courage, staying grounded in our values even when faced with challenges or resistance. It's the courage to act from a place of integrity, even when it's difficult.

It's here that we step into the Broadwell's stage of "Unconscious Competence," where our skills and awareness become so ingrained that we no longer need to think about them. This is the stage where power-consciousness becomes effortless. We've internalized the "power-with" paradigm to the point where it's simply how we operate.

However, it's important to note that integration is not a static endpoint, but an ongoing process. Even as we move into unconscious competence, we must remain open to feedback and willing to adapt as new challenges arise. When we fail to do this, we can easily fall into the trap of thinking we're always right (because we've reached the Integration Phase). Then when we encounter someone in an earlier phase or in a cycle beyond our own, we may react with judgment or even fear—which brings us right back to the Denial phase—where we start to protect our newfound wisdom. And the cycle begins again.

These phases reveal our very human push/pull of wanting to stay in the familiar but also wanting to grow. It's a journey that requires courage, persistence, and a willingness to stay present with the messiness of change. Ultimately, power-consciousness is not a destination, but a lifelong practice of cultivating our personal power. In order to keep moving forward on the journey, it is helpful to know some strategies that you can use for yourself or to aid your own knowledge in supporting others on their journey.

22

Strategies for the Phases

When I was home for a visit some years ago, politics came up as a topic of conversation—and didn't end for several hours. Anyone who has family members that have very different political views, religious beliefs, or just values in general knows what this means—it's a shit show. I have expertise in both power and conflict, and yet somehow, when I am with my family of origin, I can get triggered and my personal power and skills for navigating conflict can go offline. However, it is because I come from a place very different from where I am now that I am able to do the work that I do. I was fortunate enough to have a father who would listen intently and with curiosity to beliefs and opinions that were very different from his. He taught me we can be with one another across difference in a way that is loving and still disagree. He taught me that conflict is a part of relationship and difference isn't wrong. This is perhaps one of the greatest gifts I received as a young person. Of course, we had our share of heated arguments, but in the end, there was always love there.

I'm not naive enough to believe that all conflict and disagreements can end this way. In fact, some things that get framed as disagreements are actually unchecked oppressive behaviors. For this reason, I think the number one skill for engaging across difference, particularly when there is a power differential, is discernment. We have to be aware enough of our own stuff (biases, triggers, boundaries), and aware of the differences between conflict, harm, abuse, oppression, etc., so that we can navigate relationship with wisdom.

Power-consciousness is not about achieving perfection, but about cultivating a deep, embodied awareness of how we engage in power and our impact on others. And—its not easy to become more power-conscious. It's a journey that takes us through different phases, each with its own challenges and opportunities for growth. Part of the inspiration for creating the Phases of Power Consciousness is so that I could cultivate more understanding around why we miss each other so much when we're in conflict. It goes beyond just having different views and cognitive errors—we are also in different phases of *development in power-consciousness*. After we identify where we are in terms of the phases, it can be helpful to have strategies for relating to ourselves or others in each phase. In this chapter, I've outlined some strategies to help us move forward—to help us get unstuck. Whether you're just starting to question your relationship with power or you're well on your way to embodying it more authentically, these strategies can help you navigate the ups and downs of this process.

STRATEGIES
FOR WORKING WITH EACH PHASE

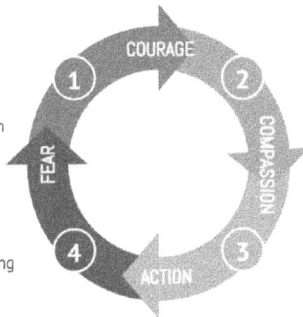

DENIAL
Emotion Regulation
Question w/Curiosity
Find similarities
Mentoring from others with
similar identities

CURIOSITY
Mindfulness Practice
Compassion
Feedback Practice
Learning
Exposure to diverse
identities/perspectives

INTEGRATION
Collaboration
Systemic Perspective Taking
Facilitation
Self-care
Community across difference

TRANSFORMATION
Holding complexity
Courage & Acceptance
Conflict Practice
Relationship with
diverse others

COURAGE
COMPASSION
ACTION
FEAR

1 2 3 4

Strategies for The Denial Phase: Breaking Through the Comfort Zone

When we're in the Denial Phase, we're often clinging to what feels safe and familiar. We might defend our current beliefs, avoid uncomfortable truths, or even feel anger or numbness when confronted with new perspectives. This is the stage of unconscious incompetence, where we don't yet realize how much we don't know. Of course, growth starts with breaking through this denial. But here's the thing: it's also a necessary phase. It is a place where we can be in safety until we are ready to be vulnerable. I think of the denial phase as similar to a hermit crab deciding when to change its shell. As they grow, hermit crabs must seek out larger shells to accommodate their increasing size. The decision to change shells is not taken lightly. A hermit crab will spend time carefully inspecting potential new shells, using its claws to assess the size, shape, and condition. It may even try on a few shells before committing to one, ensuring the fit is just right. The crab's behavior during this process is cautious and deliberate, as it must balance the need for a better shell with the risk of being exposed to predators during the transition.

Understanding that safety is number one can really help when we are dealing with the Denial Phase. How can you help yourself or the other person be vulnerable? When is it the right time to move to a new shell? When we are moving from one perspective, reality, or belief to another, it is a vulnerable process. We often hang our identities on our understanding of the world. When our understanding gets shaken, or we are confronted with a new reality, it can be scary—it feels like our very sense of self is under threat. Taking the time to make sure a new shell is suitable—-trying it on and being cautious—- is all part of the process.

This is a useful metaphor with one major difference: we're usually not seeking larger shells! Humans tend to avoid cognitive dissonance and discomfort—often growing in awareness only when we are forced to. However, if we *seek out* growth, then we have more control over the shell switching process than when we are *forced* into it. For example, a parent who is transphobic may sit safely inside their belief that transgender people are wrong or bad in some way. They can avoid learning about trans issues, trans lives, what trans people face—until, for example, their child comes out as trans. And then there is a choice: you can dig your head deeper into the sand and cling to your shell that is now too small (which the vast majority opt for), or you can look for a bigger shell that can accommodate both you and your child's reality. Either way, you are confronted with something that forces a choice. This is often the impetus for moving to the Curiosity Phase. Something has happened that has forced you into considering one or more different perspectives other than your own.

We cannot successfully move into the Curiosity Phase without one key ingredient: courage. Because we are vulnerable in this phase and more susceptible to the shadows of power, we have to intentionally cultivate the strength to face the unknown. Here are some strategies to help:

Emotion Regulation: When we're in denial, we are scanning the environment for threats, and our emotions are heightened. Anger, defensiveness, rage, or even numbness arise here often. Learning what we need to emotionally regulate can be really helpful when we feel defensive or when we encounter someone else who is being defensive. Whether it's you or another person in this phase, its helpful to take a moment and do something that helps you connect with your personal power. Take a deep breath, pause, and see if you can bring in any amount of curiosity. If not, go back to self-regulation techniques. One of my favorite regulation techniques is water—washing my hands, taking a bath, getting in a hot tub. Self-regulation is different for different people. I taught a workshop involving self-regulation techniques and one of the participants share that having a cat in their lap helped their nervous system. What are your go-to techniques?

Find Similarities & Values Affirmation: It's easy to see differences and feel threatened, but try to find common ground. What values or goals do you share with others, even if you disagree on the details? This can help reduce defensiveness and build connection. It can even work for yourself by exploring and deepening your understanding of your own values. Cohen[1] explores how values affirmations can be a powerful tool for reducing bias. The idea is simple yet profound: when people take a moment to reflect on their core values—whether it's creativity, family, or kindness—it boosts their sense of self-worth and resilience. This self-affirmation helps counteract the negative effects of stereotypes and biases, both in how we see ourselves and how we interact with others. Cohen explains that when people feel secure in their own identity, they're less likely to feel threatened by differences and more open to engaging with diverse perspectives. The beauty of values affirmations is that they're not about ignoring bias or pretending it doesn't exist; they're about building the inner strength to confront it with empathy and openness.

Question with Curiosity: Instead of shutting down or defending your position, try asking questions. If someone challenges your perspective, ask, "Can you tell me more about why you see it that

---

1. Cohen, G. L. (2022). Belonging: The Science of Creating Connection and Bridging Divides. W. W. Norton & Company, p.135-136.

way?" This opens the door to learning rather than resisting. Curiosity is the key ingredient when asking questions. If you aren't able to access curiosity, better to go back to emotion regulation first and then try again. Other questions: Why do you think this happened? Do you think this could be another way? What else might be at play here? Is there anything else we should be considering?

Mentoring from Others with Similar Identities or Perspectives: Mentoring from others who share your identity or perspective can be a transformative experience, especially when it comes to navigating the complexities of self-doubt or shifting beliefs. There's something uniquely powerful about hearing from someone who has walked a similar path but has moved beyond the initial stages of denial or resistance. They can offer a sense of validation and clarity, showing you that questioning your beliefs isn't about losing yourself—it's about evolving. When we're in the company of people who "get" us, there's a natural sense of comfort and emotional regulation that allows for deeper introspection. Affinity groups, or spaces where people with shared identities or experiences come together, create an environment where vulnerability feels safer. In these spaces, we're more likely to let our guards down, explore uncomfortable truths, and engage in meaningful growth. It's not just about feeling understood; it's about leveraging that understanding to push past our limits and embrace change. When we're surrounded by people we relate to, we're not just talking—we're truly connecting, and that's where the real work happens.

Strategies for The Curiosity Phase: Opening Up to New Possibilities

The Curiosity Phase is a pivotal yet delicate stage where we begin to emerge from the fog of denial and start to see the world—and ourselves—in a new light. It's a time of awakening, where the seeds of awareness are planted—-but the process can feel chaotic and overwhelming. We're no longer clinging to the comfort of old beliefs, but we're not yet grounded in new understandings either. This phase is marked by a willingness to explore, to ask questions, and to challenge the narratives we've taken for granted. However, as we start to peel back the layers, we may also encounter feelings of guilt or shame as we realize how much we've overlooked or misunderstood in the past. The weight of this realization can be heavy, especially as we become conscious of the harm we may have inadvertently caused during the Denial Phase.

The key to navigating the Curiosity Phase is to embrace the discomfort rather than shy away from it. It's okay to feel over-whelmed or unsure—these emotions are part of the process. What's important is that we stay open, that we allow ourselves to sit with the uncertainty and resist the urge to retreat back into denial. This is where growth happens, in the messy, uncertain space between what we once believed and what we're beginning to understand. It's a phase of transformation, and while it may feel fragile, it's also full of potential. By leaning into curiosity, we're taking the first steps toward a deeper, more nuanced understanding of power, privilege, and our place in the world. And this takes an incredible amount of courage and compassion.

Mindfulness Practice: Mindfulness Practice is a powerful strategy for navigating the Curiosity Phase, where awareness begins to blossom but the journey can feel unstable. As we open ourselves to new ideas and perspectives, curiosity demands presence—a will-ingness to stay engaged with the moment rather than retreating into old patterns of defensiveness or judgment. Mindfulness helps us stay grounded in this exploration by fostering a non-reactive awareness of our thoughts and emotions. It allows us to notice when we're feeling overwhelmed, guilty, or triggered, and gently guides us back to a state of openness. By practicing mindfulness, we create a mental space where we can observe our reactions without immediately acting on them, giving us the clarity to approach new information with curiosity rather than fear. This practice not only supports our growth during this delicate phase but also helps us build the resilience needed to continue moving forward with intention and self-compassion.

Compassion: Much like mindfulness, compassion is an essential companion during the Curiosity Phase, as the process of uncovering blind spots can often bring up feelings of guilt or shame. It's important to remember that these emotions are a natural part of growth and don't have to define or paralyze you. Instead of being harsh on yourself for what you didn't know, try to treat yourself with the same kindness and understanding you'd offer a friend who's learning something new. Self-compassion allows you to acknowledge your mistakes without letting them overshadow your progress. By being gentle with yourself, you create a safe emotional space to continue exploring and growing, even when the journey feels uncomfortable. This mindset helps you move forward with resilience and a willingness to keep learning. Be kind to yourself and others in this phase. It's normal to feel guilt or shame as you become more aware of your blind spots, but these emotions don't have to paralyze you. Treat yourself with the same compassion you'd offer a friend who's learning something new.

Feedback Practice: Compassion gives us the foundation to enter into generative conversations. Feedback is another crucial strategy for navigating the Curiosity Phase. Actively seeking out feedback, especially from those who have different perspectives or experiences than your own, can be incredibly insightful—if you let it be. The key is to listen without defensiveness, even when the feedback challenges your self-image or beliefs. This practice requires humility and a genuine desire to understand how others perceive you and the world around you. By opening yourself to feedback, you gain valuable insights that can help you see beyond your own limitations and expand your understanding. It's an opportunity to learn from others' lived experiences and to grow in ways that might not have been possible on your own.

Learning: Learning is the heart of the Curiosity Phase, and actively engaging with new ideas is essential for growth. Dive into books, podcasts, workshops, or any resources that challenge your assumptions and expose you to diverse identities and perspectives. This phase is about expanding your worldview, and that requires intentional effort to seek out voices and stories that differ from your own. Learning in this way helps you see the world through new lenses and deepens your understanding of complex issues. It's not just about accumulating knowledge—it's about transforming how you think and relate to others. By immersing yourself in learning, you're taking proactive steps to move beyond your comfort zone and embrace the richness of a more inclusive perspective.

Strategies for The Transformation Phase: Embracing the Hard Work of Change

The Transformation Phase is where the seeds of awareness planted in earlier stages begin to bear fruit, but it's also where the real work of change takes place. By this point, we've gained clarity and acceptance of the issues at hand, but now we must move beyond understanding and into action. This phase requires us to adapt, take active responsibility, and consciously work to integrate new skills, behaviors, and perspectives into our daily lives. It's not enough to simply *know* better—we must *do* better. This stage is often marked by a sense of grief as we let go of old ways of thinking and being that no longer serve us or align with our growing awareness. Letting go of these familiar patterns can feel like losing a part of ourselves, even if we know they were flawed or harmful. This grief is a natural part of the process, as we mourn the comfort of the past while stepping into the uncertainty of a new way of being.

This phase can feel awkward or challenging at first, as we're essentially rewiring old habits and thought patterns. It's a time of trial and error, where we may stumble or fall back into old ways, but each misstep is an opportunity to learn and grow. The key is to stay committed to the process, even when it feels difficult, and to celebrate the small victories along the way. It is about building the muscle of conscious change, and like any muscle, it takes time and effort to strengthen. Ultimately, the Transformation Phase is about stepping into a new version of yourself—one that is more aligned with your values, more aware of your impact, and more committed to creating positive change in the world. It's a challenging but deeply rewarding stage, where the work you put in begins to shape not only your own life but the lives of those around you.

Holding Complexity: This is a critical strategy during the Transformation Phase, as this stage often requires us to grapple with multiple, sometimes conflicting truths. For example, you might need to acknowledge the harm you've caused in the past while also recognizing your capacity for growth and change. This isn't easy—it can feel uncomfortable to sit with the discomfort of your own imperfections. However, holding space for these dual realities is essential for true transformation. It allows you to take responsibility for your actions without becoming paralyzed by guilt or shame. By embracing complexity, you can move forward with a more nuanced understanding of yourself and your impact on others, which is key to making meaningful, lasting change.

Courage & Acceptance: These are vital companions as you navigate the Transformation Phase. Change is rarely linear, and it takes courage to step into the unknown and challenge deeply ingrained habits or beliefs. Along the way, you're likely to make mistakes—and that's okay. What matters is not perfection but connection—to yourself and others. Accepting that missteps are part of the journey allows you to approach transformation with self-compassion and resilience. Courage means showing up even when it's hard, and acceptance means giving yourself grace as you do the work. Together, they help you stay committed to the process, even when the path feels uncertain.

Conflict Practice: This stage often involves both internal and external conflict. Internally, you may wrestle with guilt, doubt, or resistance to change. Externally, you might encounter difficult conversations with others who challenge your views or actions. Practicing how to engage in these conflicts with openness and respect is crucial. Instead of avoiding or escalating tension, approach these moments as opportunities to learn and grow. By developing the skills to navigate conflict effectively, you can better understand power dynamics, build stronger relationships, and create space for mutual understanding. Conflict, when handled with care, can be a powerful catalyst for transformation.

Relationship with Others Across Difference: In this phase, we are just being exposed to others who are different from us in some significant way; we are intentionally building connections with people who have different identities, experiences, and perspectives from our own. These relationships can challenge your assumptions, broaden your worldview, and deepen your empathy. Transformation isn't just about changing your own behavior—it's about understanding how your actions impact others and learning how to be in relationship with people who see the world differently. By engaging with others who are different from you, you gain new insights that can help you navigate complex social dynamics and become a more inclusive, thoughtful person. These relationships are not just about learning from others; they're about creating meaningful connections that enrich your journey of growth.

Strategies for The Integration Phase: Embodying Power with Authenticity

By this stage, we've reached a place of authenticity and skill, where our new awareness and behaviors have become second nature. The shifts we've made in how we think, act, and relate to others are no longer forced or awkward—they're woven into the fabric of who we are. We're no longer consciously thinking about every step; instead, we're living out our values and principles in a way that feels intuitive and aligned with our true selves. However, integration isn't the end of the journey; it's an ongoing process of living out our values and using our power responsibly.

This phase is about consistency and commitment, ensuring that the changes we've worked so hard to achieve are sustained over time. It's not enough to simply reach this stage and then coast—integration requires us to stay engaged and mindful. We must continue to reflect on our actions, check in with ourselves, and remain open to further growth. Life is dynamic, and new challenges will inevitably arise that test our ability to stay true to our values. Integration is about being prepared to meet those challenges with the same level of awareness and intentionality that brought us here.

In this phase, it's also important to celebrate how far we've come while acknowledging that growth is a lifelong process. We've likely overcome significant internal and external obstacles to reach this point, and taking time to honor that progress can be deeply affirming. At the same time, Integration doesn't mean we've "arrived" at a final destination; it means we've built a strong foundation that allows us to continue evolving.

When we reach this stage, there's a risk of slipping back into a new Phase of Denial—one where we become overly attached to our new way of thinking and shut ourselves off from further growth or feedback. We might start to believe we've "figured it all out," closing the door to new perspectives or dismissing challenges to our views. This rigidity can be just as limiting as the resistance we experienced in earlier phases, because it prevents us from staying open and adaptable. True integration requires humility and a willingness to remain curious, even when we feel confident in our progress. It's about staying flexible enough to evolve as we encounter new situations, people, and ideas, ensuring that our growth remains dynamic and responsive rather than static and complacent.

Collaboration: Collaboration is a key strategy in the Integration Phase, where the focus shifts from personal growth to collective impact. Now that you've developed a deeper understanding of power and privilege, it's important to use that awareness to collaborate with others, especially those down-power from you. True integration means moving beyond individual success and leveraging your power to uplift others. By working together, you can ensure that your actions contribute to the collective good rather than just personal gain. Collaboration fosters mutual learning, shared responsibility, and a more equitable distribution of power.

Systemic Perspective Taking: Remember to bring your understanding of systems with you, as it challenges you to look beyond individual actions and consider the larger dynamics at play. While personal growth is important, true transformation requires addressing the structural and institutional forces that perpetuate inequity. How can we use our power to challenge these systems and create more just structures? This might involve advocating for policy changes, supporting organizations that work toward systemic reform, or using your influence to shift cultural norms. By taking a systemic perspective, you can move beyond surface-level solutions and contribute to deeper, more lasting change.

Facilitation: As someone who has navigated the journey of power consciousness, you have valuable insights to share with others who are just beginning their own paths. Facilitation involves creating spaces—whether through mentorship, workshops, or community dialogues—where others can explore their understanding of power, privilege, and identity. By guiding and supporting others, you not only help them grow but also reinforce your own learning. Facilitation is about paying it forward, ensuring that the lessons you've gained continue to ripple outward and inspire collective transformation. It's a way to use your power to empower others, fostering a culture of awareness and accountability.

Self-care: Integration can be demanding, so don't forget to take care of yourself. It is crucial in the Integration Phase to focus on your health, boundaries and capacity, as sustaining your ability to make a positive impact requires ongoing energy and resilience. As you take on larger responsibilities and navigate complex systems, prioritizing self-care is essential—it helps prevent rigidity or burnout, keeping you open to new ideas and adaptable to change. By taking care of yourself, you ensure that you can continue to show up fully and authentically, both for yourself and for the communities you serve.

Community Across Difference: Building and supporting communities across difference is a strategy for staying grounded and connected during the Integration Phase. Building communities that bridge differences—whether in identity, perspective, or experience—helps you stay connected to the shared humanity that underpins all power dynamics. These connections challenge you to remain humble, curious, and open to learning, even as you grow in confidence. Communities that embrace diversity also provide a space for mutual support and accountability, reminding you that transformation is a collective effort. By co-creating communities that promote diversity, you create a network of solidarity that strengthens your ability to navigate power dynamics with empathy and integrity. This strategy ensures that your growth remains rooted in connection and collaboration, rather than isolation or rigidity.

The journey through these phases isn't linear—we might move back and forth as we encounter new challenges and opportunities. But each phase offers its own lessons and strategies for growth. By staying curious, compassionate, and committed to learning, we can move toward a more conscious and ethical relationship with power. Remember, it's not about perfection; it's about connection. Along the way, we'll make mistakes, face discomfort, and grapple with complexity, but these are all signs that we're growing. The goal isn't to reach a final destination where we have all the answers, but to cultivate a mindset of continuous learning and humility. Power consciousness is a lifelong practice, one that requires us to stay engaged, adaptable, and open to the perspectives of others.

As we integrate these strategies into our lives, we begin to see that power isn't just something we wield—it's something we share. Whether we're collaborating with others, challenging systemic inequities, or facilitating growth in those around us, we're contributing to a larger movement toward justice and equity. The work of power consciousness is deeply personal, but it's also profoundly collective. It's about how we show up in the world, how we use our influence to uplift others, and how we remain accountable to the communities we're part of. By embracing this journey with intention and care, we not only transform ourselves but we also become more capable of shaping power for good.

We are at the end of Part Two of the book. In Part One, we developed a foundational understanding of power. We now have a shared language that encompasses different types of power that can help us more effectively communicate with others. In Part Two, we explored what gets in the way and what supports our development of power consciousness. This consciousness helps us be more intentional about how we navigate power differentials, which is a critical component of right-relationship. From here, I invite us to step into Part Three where will explore a model for leveraging wayfinding techniques to increase our ability to find our way to right-relationship.

-Part Three-

Wayfinding to Right-Relationship

23

Wayfinding

"We are participants in a vast communion of being, and if we open ourselves up to its guidance, we can learn anew how to live in this great and gracious community of truth. We can and we must—if we want our sciences to be humane, our institutions to be sustaining, our healings to be deep, our lives to be true." - Parker Palmer

"The journey of wayfinding is not about reaching a destination, but about discovering who you are along the way." - David Whyte

With a nuanced language and framework for navigating power, we now have a foundation for the journey we take toward right-relationship: wayfinding. Wayfinding in relationship is the delicate process by which we find right-relationship *through* power-consciousness *and* a commitment to being present to *what is* (not just what we want it to be). Wayfinding toward right-relationship—both with ourselves and others—is a journey that requires self-awareness, compassion, and commitment.

In this section of the book, I have created a compass of sorts called **The Right-Relationship Spiral** to help guide us in finding right-relationship with ourselves, each other, the land, and universal power. The following chapters will explore that spiral and the wayfinding process. But, before we begin, I'd like to surface a few reminders about wayfinding:

1. You can't be a wayfinder if you already know the way.

Wayfinding is about navigating an uncertain path. It's not about having a map with every turn marked out, but about developing the skills, mindset, and principles to move forward even when the path isn't clear. Being present, we have to listen for what arises in the moment, and respond from awareness. Bringing back the jazz metaphor feels appropriate here. In jazz, musicians don't just play; they listen to each other, to the rhythm, to the energy of the room. This deep listening allows them to harmonize, to find the right moment to step forward or to hold back. In wayfinding, listening is equally crucial. You listen to your intuition, to the environment, to the people around you. This kind of attentive awareness helps you make decisions that are in tune with the moment, rather than forcing a pre-planned route.

Both wayfinding and jazz are about trusting the process. They remind us that life isn't a straight line; it's a series of improvisations, a dance between structure and spontaneity. Whether you're navigating a melody or a life path, the key is to stay present, stay curious, and embrace the beauty of the unknown. As the great jazz musician Miles Davis once said, "Don't play what's there; play what's not there." In the same way, wayfinding invites us to explore what's not yet mapped, to find our way by listening, adapting, and creating as we go. Relationships don't exist in rulebooks.

2. The journey starts where you are.

So many of us believe that we have to be somehow different from who we are to start on the path—we need to read more books, take more workshops, be more certain, have more security. But the truth is that we can start right now, right as we are. My favorite scene in Moana is when she is alone in the middle of the ocean, on a journey, when everything goes wrong, and she completely gives up. She is filled with doubt and calls on her ancestor, her grandmother, for guidance. Her grandmother's message is:

Sometimes the world seems against you
The journey may leave a scar
But scars can heal and reveal just
Where you are
The people you love will change you
The things you have learned will guide you
And nothing on Earth can silence
The quiet voice still inside you
And when that voice starts to whisper
"Moana, you've come so far
Moana, listen
Do you know who you are?"

The starting place for wayfinding always starts with us. Moana's grandmother doesn't tell her what to do or where to go. Instead, she points to Moana and asks, "Who are you?" By remembering who she is and why she started the journey, she can get back on track. Right-relationship requires us to be in touch with who we are—that is where true authenticity arises. When we are in contact with our personal power, then we can tap into our connection to universal power and our "why," which can help us begin or start again.

One of the most important truths about moving toward right-relationship is that it's rarely a straight line. You'll have moments of clarity and progress, but you'll also face setbacks, detours, and plateaus. This isn't a failure—it's part of the process. Growth often happens in cycles, where you revisit old lessons with new perspectives. It's easy to get caught up in regrets about the past or anxieties about the future, but the only place you can truly start is right here, right now. Wayfinding is about being present with where you are, even if it's not where you want to be. From this place of presence, you can make intentional choices that move you forward.

The lasting wisdom of this principle is that we can't find right-relationship with others if we're not also aiming toward right-relationship with ourselves. This means cultivating self-awareness, self-compassion, and self-acceptance. It's about understanding your own needs, values, and boundaries, and honoring them in your interactions with others. Embrace where you are—with all of the twists and turns; that is the best place to start.

3. Discomfort and conflict are part of the path.

Honestly, if you're comfortable all the time, you're probably not growing. Wayfinding means stepping outside your comfort zone, confronting fears, and facing parts of yourself you'd rather ignore. That discomfort? It's not a sign you're doing something wrong; it's a sign you're growing. It's like stretching a muscle—it might feel a little awkward or even painful at first, but that's how you build strength and flexibility. As the saying goes, "A ship in harbor is safe, but that's not what ships are built for." You weren't built to stay anchored in the familiar; you were built to explore, to grow, to transform.

Similarly, in the process of wayfinding toward right-relationship conflict is inevitable. It's not a sign that something's broken or that you've failed at relationships. Instead, think of conflict as the natural result of the presence of difference. This is how I define conflict, as simply the presence of different needs, beliefs, expectations, and/or commitments—and this can happen internally with ourselves or externally with others. When thought about this way, we are essentially always navigating conflict! So we might as well learn how to navigate conflict well. The key is to stop seeing all conflict as something to avoid and start seeing it as something to lean into when appropriate. Conflict, when approached with curiosity and openness, can be a catalyst for growth[1]. It's an opportunity to learn, to understand, and to find new ways of being in relationship—with yourself and with others.

The challenge, of course, is tolerating the unknown and the cognitive dissonance that comes with conflict. That feeling of "Wait, I'm not sure what's right here" can be unsettling, but it's also where the wisdom arises. If you can sit with that discomfort long enough—without rushing to resolve it or shut it down—you'll often find a deeper understanding on the other side. It's like untangling a knot: you have to be patient, willing to work through the mess, and open to discovering something new.

4. You can't do it alone.

You remember the hermit crab metaphor? One of the most fascinating aspects of hermit crab behavior is the "shell exchange chain." This is when a group of hermit crabs, all in need of new shells, gather together in what looks like a carefully choreographed dance. The largest crab kicks things off by finding a new, roomier shell and

---

1. . This is, of course, when it is true conflict, not oppression or abuse disguised or labeled as "conflict."

moving in, leaving its old shell behind. The next largest crab, seeing the newly vacated shell, quickly claims it as its own, leaving *its* old shell empty for the next crab in line. This domino effect continues down the line, with each crab trading up to a better-fitting shell, until everyone has found a home that suits them. It's like a game of musical chairs, but with shells—and everyone wins.

What's truly remarkable about this process is how efficient and organized it is. Hermit crabs don't fight over shells or try to hoard the best ones for themselves. Instead, they work together in a way that ensures the whole group benefits. This behavior highlights a deep, almost intuitive understanding of mutual aid—the idea that helping others ultimately helps you. It's a lesson in cooperation that feels especially poignant in a world that often prioritizes competition over collaboration.

In a broader sense, the shell exchange chain is a metaphor for how we can support each other in the wayfinding process. Just as hermit crabs pass shells down the line, we can share resources, knowledge, and encouragement to help each other grow. Wayfinding is such a deeply personal journey, but you are never alone in it—we are interconnected, whether we want to be or not. And if it feels like you are alone, seek a community, mentorship, or support. They are closer than you think. And when you feel up-capacity and have a sense of abundance, share it with others. Reach out to those who might be struggling *(hint: it's usually the caretakers and the people who are being strong for others)*.

5. Rooted personal power is the navigator.

When it comes to finding right-relationship—with yourself, with others, or with the world around you—there's no GPS, no step-by-step manual. The journey is yours to navigate, and the compass you need is rooted personal power. It's about being deeply connected to something larger than yourself while also staying firmly grounded in your own agency. It's about knowing who you are, what you stand for, and trusting that you have what it takes to steer your own ship.

In the midst of uncertainty, your values can serve as a guiding light. What truly matters to you? What kind of person do you want to be? What do you stand for? What brings you alive? What allows you to feel grounded in your inherent belongingness? These questions aren't always easy to answer, but they're essential for cultivating your personal power. When you're aligned with these things, decisions become clearer, even when the path ahead is foggy or the world feels chaotic.

Of course, you can—and should—seek guidance from trusted mentors and other external wisdom and resources. They can offer valuable insights, but ultimately *you're the one at the helm*. No one else can tell you exactly what path to take or what decisions to make. This is where rooted personal power comes in. It's about taking ownership of your choices, learning from your mistakes, and trusting your inner compass. It's about balancing the wisdom you gather from the outside with the intuition and values that live inside you. Think of it as a dance between listening to others and listening to yourself. Wayfinding to right relationship must include a grounding in your rooted personal power.

6. The journey is also the destination.

Finally, remember that wayfinding isn't about reaching some final, perfect relationship. It's about the process itself—the lessons you learn, the person you become, and the connections you make along the way. Wayfinding is about embracing the journey as an ongoing adventure, rather than a race to a finish line. And part of the process in any journey is losing your way.

Have you ever been traveling, lost your way, and decided to just go with it? In those moments, when I'm able to embrace the adventure, the times I have gotten lost in another country have been my most meaningful and fun travel experiences. Similar to reframing conflict and discomfort, we can reframe getting lost as just part of the process—perhaps even a very important part of the wayfinding process. One of my favorite poems, *Lost*, by David Wagoner, communicates this well:

> *Stand still. The trees ahead and the bushes beside you*
> *Are not lost. Wherever you are, is called Here,*
> *And you must treat it as a powerful stranger,*
> *Must ask permission to know it and to be known.*
> *Listen, the forest breaths. Listen. It answers,*
> *I have made this place around you.*
> *If you leave it, you may come back again, saying Here.*
> *No two trees are the same to the Raven.*
> *No two branches the same to the Wren.*
> *If what a tree or a bush does is lost on you,*
> *You are surely lost. Stand still. The forest knows*
> *Where you are. You must let it find you."*

It is a counter-intuitive thing to allow yourself to be found when you are lost—or to stand still and find yourself. When we have a sense that the journey is also the destination, being "lost" loses its meaning. In a sense, every place we find ourselves is another valid and meaningful step on the path. It's about trusting the process, believing that even in moments of uncertainty, we're exactly where we need to be. By letting go of the need to control and instead allowing the world to guide us, we can find our way not by escaping, but by deepening our understanding of where we are.

While getting to right-relationship, you might feel lost, uncertain, uncomfortable, and full of doubt, but keep going. Wayfinding toward right-relationship with ourselves and others is a lifelong journey. It's about cultivating self-awareness, authenticity, and compassion, while also fostering connection, respect, and mutual growth. It's not about perfection, but about showing up with intention and care, even when it's hard. In other words, the journey itself is where the magic happens.

24

The Right-Relationship Spiral

"One of the powerful things about purpose is that we can always choose to have one, no matter how harsh our circumstances." - Geoffrey Cohen

"He who has a why to live for can bear almost any how." - Friedrich Nietzsche

"The only true antidote to the despair, nihilism, and hopelessness is action." - Hannah Arendt

While some wayfinding practices involve well-designed maps, we don't generally receive a map for navigating relationships. Relationships are diverse, and each one requires a different path. But it can be helpful to have some guideposts or cues to help us along the way. Nautical wayfinders traditionally use the stars, the wind, the birds, the waves, and even the color and temperature of the water to help them navigate. But perhaps the most important reference point is the oral traditions and ancestral knowledge passed down through generations, encoded in chants, stories, and songs, and of course, their intuition and experience. After years of practice, they develop a "feel" for the ocean —an almost instinctive understanding of its rhythms and moods. This inner compass, honed through countless voyages, allows them to navigate even in challenging conditions.

Ultimately, wayfinders use a holistic approach, combining all these elements to navigate the vast and unpredictable ocean. It's a testament to human ingenuity and our deep connection to the natural world—even when the path isn't clear, there are always signs to guide us—if we know how to look.

It is the learning-how-to-look-part that is the challenge—especially in modern times and Western culture. Many of us didn't have ancestral knowledge like this passed down to us. Most of us did not have "right-relationship" prioritized in our learning, and if it was, it was more likely to be based in rules rather than intuition and presence. Tyson Yunkaporta said:

> "You only need to have enough awareness to see or hear or feel the pattern of the system, and everything you need is always nearby. This requires installing some sacred mind updates, though, and the sacred is hard to trust because it can't be observed and replicated in controlled conditions, so any data you might collect on it will always be invalid. Sill, the sacred mind does let you see the pattern, see the things land gives you—always exactly the things you need. These are the things that let you know what you're supposed to be doing today. This way of being isn't always conducive to holding down a job or meeting a deadline. In a world of Reason and tinkered metrics and forensically designed histories, the sacred mind condemns you to limbo."[1]

---

1. Yunkaporta, T. (2019). Sand Talk: How Indigenous Thinking Can Save the World. HarperOne, p. 50.

In some ways, we have to unlearn a lot of what we were taught about human relationships and power if we are going to make it any distance on the path to right-relationship. For those of us trapped in modern, Western culture—in deadlines and rigid systemic structures—we may be condemned to limbo, but it is not hopeless. We have been given too many gifts as human beings to squander them on hopelessness.

Like many around the world, I have been deeply moved and inspired by the work of Joanna Macy—specifically the work she named, "The Work that Reconnects." Drawing from indigenous wisdom (human ancestral knowledge), she created a spiral of steps to help us reconnect with our interdependent nature. It is a simple and powerful way to keep moving toward connection. Also, inspired by her experience with indigenous elders, Dr. Barstow created The Power Spiral for the Right Use of Power—one that reveals the different dimensions of power and how we can access each of them. I recommend exploring both, as they offer helpful steps toward greater connection with ourselves and each other.

After steeping myself in many spiral models and spending time fasting on the land, what came through was an image and a dream. I've done my best to interpret that image into a step-by-step path toward right-relationship which I call "The Right-Relationship Spiral." It is a sort of wayfinding compass that can keep us on the journey of developing deeper power-consciousness. Ultimately, the Right-Relationship Spiral is a practice of interdependence. The biggest message of interdependence is that we each belong—we each have a natural sacred place on Earth.

The Spiral begins with "Connecting with our Roots," which leads to "Listening," and then to "Turning Toward" (rather than away from) our interdependence. Once we've faced "what is," we are encouraged into "Grieving and Resourcing" ourselves, which

will give us space for "Dreaming and Imagining." Finally we are
called into "Manifesting" and "Practicing" which brings our commitment into action. Entering the spiral itself is a commitment.
Wayfinding to right-relationship cannot happen without this commitment. Before you step into the spiral, take a moment to name
your own commitment for your journey toward right-relationship
with yourselves and others. Why do you want to do this work?

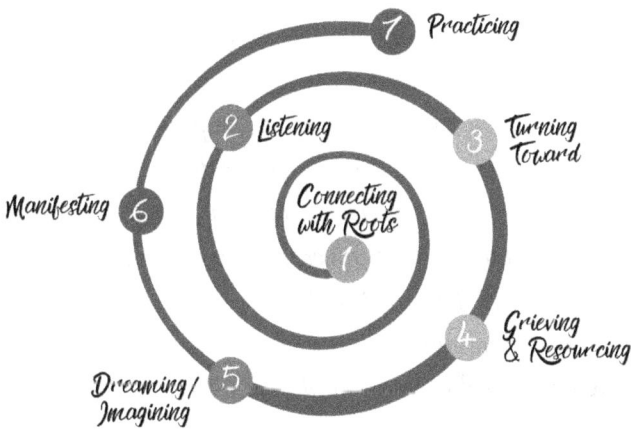

The Right Relationship Spiral

25

Connecting with Roots

"For those who do not belong to a religious community, are interspiritual, or spiritual but not religious, one may feel lost without the ideals of an established tradition. Yet, there is a sacred path, interior to every person, an organic constellation of wisdom imprinted in each soul. This universal process or path is occurring in our depth. It involves spiritual transformation—purifying old habits, stages of growth, and opening one's heart to love. The motivation of inner transformation is to receive and act upon the presence of the sacred within us, thus opening ourselves to a life of wisdom and meaning." — Beverly Lanzetta, "Turning One's Life Around," Unpublished Lecture, April 13, 2022.

"Aunty says, 'The first step is realising that the self is in relation.'" - Tyson Yunkaporta

"The intelligence that evolved us from star dust and interconnects us with all beings is sufficient for the healing of our Earth community, if we but align with that purpose." – Dr. Joanna Macy

"If we surrendered to earth's intelligence we could rise up rooted, like the trees." - Rainer Maria Rilke

I used to have a picture of our solar system as the wallpaper on my computer. I liked being reminded of how inconceivably small I am in relationship to the rest of existence—somehow it helped me to have perspective when my problems seemed really big. The vastness also prompted a sense of awe, that somehow I was a tiny speck, but a tiny speck that was a part of something so inconceivably huge, complex and special.

It turns out that viewing oneself as part of something bigger can be profoundly important, not just to adjust our perspective. When we see ourselves as part of a larger whole —be it a community, society, or the universe —it gives us context, purpose, and even direction in our lives. It impacts our social relationships, ethical perspectives, and overall wellbeing. Research shows that it can even reduce anxiety and stress and promote social well-being[1] . When we realize we are part of something larger, it becomes easier to show up, to be response-able, and to access our rooted personal power.

Of course, everyone perceives the "something bigger" differently, which makes it hard to discuss in diverse groups. I wanted to find a word or phrase that could capture this grounding element and be inclusive of all our perceptions. Perhaps this is not possible, and I'll fall miserably short, but I don't want to keep saying "something bigger" because it is an annoying way to speak, and it just feels…inadequate. So I've taken to calling it the "Sacred Fifth" after the Living Myth Podcast episode I shared at the end of the Universal

---

1. Steger, M. F., Kashdan, T. B., & Oishi, S. (2008). Being good by doing good: Daily eudaimonic activity and well-being. *Journal of Research in Personality*, 42(1), 22-42. & Kashdan, T. B., & McKnight, P. E. (2013). Commitment to a purpose in life: An antidote to the suffering by individuals with social anxiety disorder. *Emotion*, 13(6), 1150-1159.

Power chapter. Across cultures, the Sacred Fifth, or fifth direction, often symbolizes a spiritual center or focal point. It represents the space where the physical and spiritual worlds meet and integrate, offering balance, connection with "something bigger," and a sense of wholeness or interdependence.

No matter what we call it, this connection to Universal Power seems to have a sacred element. Sacredness need not be "spiritual," but it does accompany a deep sense of reverence, respect, and connection. So why is being in touch with that which is "sacred" important? Many religions have much more sophisticated answers to that than I have, but I do notice that the lack of the consciousness of the Sacred Fifth or at least the loss of connection with what is "sacred" seems to contribute to our general disconnection from ourselves and each other. Charles Eisenstein said, "Today we live in a world that has been shorn of its sacredness, so that very few things indeed give us the feeling of living in a sacred world. Mass-produced, standardized commodities, cookie-cutter houses, identical packages of food, and anonymous relationships with institutional functionaries all deny the uniqueness of the world. The distant origin of our things, the anonymity of our relationships, and the lack of visible consequences in the production and disposal of our commodities all deny relatedness. Thus we live without the experience of sacredness."[2] Recognizing something as sacred involves acknowledging its deeper connection to what is real or eternal (meaning beyond the comings and goings of fashion, trends, or even models of governance). So much of our world is manufactured, touched-up, or seems terrified of going beyond the surface. But why?

---

2. Eisenstein, C. (2011). Sacred Economics: Money, Gift, and Society in the Age of Transition. Evolver Editions, p. 6.

In my experience, I have noticed that when people or groups want to stay on the surface of things, it's usually because they don't want you to see what's underneath. The fool's gold of social construction wants you to be satisfied with what's on the surface. If we were to connect with the truth of our interdependence, it would be much harder to be productive, to fit people into boxes, to collapse into binary thinking, and to simplify things so much that it becomes possible to control a lot of people at once. The damage that not diving deep has done to our culture is immense.

So how do we go deep and find the sacred together when we come from different Systemic Lenses and have different conceptions of what we are rooted in, or perhaps no conception that we're rooted in something bigger at all? This is an incredibly hard question that strikes at the heart of why I have invested so much of my life's energy into exploring power and how to use it well. I hold this question with me wherever I go. And while I do not believe there is a single "right" answer, just asking the question helps me expand my perspective. It promotes my search beyond what I already know and it is entirely dependent on who I am in relationship with in any given moment. So, what I know to be true in response to this question is that when I take the time to connect with my roots, I have more capacity, resilience, patience, and spaciousness to attempt to connect across difference. This is a useful step in the direction of right-relationship.

Below, I've included many different ways to connect to this first, very important foundation of the spiral. Each of the ways outlined below is an element of what I mean by "connecting with roots." But do what works for you. If one metaphor or way of understanding doesn't land for you, let go of it and cultivate another one that does.

Roots in the Earth

Connecting to roots can refer to the literal roots in the ground. When we are connected with the natural world, we feel more connected to ourselves. And this isn't only because we feel connected to something larger than ourselves, it's also because we are not separate from nature. We are made up from the substances of the universe—literally. The elements that make up the human body—like carbon, oxygen, nitrogen, and hydrogen—were forged in the hearts of stars through nuclear fusion. When massive stars exploded in supernovae billions of years ago, they scattered these elements across the universe, eventually forming the building blocks of planets, life, and us. The saying "we are made of stardust" is scientifically accurate. But the science of it doesn't really matter—does it? The part that matters in terms of coming closer to right-relationship, is that being fully in nature (and away from all of the ways we cover over nature) allows us to come closer to ourselves. As Rick Rubin said, "The closer we can get to the natural world, the sooner we start to realize we are not separate. And that when we create, we are not just expressing our unique individuality, but our seamless connection to an infinite oneness."[3] The natural world is naturally interdependent.

One of the reasons I love to use the word "roots" is that it is the way in which roots support the life of the plant. Roots are the unsung heroes of a plant's life, quietly anchoring it in place while playing a crucial role in its survival. They absorb water and essential nutrients from the soil, acting like a plant's lifeline. But roots do more than just feed the plant—they're also part of a fascinating underground network. Through a symbiotic relationship with mycelium (the thread-like structures of fungi) roots connect to a vast mycelial web. This network acts like nature's internet,

---

3. Rubin, R. (2023). The creative act: A way of being. Penguin Press, p . 52.

allowing plants to "communicate" with each other, share nutrients, and even send warnings about threats. It's a hidden, interconnected world that supports not just individual plants, but entire ecosystems. Just like plants, our roots allow us to be grounded and to connect to the reality of our interdependence.

Tyson Yunkaporta said, that there is "....a Law of relationality that you can only learn from the land. The first relation is between land and people, and the second relation is between people and people. The second is contingent on the first." We have lost touch with our connection to the land in the modern Western world. And it is land we must connect with first if we are to find right-relationship.

Inherent Belongingness

When I first created the material around personal power, I was coming from time on the land—a wilderness vigil, as I have mentioned before. The primary experience I had at that time, when everything dropped away except for me and the land, was a feeling of inherent belonging. I was not separate, as I often feel when I'm around other people or caught in the complexities of human systems. There were no expectations or demands that I be different. I was able just to be—exactly as I was. This is when I realized that feeling a part of something is very different than relating to something. My whole life, I was taught to relate to the natural world as if it were separate, and here I was—just a part of it. That had a profound impact on my understanding of my place in the world, and it allowed me to finally root into my natural and inherent personal power. Not the surface, socialized "confidence" or "agency" but a rooting into the stability of my inherent belonging.

There is a concept in psychology called "the belonging effect," which refers to the positive impact that a sense of belonging has on an individual's well-being, motivation, and behavior. It highlights how humans have an innate need to feel connected to others and to be part of a group or community. When people feel that they belong, they experience greater emotional security, self-esteem, and purpose, which can lead to improved mental health and increased resilience in various areas of life. Geoffrey Cohen said:

> "In a study involving a nationally representative sample of over 12,000 teenagers, the most powerful protective factors for every form of adolescent risk behavior and distress—including emotional distress, drug abuse, violence, and suicidality—were how strong a sense of belonging they had in school and how strong a sense of belonging they had at home. The 'belonging effect' surpassed the effects of academic performance, self-esteem, religiosity, being held back a grade, parental absence, and household access to guns. Many of these risk factors capture our attention because they are visible, but the importance of connection, being harder to 'see,' too often eludes our attention."[4]

Our sense of inherent belongingness is similar to the Buddhist concept of "basic goodness" which suggests that at our core, all beings possess an innate purity and potential for wisdom, compassion, and clarity. It's not about being morally perfect or free from flaws, but rather recognizing that beneath our conditioned habits and negative emotions, there's a fundamental wellspring of goodness

---

4. Cohen, G. L. (2022). Belonging: The Science of Creating Connection and Bridging Divides. W. W. Norton & Company, p.232.

that connects us all. This idea invites us to trust in our own nature and the nature of others, even when life feels messy or chaotic. Basic goodness isn't something we need to earn or create—it's already there. While at times we have a sense of our basic goodness or inherent belongingness, sometimes it can feel like we've lost both. But they remain a fact of our existence—even if we've lost touch with it. Just like the sun doesn't cease to exist just because it is occasionally cloud-covered. Our inherent belongingess and basic goodness are always there—no matter how lost we might feel, we always have the potential to return to this sense of wholeness and openness.

Rooting Down: Connecting with your Sacred Fifth

As we discussed in previous sections, the Sacred Fifth is whatever is larger than us and reminds us of our deep connection with one another. Rooting into the Sacred Fifth is the source of our Inherent Belongingness. Connecting to roots may seem like just another thing "to do," but it is more of a letting go or a surrender than something you have to create or effort to do.

I was just at a retreat recently, and the theme was loving kindness. We talked a lot about compassion. What seemed helpful to many participants was recognizing that, because of our inherent belongingness and basic goodness, there is a field of compassion that exists between and through us. When we struggle to bring compassion to our experience or our relationships, it is often because we are trying to generate it on our own rather than tapping into the field of compassion all around us. Realizing that there is this natural context of compassion that I can relax into is very helpful for me. Instead of trying to create our connection with the Sacred Fifth, we can just relax into it. It is already there. In fact, this is probably the most significant gift of connecting with our roots: it allows us to be held so that we can be more resourced. When we are more resourced, all kinds of things that normally seem burdensome start to arise naturally, like gratitude, responsibility, and helping one another. One of the teachers at the retreat, Judith Simmer-Brown, said, "Compassion practice is the activism of our time." I just love this. Because compassion practice helps us tap into an expansive container (the field of compassion), we are resourced and aware enough of our interconnection for the natural arising of responsibility, without it feeling like a burden. Resting in the field of compassion, we have the capacity not only to be aware of our relational responsibilities but also to act on them. True compassion is active. As Simmer-Brown puts it, compassion is the link between mindfulness and activism.

Another thing that naturally arises from our sense of interconnection is gratitude. My dear friend, Ian Sanderson, who is from the Mohawk Nation, Turtle Clan, shared with me that when his clan gathers, before doing anything else, they spend over an hour just giving gratitude—gratitude to and for all things. Gratitude is considered "the words that come before all else." When I first heard this, my white self thought, "wow...how laborious!" So often in modern Western culture, gratitude is an afterthought, not a starting place. But what I have since realized is that being in a state of gratitude also helps us to root—so it is a symbiotic relationship. Natural gratitude arises when we feel connected, and cultivating gratitude can deepen our connection. What a wonderful way to start anything—especially if it is a gathering of humans.

When we begin rooted, we can access our authentic self and our authentic connection with others. This is what the world most needs. Not for you to be like other change-makers, or a hero, or a martyr - just *you*, rooted. Dominant culture can be all encompassing, influencing every moment. Being rooted in this way helps us to find our way to right-relationship. This poem by Rumi perfectly encapsulates this first step in the spiral:

The Root of the Root of Yourself - by Rumi

Don't go away, come near.
Don't be faithless, be faithful.
Find the antidote in the venom.
Come to the root of the root of your Self.

Molded of clay, yet kneaded
from the substance of certainty,
a guard at the Treasury of Holy Light —
come, return to the root of the root of your Self.

Once you get hold of selflessness,
you'll be dragged from your ego
and freed from many traps.
Come, return to the root of the root of your Self.

You are born from the children of God's creation,
but you have fixed your sight too low.
How can you be happy?
Come, return to the root of the root of your Self.

Although you are a talisman protecting a treasure,
you are also the mine.
Open your hidden eyes
and come to the root of the root of your Self.

You were born from a ray of God's majesty

and have the blessings of a good star.
Why suffer at the hands of things that don't exist?
Come, return to the root of the root of your Self.

You are a ruby embedded in granite.
How long will you pretend it isn't true?
We can see it in your eyes.
Come to the root of the root of your Self.

Connecting with roots means many different things to each of us, but they all lead to the same result: cultivating our sense of the interdependence of all things—our place in the web of life. It is finding whatever is sacred in the moment and coming from that place. So this is where we begin—with our Sacred Fifth—as frequently as possible. We find our roots and we connect with what is underneath (and all around) us, supporting us—the root of the root of yourself. We feel it holding us, providing us with space, support, strength, and ease.

A Note About Spiritual Materialism and Bypassing

While cultivating familiarity with universal power and greater comfort with mystery, it can feel alluring to use spiritual practices, beliefs, or achievements to bolster our ego. This can manifest as seeking spiritual experiences, titles, or insights to feel special or superior, rather than addressing the imbalances in our psyche, our relationships and our communities. Chögyam Trungpa Rinpoche, a Tibetan Buddhist teacher, defined this as spiritual materialism. He said, "We may deceive ourselves into thinking that we are developing spiritually when instead we are

strengthening our egocentricity through spiritual techniques."
Unfortunately, none of us is immune to this temptation, including Trungpa.

John Welwood also addressed a similar dynamic called spiritual bypassing. Spiritual bypassing is the use of spirituality
to avoid dealing with psychological or emotional challenges.
When we say we are connecting with our roots, we aren't using
it as a way to bypass the challenges of the world, but to better
prepare us for them. It is important not to confuse this first step,
or we will end up going on a very different path.

Reflection Questions:

1. What does rooting into the "Sacred Fifth" or "Something
   Bigger" look like for you?

2. When you are connected to your version of the Sacred
   Fifth, what becomes possible for you?

3. What does the word "sacred" mean to you? What people,
   places, or experiences do you consider sacred? When do
   you feel most disconnected from that which you consider
   sacred?

4. What small, actionable step can you take today to deepen
   your connection to your roots or the Sacred Fifth?

26

Listening

"There must be nothing inside you but a great willingness to hear, to listen. . .It's as if you are nearly starving and someone is offering you food. When you listen like that, then you can truly hear." - Paula Underwood

"Before you charge in to make things better, pay attention to the value of what's already there." - Donella Meadows

"Eventually we realize that not knowing what to do is just as real and just as useful as knowing what to do. Not knowing stops us from taking false directions. Not knowing what to do, we start to pay real attention. Just as people lost in the wilderness, on a cliff face or in a blizzard pay attention with a kind of acuity that they would not have if they thought they knew where they were. Why? Because for those who are really lost, their life depends on paying real attention. If you think you know where you are, you stop looking." - David Whyte

At the heart of any meaningful journey toward right-relationship lies a simple yet profound act: listening. Once we have connected with our roots, our task is to open ourselves fully to the world around and within us. Listening is the bridge that connects us—to ourselves, to each other, and to the larger web of life. It's how we begin to understand, to heal, and to move forward together. But listening, in its deepest sense, is not always easy. It requires presence, patience, and a willingness to be changed by what we hear. It's an act of humility and courage, one that starts with being rooted in who we are and where we come from.

There are four directions of listening that are relevant for moving toward right-relationship:

1. listening to the Sacred Fifth (the unseen, the divine, or the larger mystery that connects us all),

2. listening to ourselves (our inner truths, fears, and desires),

3. listening to one another (the voices, stories, and experiences of those around us), and

4. listening to the in-between (the spaces, silences, and tensions that exist between us).

These directions are not separate; they are interconnected, each one informing and enriching the others. When we listen in this holistic way, we begin to see the threads that bind us together, and we move closer to right-relationship. But here's the thing: listening deeply is only possible when we are rooted. If we're not grounded in our own sense of self, our own personal power, or our connection to something larger, our listening can become shallow or distorted. We might hear only what we want to hear, or we might become overwhelmed by the noise around us. That's why, if you haven't rooted yet—or if you've lost your connection—it's essential to go back and do that first. Rooting gives us the stability and clarity we need to listen with openness and discernment.

As we embark on this step in the spiral—this movement toward right-relationship—we'll explore how listening, in all its dimensions, can guide us. We'll see how it helps us navigate the complexities of human connection, how it brings us closer to understanding the sacredness of life, and how it opens the door to transformation. Listening, when done with intention and care, is not just a skill; it's a way of being in the world. It's how we begin to weave the fabric of right-relationship, one thread at a time. So, as we move forward, let's remember to listen—not just with our ears, but with our whole selves.

Listening to the Sacred Fifth

When I was 22, I lived in Costa Rica with my then-boyfriend, Alex, who was a surfer from Venezuela. On the days he surfed, he would get up just as the sun was rising, and he would sit still and look at the ocean for what seemed like a long time. He just stared at it. When I first observed him doing this, I didn't understand. Since I was raised in the United States, my inclination was to "just do it." Day after day, I watched him as he watched the waves, often for up to half an hour at a time. After a while, I realized that he was attuning himself to the ocean—listening with his whole being. Only after he had a felt sense of the waves would he grab his surfboard and enter the water.

Alex had a natural sense of the Sacred Fifth. He knew how to root himself in it and listen to what it was offering in the moment, whether it was the pull of the tide, the energy of the waves, or the stillness of the horizon. His ability to listen deeply to the Sacred Fifth allowed him to move in harmony with the ocean, rather than forcing his way through it. This is the essence of listening to the Sacred Fifth: being sourced by something greater than ourselves, something that guides us when we open ourselves to it.

When we can connect with this universal power and listen to it deeply, we are better able to access our unique selves and offer our inner genius to the world. This isn't about grand gestures or dramatic revelations; it's about the quiet, intimate act of tuning in to the present moment—to the place, the beings, and the energy around us.

There are countless ways to listen to the Sacred Fifth, and many of the world's religions and spiritual traditions have developed practices to guide this kind of listening. I have found, though, that it is an intimate and personal process. We can learn meditation techniques or recite prayers, but the real work happens in the quiet space between us and the universal power we're connecting with. It's about how we open ourselves—how we soften, how we attune, how we receive. How can we open ourselves to receive what this wisdom is offering to us, right now, in this moment?

Listening to the Sacred Fifth starts with slowing down, with creating space in our lives for stillness and reflection. It requires us to let go of the need to "just do it" and instead to simply *be*—to observe, to feel, to listen. I have found when I can relax and trust in my relationship with the Sacred Fifth—to universal power, I receive guidance by a wisdom greater than mine. This is the gift of listening to the Sacred Fifth: it connects us not only to the world around us but also to the deepest parts of ourselves, allowing us to move through life with greater clarity, purpose, and grace.

Listening to Ourselves

Once we've opened ourselves to universal power, the next step is to turn inward and listen to what's happening within us, right here, right now. This is where the real work begins. If we rely too heavily on lists of rules, maps drawn by others, or societal expectations, we risk losing touch with our true selves. Worse, we might try to shrink, twist, or reshape ourselves to fit into molds that weren't made for us. When we do that, we miss the opportunity to manifest what we're uniquely here to give—something that only we can offer in this specific place and moment in time.

Listening to ourselves is about more than just self-awareness; it's about self-trust. This self-trust allows us to move through the world with clarity and purpose, offering our gifts in a way that no one else can. This is the foundation of presence—the act of fully inhabiting the here and now. When we listen deeply to ourselves, we begin to uncover our authentic essence—the qualities, talents, and insights that are uniquely ours.

Cultivating this kind of presence isn't always easy. It requires us to slow down, to pause, and to really listen. It asks us to let go of the need to conform or perform and instead to trust in our own unique shape. This is where authenticity begins. When we listen to ourselves and embrace our true nature, we're able to show up in the world as we truly are, not as we think we should be. And in doing so, we create space for others to do the same.

Listening to One Another

Once we've practiced listening to ourselves from a place of rooted personal power, we can begin to authentically listen to others. Listening is something we often assume we're good at, but in reality, we rarely do it well. While we might hear words, pay attention, or even retain information, the process often gets clouded by our assumptions about the other person—what we think they'll say, what we believe they mean, or the idea that listening only involves our ears. True listening goes beyond that. It requires letting go of the urge to fill the space with our own words or solutions and instead simply being present to receive. When we listen this deeply, we create a space where the speaker feels truly heard and understood—but more importantly, where we feel our interconnection.

The starling murmuration is a breathtaking example of this kind of listening, where thousands of starlings move in synchronized harmony, almost as if they were one entity. If you've never seen this, I encourage you to look up a video of it. Each starling isn't just reacting to its immediate surroundings; it's deeply attuned to the movements of the entire flock, listening with its whole being—eyes, instincts, and even the subtle shifts in air currents. No single leader is dictating the flow; instead, every bird responds to the collective energy, creating a fluid, ever-changing dance. This phenomenon mirrors the essence of whole listening, where we tune in not just to the words being spoken, but to the broader context, emotions, and unspoken signals. Like the starlings, whole listening requires us to be fully present, attuned to the bigger picture, and responsive to the subtle shifts in communication. It's about being part of a larger flow, where listening becomes a dynamic, interconnected act. This kind of listening is what allows for right-relationship.

Listening to the In-Between

Listening to the in-between is about tuning in to the subtle, often unspoken layers of communication beneath the surface. It's not just about hearing the words someone says; it's about reading between the lines—catching the tone, the body language, the pauses, and the emotions that linger in the spaces between words. This kind of listening is part of the skill practice of Zooming In & Zooming Out—shifting our focus from the minute details to the broader context, and back again. It's about noticing the little things —like a fleeting expression or a shift in posture —while keeping an eye on the bigger picture: the overall energy of a conversation or the dynamics at play in a room.

There are many ways to listen. We can listen up-close, tuning into the immediate, visceral details of a moment. We can listen internally, paying attention to our own reactions and feelings. We can listen externally, picking up on the cues and signals from others. And we can listen from a distance, taking in the broader context or the long-term patterns that shape a situation. Each perspective offers a different vantage point, and together, they create a more complete understanding. As Shawn Ginwright wisely puts it, "We have to learn to be close up, to see and smell the sweat, yet far enough above to really see why people are sweating. Both vantage points are important, and neither is right nor wrong, but rather together they are more complete."[1]

True listening isn't just about accuracy; it's about depth. And

---

1. Ginwright, S. (2022). The Four Pivots: Reimagining Justice, Reimagining Ourselves. North Atlantic Books, p.164.

to listen deeply, we need to engage as many perspectives as we have capacity for in the moment. We need to use our eyes to observe body language, our intuition to sense what's unsaid, and our empathy to connect with the emotions behind the words. For example, someone might say, "I'm fine," but their slumped posture, hesitant tone, or lack of eye contact could tell a completely different story. It's in these moments that listening becomes an art—a way of sensing what's not being said, of tuning into the in-between.

One of the most transformative approaches to this kind of listening is Nonviolent Communication (NVC). When practiced with an awareness of power dynamics, NVC helps us dig beneath the surface of words to uncover the feelings and needs that are aching to be understood. It's not always easy—communication can be messy and fraught with misunderstandings—but the key lies in the listening, particularly in the in-between. Can we listen beyond the words and connect with the deeper human experience that's yearning to be heard?

As the poet David Whyte suggests, the art of listening to the in-between is best cultivated in the *not-knowing*. It's in the moments of uncertainty, confusion, or silence that we get to practice this skill. When we're lost, when it seems like no messages are coming through, when we're unsure of what's happening—these are the moments that invite us to vary our attention, our focus, our perspective. There is always something there, even in the quiet, even in the chaos. The question is, can we let what's there find us?

Reflection Questions:

1. Which of the Four Directions of Listening (Sacred Fifth, yourself, others, the in-between) do you find most chal-

lenging? Why?

2. How do you listen to your inner voice or intuition?

3. What societal expectations or external pressures make it difficult to listen to yourself? How can you challenge these?

4. How do you balance paying attention to the details (zooming in) with seeing the bigger picture (zooming out) when listening?

5. What is one small, actionable step you can take today to listen more deeply?

27

Turning Toward

"*Not everything that is faced can be changed, but nothing can be changed until it is faced.*" - James Baldwin

"*There is a kind of deep, visceral betrayal of human trust that can magnify harm significantly, when those around you do not even perceive it occurring. And yet that is precisely how normalized systemic violence works: it renders the harm normal, and all resistance to harm "disruptive."*" - Nora Samaran

"*The replacing of numbness with compassion, that is, the end of cynical indifference and the beginning of noticed pain, signals a social revolution.*" - Walter Brueggemann

In the spiral, after we listen deeply, we turn toward that which needs facing. Whether it is a conflict, a microaggression, destruction and chaos, an ethical breach, an illness, death, a person who is misusing their power, poverty, the person we want to cancel, or any other painful or disturbing thing, we choose to Turn Toward it instead of away from it. Since turning away is more of a natural impulse for most of us, Turning Toward must be intentional and requires tolerating discomfort to some degree. As we practice it though, it becomes easier.

In my early thirties, I started doing parkour. Parkour is the art of moving through your environment with efficiency, creativity, and fluidity. It's about overcoming physical obstacles—whether walls, rails, or gaps—by running, jumping, climbing, and vaulting. And it looks kind of funny to people who haven't tried it—it's been made fun of a lot in popular culture. But parkour isn't just about physical skill; it's also a mindset of adaptability, problem-solving, and pushing personal limits. At the time I joined a parkour gym, very few women were doing it, so my classes consisted primarily of teenage boys and young men. A lot of people asked me incredulously why I was doing such a thing, and I never knew how to respond. At first, I started it to improve my agility, primarily for my martial arts practice. But in every class, I realized that what the teacher was asking me to do sounded completely insane. I was terrified in every class. But I did it anyway. Then I realized it was a practice in facing my fears. I was intentionally cultivating courage every time I leaped on a wall or across a gap. Perhaps not everyone needs a physical way to practice courage, but for me, it became both a psychological and a physical practice of turning toward the uncomfortable.

Beyond courage, Turning Toward can look like curiosity, finding points of connection, holding differences, dropping assumptions, or just showing up. A whole other book could be written about just this spot on the spiral, but I want to address a few primary aspects: moving out of numbness, feeling-with, the courage to be vulnerable, and responsibility.

Moving Out of Numbness

One of the things we have to do before we can start Turning Toward is to move out of numbness, which is mostly a survival or coping mechanism. It's a way of protecting ourselves from the overwhelming weight of injustice, suffering, and trauma that exists in the world. But while it may offer temporary relief and help us to survive in the moment, numbness as a sustained state over time comes at a cost: it disconnects us from our own humanity, from our ability to feel, to care, and to act.

I remember a time when I was in the early stages of middle school, when my older brother shared at the dinner table about a book that he was reading in school. He described a story in it about the lynching of a Black man. I was horrified by the injustice and started sobbing at the table. I assumed everyone else would be crying as well. I was confused when they just looked at me uncomfortably. Embarrassed, I ran to my room, where my sobbing continued. My mom came in after me, held me in her arms, and said, "Honey, you can't let things like this upset you so much."

While I appreciated the comfort my mother was trying to offer, I also continued to feel confused. *How is it that she wasn't as upset as I was?* This moment illustrates two important truths: first, I clearly wasn't exposed to the accurate reality of our United States history early enough; and second, everyone else had accepted the injustice as just the way of things "back then." Both of these points reveal the consequences of collective and personal avoidance—the ways in which we turn away from discomfort and pain, often without even realizing it.

Instead of turning toward the injustices, pain, and atrocities that have occurred—and continue to occur—in various forms across the world, we often choose to turn away. War, famine, poverty, disease, natural disasters, genocide—these are overwhelming realities. They're so vast, so complex, that it's easy to feel powerless in the face of them. What's the point of turning toward them when there is nothing we can do? But the truth is, the very act of turning away is what renders us incapable of doing anything.

Numbness incapacitates us. It strips us of our connection to our personal power, to our empathy, and to each other. So, what do we do instead? How do we move out of numbness and begin to turn toward the discomfort that we've been avoiding?

The first step is to acknowledge the numbness itself. We have to recognize when we're shutting down, when we're distracting ourselves, or when we're choosing not to feel. This isn't about judging ourselves; it's about becoming aware of the ways in which we've learned to cope with overwhelming emotions. The next step is feeling-with—allowing ourselves to feel, which is often the hardest part.

Feeling-With

I have come to start saying the phrase, "feeling-with is power-with" because I have witnessed this practice create the possibility for right-relationship over and over again—even in cases where I didn't think it possible. In one of my wilderness vigils, I had nightmares every night. It was as if I were touring the world, experiencing all the suffering in its various forms in every place on the planet. There were different cultures, languages, and circumstances, but the commonality among them was tremendous pain. It was excruciating. I woke every morning disturbed but happy to have woken up in the peace of my surroundings. Throughout each day, I would try to set aside the nightmares and focus on the present. But the feelings kept building. Then, on the last night of my vigil, I had the same kind of nightmare. But this time, when I awoke, my heart utterly broke. I was broken open by the pain and suffering of the world. I let the tears come, I let myself be flooded with the pain, the feelings of betrayal, the anger, the sadness. I thought these feelings might never subside. But after a time what arose was a profound feeling of compassion. I realized we are all suffering. Those who have betrayed me have been betrayed. Those who have hurt me have been hurt. Then what came was forgiveness. I forgave each person and every hurt I was holding on to. It was an intense experience, but one that ended in an incredible peace. What was even more amazing was that in the few weeks that followed that vigil, two people from two different parts of my life who had hurt or betrayed me in different ways, sent me a letter apologizing—completely out of the blue. In both cases, the betrayal happened years prior. I wish I could say that I magically and instantly found right-relationship with them both at that point, but it doesn't quite work that way. What it did offer was a healing experience, an opening to a new kind of relationship with each of them, and a step closer to understanding my part in hanging on to the pain by avoiding it.

There is something about our willingness to *feel-with* one another—to allow the hurt feelings through, whether it's our own or someone else's. It has the capacity to transform us and our relationships. This is more than just empathy. It is allowing yourself to be impacted, to let in the experience of feeling—without trying to understand it or do anything about it—but allowing the feeling to be its own experience. Prentis Hemphill said, "A significant part of feeling is not allowing ourselves to fall too quickly into naming or categorizing what we feel, but to allow and witness."[1] This is such an important reminder for me. My mind jumps so quickly to trying to understand that I often forget the feeling part. This has been my training: avoid the feeling, try to learn the lesson, and move on. This training contributes to a sense of being trapped. So

---

1. Hemphill, P. (2023). What It Takes to Heal: How Transforming Ourselves Can Change the World. Random House, p.81.

I turn to the words of Audre Lorde: "The white fathers told us: I think, therefore I am. The black goddess within each of us - the poet - whispers in our dreams: I feel, therefore I can be free."

The Courage to Be Vulnerable

At the heart of Turning Toward lies a profound act of courage: the willingness to be vulnerable. Vulnerability is often misunderstood as weakness, but in truth, it is one of the most powerful forces for connection and transformation. It's about showing up as we truly are, and opening ourselves to the discomfort that comes with being honest, raw, and exposed. In his book, *Healing Resistance: A Radically Different Response to Harm*, Kazu Haga said, "Courage means that I have the internal fortitude to honestly speak from my heart and to act in congruence with the content of my heart."[2] This kind of courage is essential if we are to turn toward the uncomfortable—whether it's confronting our own biases, acknowledging our mistakes, or facing the pain and injustice in the world around us.

Turning toward the uncomfortable requires vulnerability because it asks us to confront truths that are often painful or difficult to face. We have to be vulnerable enough to feel the pain of others, to let it touch us, and to allow it to move us to action. It's about being willing to sit with the discomfort of not knowing what to do, of feeling helpless or overwhelmed, and still choosing to show up. It might mean admitting that we've been complicit in systems of oppression, acknowledging the ways we've hurt others, or simply sitting with the discomfort of not having all the answers. These are not easy tasks, and they often bring up feelings of shame, guilt, or

---

2. Haga, K. (2020). *Healing Resistance: A Radically Different Response to Harm.* Parallax Press, p. 100.

fear. But it's precisely in these moments of discomfort that growth and transformation become possible. When we allow ourselves to be vulnerable, we create space for honesty, empathy, and healing.

To be vulnerable is to step into the unknown, to risk being seen in our imperfection, and to embrace the possibility of rejection or judgment. And it is not a one-time act; it's a practice. It's something we must cultivate and nurture over time. It requires us to be gentle with ourselves, to recognize that vulnerability is not about perfection but about authenticity. It's about showing up, again and again, even when it's hard, even when we're scared, even when we're not sure we're doing it right. Shawn Ginwright shared:

"I suspect that is the purpose of vulnerability in our relationships with others: to not take each other for granted and to show up in ways that matter. Vulnerability is like a portal to our humanity. When we open it up, what flows out is the beautiful mess and confusion that makes us human. When that happens, we can see each other more clearly, without the clutter of all the bullshit that we carry around. We use our titles, degrees, positions, and authority to determine how we show up and form relationships. But remember, when we interact with people based on our titles, we just reinforce transactional relationships."[3]

In the end, vulnerability is the bridge that allows us to move toward right-relationship. It's what enables us to connect with others on a deeper level, to confront the uncomfortable truths that keep us apart, and to create the kind of relationships that are rooted in honesty, empathy, and mutual respect. It's not easy, but it's essential. And it's through this courage—the courage to be vulnerable—that we can begin to heal ourselves, our relationships,

---

3. Ginwright, S. (2022). The Four Pivots: Reimagining Justice, Reimagining Ourselves. North Atlantic Books, p.134.

and our communities.

Responsibility

Turning Toward is not just about facing discomfort or acknowledging pain—it's also about stepping into responsibility. When we turn toward our mistakes, our harmful cultural norms, and the moments when our impact doesn't align with our intentions, we create the conditions for accountability. Responsibility, in this sense, is not about blame or guilt; it's about recognizing our role in the larger systems we're part of and taking action to repair harm and foster growth. It's about owning our choices, learning from our errors, and committing to do better.

Don Michael, a social scientist and systems thinker, offers a profound insight into this process. He argued that "error-embracing is the condition for learning." This means that instead of shying away from our mistakes or hiding our vulnerabilities, we must actively seek out and share information about what went wrong. Only by embracing our errors can we truly learn from them. Michael also emphasized that living with uncertainty and vulnerability is essential for taking responsibility. In a world that often encourages us to mask our flaws and project confidence, this can feel counterintuitive. But Michael believed that to be the kind of person who truly accepts their responsibility, we must have a deep understanding of ourselves—a level of self-awareness that goes beyond what many of us are accustomed to.

Turning Toward, then, is an act of courage and humility. It requires us to confront the parts of ourselves and our societies that we'd rather ignore. It asks us to acknowledge that we are not perfect, that we have caused harm, and that we are capable of change. This is not easy work. It's uncomfortable to sit with the reality of our mistakes, especially when they've hurt others. But it's precisely in this discomfort that growth happens. When we turn toward our errors, we create the possibility for healing—not just for ourselves, but for the relationships and systems we're part of.

Responsibility also involves a willingness to live with uncertainty. In a complex world, we can't always predict the outcomes of our actions. We don't always know the "right" thing to do. But instead of retreating into inaction or denial, we can choose to move forward with humility and openness. We can commit to learning as we go, to listening to feedback, and to adjusting our course when necessary. This is the essence of responsibility: a willingness to stay engaged, even when the path is unclear.

James Baldwin (in the way only he could do) offers a stark reminder of what's at stake when we fail to turn toward the uncomfortable reality of our human shortcomings: "People who shut their eyes to reality simply invite their own destruction, and anyone who insists on remaining in a state of innocence long after that innocence is dead turns himself into a monster." To remain in a state of innocence—to refuse to see the harm we've caused or the systems we've perpetuated—is to deny our humanity. It's to become complicit in the very systems of oppression and destruction we claim to oppose. Baldwin is clear: turning away from reality is not just a personal failing; it's a collective one.

When we can turn toward reality—and taking responsibility for our role in it—it is an act of liberation. It frees us from the illusion of innocence and allows us to step into our full humanity. It's a way of saying, "I see the harm that's been done, and I'm committed to being part of the solution." This is the heart of responsibility: a willingness to face the truth, to learn from our mistakes, and to take action toward a more just and equitable world. This is what shaping power for good is all about.

Turning Toward Responsibilities & Vulnerabilities

Engaging in conversations about responsibility and vulnerability can have profound benefits and can help move us toward right-relationship. Unfortunately, conversations about responsibility and vulnerability are rarely comfortable, especially when power differentials are involved. But if we want to build healthy relationships in power-imbalanced dynamics, we need to lean into these difficult conversations. I've outlined a few prompts to help with navigating the power differential below.

The First Step: Awareness

The first thing to consider when you find yourself in a power differential is to pause and reflect:
- What power differentials are present here?

- What are my vulnerabilities?

- What are my responsibilities?

- Where is my focus—am I avoiding something?

The Second Step: Engage your Personal Power:

- Self-Regulation: What do you need to feel grounded and regulated right now?

- Rooting: How can you connect with what is larger or sacred to you right now?

- Needs: What or who do you need to feel supported right now?

- Boundaries: What boundaries do you need to create, communicate, or re-state right now?

- Communication: How can you communicate your needs & boundaries? What support do you need in doing so?

- Self-Care: How can you express or experience care for your: body, mind, emotions, and/or spirit right now?

If you are Up-Role:

- Responsibilities: What responsibilities do you have in this role? Are you saying "yes" to your up-power or are you avoiding your responsibilities in some way?

- Right-Relationship: What conversations need to be had about our power, responsibilities, and vulnerabilities to move closer to right-relationship?

- Vulnerabilities: What vulnerabilities might the person down-role from you be experiencing right now?

- Shadow: How are you tempted to misuse, under-use, or over-use your role power? Where might up-power fragility show up for you? What negative impacts might you have had on the down-power person that you've overlooked or ignored?

- Perspective: How can you zoom-in and zoom-out right now? For example, can you have empathy while also holding a larger view?

- Trust: How are you earning (or continuing to earn) trust from the person down-power from you?

- Right Use of Power: Can you stand in your strength AND stay in your heart?

If you are Down-Role:

- Connection to Personal Power: Where is your center? Your roots? What capabilities can you use?

- Assessment: What is your capacity, and how much do you want to invest in this relationship? Are you idealizing or devaluing the person who is up-role from you? Are you saying "yes" to your down-role? Why or why not?

- Interventions: If you want to invest or you are saying "yes" to your down-role, how can you make the invisible, visible? What kinds of feedback can you offer?

- Type of Issue: Is this a personal, interpersonal, and/or systemic issue?

- Needs: What outcome do you want/need? Is the timing right?

- Support: Do you have the clarity, direction, and support you need to fulfill your position? Are allies needed? Can you use collective power?

- Right Use of Power: Can you stand in your strength AND

stay in your heart?

If you are Up-Status:

- Responsibilities: How can you bring awareness to your 150% responsibility in this relationship? How are you tending to the health of the relationship? What vulnerabilities might the person down-status from you be experiencing?

- Shadow: How are you tempted to deny or defend your up-status power? How might you be centering yourself instead of the down-status person? What are ways that up-power fragility is showing up for you?

- Perspective: How can you bring awareness to your up-status as a product of systemic power?

- Trust: How are you earning (or continuing to earn) trust from the person down-power from you?

- Right Use of Power: Can you stand in your strength AND stay in your heart?

If you are Down-Status:

- Connection to Personal Power: Where is your center? Your roots? What capabilities can you use?

- Assessment: Who/what are you willing to invest in? Is it safe to offer feedback in this relationship? What are your needs in this relationship? What is your capacity right now?

- Type of Issue: Is this a personal, interpersonal, and/or systemic issue?

- Needs: What outcome do you want/need? Is the timing right?

- Support: Are allies needed? Can you use collective power?

- Interventions: What boundaries need to be communicated? What kind of feedback can you offer? How can you make the invisible, visible? Which microinterventions can you engage (state values, educate, set limits, re-direct, etc.)?

- Right Use of Power: Can you stand in your strength AND stay in your heart?

Shawn Ginwright reminds us that "Grace is giving ourselves and others undeserved permission to be human. . .Dancing between accountability and grace is an art form. Without grace, accountability becomes social confinement, and without accountability, grace can become sentimental surrender."[4] This delicate balance is essential in both personal growth and collective healing. Grace allows us to approach ourselves and others with compassion, recognizing that imperfection is an inherent part of the human experience. It creates space for vulnerability and growth, fostering an environment where mistakes can be acknowledged without fear of harsh judgment or exclusion. At the same time, accountability ensures that we take responsibility for our actions and their impact on others, maintaining integrity and trust in our relationships. Together, vulnerability and responsibility form a dynamic interplay.

---

4. Ginwright, S. (2022). The four pivots: Reimagining justice, reimagining ourselves. North Atlantic Books, p.234.

In this dance, we find the potential for true transformation, where individuals and communities can heal, learn, and grow together.

Reflection Questions:

1. What does it mean to you to "turn toward" discomfort or pain? How does this look different from turning away?

2. How do you recognize when you're numb or disconnected from your emotions? What signs or behaviors indicate this to you? What practices help you stay connected to your feelings when you start to numb out?

3. When have you experienced the transformative power of "feeling-with" someone else's pain or joy?

4. What uncomfortable truths or realities do you need to turn toward in your life or community?

5. What is one small, actionable step you can take today to turn toward discomfort or pain in your power differential relationships?

28

Grieving & Resourcing

"Joy is not the opposite of grief. Grief is the opposite of indifference. Grief is an evolutionary indicator of love —the kind of great love that guides revolutionaries." - Malkia Devich-Cyril

"...the real criticism begins in the capacity to grieve because that is the most visceral announcement that things are not right." - Walter Brueggemann

"It was through the dark waters of grief that I came to touch my unlived life...There is some strange intimacy between grief and aliveness, some sacred exchange between what seems unbearable and what is most exquisitely alive." - Francis Weller

After we have Turned Toward, we pause. Before we engage, we reflect. What arises as we touch the pain, the chaos, the thing that is disturbing or uncomfortable? What feelings are there? What needs are there? Sadness, frustration and anger are common feelings when we Turn Toward and engage in the work of social change by seeking right-relationship. If we don't let ourselves do the work of grieving and resourcing ourselves well, we can get stuck in these emotions, either overwhelmed or numb-- both of which pull us away from right-relationship.

I will be forever grateful for Francis Weller, who wrote *The Wild Edge of Sorrow: Rituals of Renewal and the Sacred Work of Grief*. This book not only brought me and my partner, Steph, together, but it also taught me a great deal about the essential part that grief plays in wayfinding to right-relationship. Central to Weller's philosophy is the idea that grief is a form of love. When we grieve, we are acknowledging the depth of our connections—to people, places, and even the Earth itself. He argues that grief, when fully embraced, can become a source of profound aliveness and creativity. It reminds us of what truly matters and reconnects us to our humanity.

But grief work is *hard*—perhaps the hardest work I've had to do in my life. In fact, I avoided it like the plague for most of my life. And, the most profound ways I have abandoned myself in my life have been when I have avoided grief. The death of my father was a significant turning point in my life. It felt like when I became a young adult, I found myself floating in the middle of the ocean at night—disorienting and dark—but my father was like a lighthouse to me. When he died, I felt a profound sense of isolation—darkness was all-encompassing. At his single-day funeral (the only ritual my culture provided), I was still in such shock by his death (even though I knew, to some degree, it was coming—because, you know, cancer), that I wrote my eulogy as if I were talking to him, as if he were still alive. In the years immediately following his death, I made some of the worst decisions of my life. Instead of turning toward, allowing myself to grieve, and resourcing myself, I avoided grief and the pain of the loss. In other words, I abandoned myself.

When I finally got a hold of Weller's book (which was one of those bookstore moments when a book you didn't intend to buy calls you and you know you have to read it), I had done a lot of damage to my life. I was in a place where I had convinced myself that life would be less painful without relationships—that loving and grieving were just too painful to bear. And, in a way, I was right. Grieving by yourself is a painful burden. I honestly didn't know that grieving together was an option.

Weller's work emphasizes that grief is not just an individual experience but a communal one, deeply woven into the fabric of human existence. He argues that in modern society, grief is often privatized, leaving individuals to carry their sorrow in isolation. This lack of communal grieving has profound consequences, leading to emotional stagnation, disconnection, and even physical illness. Reading this was both relieving and caused more grief. How have we gotten to a place where we have abandoned each other in our grief? We even help each other avoid it!

Weller invites us to create spaces where we can grieve together, to honor our losses, and to recognize that sorrow is not a sign of weakness but a testament to our capacity for love and connection. By doing so, we can begin to heal the collective wounds of our time and restore a sense of wholeness to our lives. In Weller's words, "Grief is not a problem to be solved; it is a presence to be tended."

Attending to the presence of grief is a big part of the work in this step on the spiral. We all have grief—whether it is personal or communal, from losses recent or distant. Though it is a single step in the spiral, it is ongoing work as the presence of grief can inform our wayfinding to right-relationship. Mary Watkins and Helene Shulman, in their work on liberation psychology, challenge the conventional idea that grief should lead to closure, resolution, or a return to "normal life." Their concept of "non-redemptive mourning" acknowledges that some forms of loss—particularly those tied to historical, collective, or systemic trauma—cannot and perhaps should not be "redeemed" or neatly resolved.

At its core, non-redemptive mourning is about staying connected to the past, even when it is painful, as a way of resisting the erasure of historical and collective trauma. For example, the legacies of colonization, slavery, or genocide are not simply events that happened in the past; they continue to shape the present in profound ways. Non-redemptive mourning asks us to hold space for these ongoing impacts, not as a way of dwelling in victimhood, but as a way of honoring the suffering and resilience of those who came before us. It's a process of bearing witness—acknowledging the truth of what happened and allowing it to inform our present actions and relationships. In this way, non-redemptive mourning becomes a form of active remembrance, a way of ensuring that the past is not forgotten or denied, but carried forward with dignity and care.

Prentis Hemphill said, "More than we realize, history and power script our relationships with one another and prevent the kind of reciprocity and connection we need to heal ruptures between us." The systems many of us are in, and the ways many of us have been socialized, leave us to believe that we must endure the injustices, trauma, and loss (often caused by systems) alone. Individualistic culture has led us to an emptiness and isolation that is almost as painful as the grief itself. So how do we resource ourselves? How do we endure this pain together?

Resourcing Ourselves

Resourcing ourselves is about more than just self-care; it's about cultivating the inner and outer supports that allow us to thrive in the face of life's losses and challenges. Whether we're navigating personal struggles, engaging in social justice work, or simply trying to keep up with the demands of daily life, resourcing ourselves is essential for maintaining balance, clarity, and resilience. It's about

recognizing our needs—physical, emotional, mental, and spiritual—and taking intentional steps to meet them. This isn't a one-time fix but an ongoing practice —a way to build the capacity to show up fully in our lives and in the world. By resourcing ourselves well, we create a foundation of strength and sustainability that enables us to face whatever comes our way with grace and purpose.

At its core, resourcing ourselves is about **self-awareness**. It starts with tuning into our own needs and recognizing when we're running on empty. In a culture that often glorifies busyness and productivity, it's easy to ignore the signs of burnout or depletion. But resourcing ourselves requires us to slow down, to check in with ourselves, and to ask: *What do I need right now?* This might be rest, nourishment, connection, or simply a moment of stillness. Self-awareness allows us to respond to our needs with compassion and intentionality, rather than pushing through until we're completely drained.

Another key aspect of resourcing ourselves is **building a toolkit of intentional practices and rituals** that help us stay grounded and centered. This toolkit will look different for everyone, but it might include mindfulness, journaling, movement, or creative expression. The goal is to have a range of practices that we can turn to in different moments—whether we need to calm our nervous system, process our emotions, or reconnect with our sense of purpose. These practices are not just for moments of crisis; they're part of a daily rhythm that helps us maintain our well-being over time.

Tending to our nervous systems and developing skills in emotion regulation are foundational aspects of resourcing ourselves. Our nervous system is the body's command center, constantly responding to stressors and stimuli, and when it's out of balance, it can leave us feeling overwhelmed, anxious, or shut down. By learning to regulate our emotions and care for our nervous system, we create a more stable internal environment that allows us to respond to life's challenges with more response-ability. Although pop psychology would have us believe that there is a universal way for humans to emotionally regulate, it is actually deeply unique and personal. While our breath directly impacts our nervous system, breathing techniques might not be the go-to for someone who has had past breath-trauma (from asthma or other breathing issues), for example. I recommend that you take some time to identify ways to attend to *your* nervous system. Practices like mindfulness and grounding techniques can help calm the fight-or-flight response, while somatic practices like yoga or gentle movement can release stored tension and restore balance. Emotion regulation could also involve recognizing and naming our feelings without judgment. By tending to our nervous systems and emotions, we not only enhance our own well-being but also strengthen our capacity to show up fully in our relationships and in the world.

Equally important is **cultivating supportive relationships and tapping into our communities** (or creating them if they don't exist). We are not meant to do this work alone. Resourcing ourselves means building a network of people who can offer support, encouragement, and accountability. Whether it is friends, family, mentors, or a community of like-minded individuals, these relationships provide a safe space to share our struggles, celebrate our wins, and remind us that we're not alone. They also help us stay connected to our values and our vision, even when the path feels difficult.

Resourcing ourselves also involves **setting boundaries.** In a world that constantly demands our time, energy, and attention, boundaries are essential for protecting our well-being. This might mean saying no to commitments that drain us, limiting our exposure to negative news, or carving out time for rest and rejuvenation.

Boundaries are not selfish; they're a necessary act of self-respect. They allow us to show up fully in the areas of our lives that matter most, without spreading ourselves too thin.

Finally, resourcing ourselves is about cultivating a sense of purpose and meaning. When we're connected to a larger vision—whether it's personal growth, social justice, or community building—we're better able to navigate the challenges that come our way. Purpose gives us a sense of direction and motivation, even when the road is tough. It reminds us why we're doing this work and helps us stay committed to our values and goals. It's about creating a life that is sustainable, meaningful, and aligned with our deepest values—and it brings us closer to right relationship.

Reflection Questions:

1. How do you typically process grief or loss? What practices or rituals could help you grieve in a healthy and supportive way?

2. What practices help you tune into your physical, emotional, mental, and spiritual needs? What practices help you self-regulate and soothe your nervous system?

3. Who in your life provides you with support, encouragement, and accountability?

4. What boundaries do you need to set to protect your time, energy, and well-being?

5. What is one small, actionable step you can take today to better resource yourself?

29

Dreaming & Imagining

"*Questions stimulate the imagination, which is our most profound defense against habitual thinking and normative pressures.*" - Briskin, et al. from *The Power of Collective Wisdom*

"*'What is' offers a poor guide to 'what will be' and, I would add, an even worse guide to 'what could be.'*" - Geoffrey Cohen

"*Articulating what we want whether than what we are resisting is much harder.*" - Shawn Ginwright

As we grieve the pain of the past and present and engage in resourcing, we are creating space for something new. And unless we want to recreate the same systems with different clothes, we must engage the space beyond reason or proof. We need the space and time to dream individually and collectively, without the restrictions and constraints imposed by the system's way of doing things. As Audre Lorde said, "For the master's tool will never dismantle the master's house. They may allow us temporarily to beat him at his own game, but they will never enable us to bring about genuine change. And this fact is only threatening to those women who still define the master's house as their only source of support."

Dreaming and imagining are not just acts of creativity; they are acts of courage and resistance. In a world shaped by systems of oppression and inequality, the ability to envision alternatives is a radical and necessary step toward right-relationship. Walter Brueggaman said, "We need to ask not whether it is realistic or practical or viable but whether it is imaginable. We need to ask if our consciousness and imagination have been so assaulted and co-opted by [dominant culture] that we have been robbed of the courage or power to think an alternative thought." Too often, we are conditioned to accept the status quo as inevitable, to believe that the way things are is the way they must always be. But dreaming and imagining challenge this narrative, inviting us to envision a world beyond *what is*, as Cohen suggests—and into *what could be*.

Learned Helplessness

In our Power & Equity Challenge program, my friend and colleague, Dr. Sherri Taylor, led us in an exercise that challenged us to dream. She invited us to each complete this sentence: "I dream of a world…" It is a powerful exercise. I have since repeated her exercise with different groups, and there is inevitably pushback from at least one person who asks, "But what's the point?" This, I believe, is an expression of learned helplessness. Learned helplessness is a psychological phenomenon in which individuals come to believe they have no control over their circumstances, even when opportunities for change exist. This phenomenon often arises from repeated experiences where efforts to influence outcomes are met with failure, shame, or punishment. If this happens enough over time, people internalize the idea that they are powerless, leading to a sense of resignation and passivity.

At its core, learned helplessness is about the erosion of personal power. When we repeatedly experience situations where our actions seem to have no effect, we begin to disengage from trying altogether. So we fall into a lack of motivation, a sense of hopelessness, or even depression. Learned helplessness is particularly relevant in the context of systemic oppression. Down-status groups often face barriers that make it difficult to effect change, from discriminatory policies to social stigmatization. Over time, these barriers can lead to a collective sense of learned helplessness, in which entire communities come to believe their circumstances are unchangeable.

One of the most insidious aspects of learned helplessness is its tendency to become self-reinforcing. When people believe they are powerless, they are less likely to take action, which in turn reinforces the belief that nothing can be changed. This creates a vicious cycle in which inaction leads to stagnation, and stagnation reinforces the belief in helplessness. Breaking this cycle requires not only external changes—such as policy or structural changes that remove roadblocks and create real opportunities for successful agency and creativity—but also a mindset that fosters imagination.

Ultimately, learned helplessness is a reminder of the power of belief. Our beliefs about our own capabilities—whether we see ourselves as agents of change or as powerless victims—have a profound impact on our behavior and our outcomes. In the context of right-relationship, overcoming learned helplessness is essential. It requires us to believe in our own capacity to effect change and to support others in accessing their personal power.

Breaking Free from Conformity

Dominant culture thrives on conformity, encouraging us to accept the status quo as inevitable. It tells us that the way things are is the way they must always be, and that any attempt to imagine or create something different is naive or unrealistic. This assault on our imagination is not accidental; it is a tool of control. When we are unable to envision alternatives, we are less likely to challenge the systems that oppress us. We become passive participants in our own disempowerment, accepting the world as it is rather than striving for the world as it could be.

But what if we were to reclaim our imagination? What if we were to ask not whether an alternative is practical or reasonable, but whether it is imaginable? This shift allows us to dream boldly, to envision possibilities that defy the limitations imposed on us. As adrienne maree brown writes in *Emergent Strategy*, "All organizing is science fiction," reminding us that the work of social change, and I would add the path to right-relationship is, at its core, *an act of imagination*. When we imagine alternatives, we begin to create the conditions for those alternatives to exist.

Of course, reclaiming our imagination requires courage. It means confronting the ways in which dominant culture has shaped our thinking and challenging the narratives that tell us certain ideas are "unrealistic." It means embracing uncertainty and stepping into the unknown, trusting that even if we don't have all the answers, we have the capacity to figure them out as we go. In other words, we don't need to know how relationships are "supposed" to be; instead, we need the capacity and willingness to create them together.

Imagination as a Pathway to Right-Relationship

One day, I was driving with my daughter in the backseat. She often likes to chat and ask questions when we are driving, but on this day, she was really quiet. So I asked if she'd like to talk. She replied, "No thanks. I'm day-dreaming right now." Children are such beautiful reminders of this step on the spiral. They already live in the world of imagination that adults have lost touch with. Imagining, even creating simple images of a more just future, is potent. It is a powerful tool for creating right-relationship—both with ourselves and with the world around us. But we have to make space for it.

When we allow ourselves to dream, to envision a more just and equitable future, we tap into a source of creativity and possibility that can guide us toward meaningful change. Even the act of creating simple images of a better world—whether through art, storytelling, or mental visualization—can be profoundly transformative. But to access this creative potential, we must first let go of what is known and familiar, stepping into the unknown with curiosity and courage.

So, what helps us to dream, to imagine, to create? For many, it's about finding the right environments that inspire and nurture creativity. For some this might be finding a private, quiet space where we our imaginations are free to roam uninterrupted. For others, being around people who encourage you to dream big, challenge you to think beyond the status quo, and support you in taking risks may be more supportive of venturing into the unknown. Or maybe you need a vibrant community gathering, where the energy of collective imagination fuels our own. For others, it's about engaging with tools that unlock creativity—whether that's a journal, a paintbrush, or a musical instrument. These creative tools can help us externalize our thoughts and feelings, giving shape to the visions that live within us. Similarly, the greater-than-human beings—whether animals, plants, or the natural world—can also inspire us to imagine alternatives. Their presence reminds us of the interconnectedness of all life and invites us to think beyond human-centric perspectives.

Ultimately, imagination is not just a personal act; it is a *relational* one. Are we supporting each other in finding liberation so we can co-create new things together? Or are we confining one another and making sure we stay inside the lines? When we come together to dream and envision a more just future, we create a shared sense of possibility that can inspire and sustain us in the path toward right-relationship. So, what helps *you* to dream, to imagine, to create? What environments, tools, people, non-human beings, and internal spaces allow you to venture into the unknown or the eternal? Reflect on the questions and prompts below before moving on to the next step in the spiral.

Reflection Questions & Prompts

1. Complete the phrase: "I dream of a world…" What does a just and equitable future look like to you? Can you describe it in vivid detail—what it feels like, sounds like, and looks like?

2. What fears or discomforts arise when you imagine alternatives to the status quo? In what areas of your life do you feel a sense of powerlessness or resignation? How can you move through these fears and sense of powerlessness?

3. What tools or activities (e.g., journaling, art, music, nature) help you externalize your thoughts and dreams?

4. Who in your life encourages you to dream big and think outside the box? What environments, people, or practices help you feel most creative and inspired? How can you create more space for these in your life?

5. Who is one person in your life you can experiment with having new ways of relating? What is one step you can make toward creating right-relationship with them?

30

Manifesting

"*We had learned to stay ready, defended, our lives unfolding as a series of things that just happened to us, never something that we shaped.*" - Prentis Hemphill

"*In relationships, the little things are the big things. The way partners handle power and control in everyday interactions determines the health of the relationship.*" - John Gottman

"*Pull a thread here and you'll find it's attached to the rest of the world.*" - Nadeem Aslam

Tell me, what is it you plan to do
with your one wild and precious life?
—Mary Oliver

Manifesting is the process of embodying and making real the dreams and discoveries that emerge as we move through the spiral. It's about taking the insights, visions, and intentions that arise from rooting, listening, turning toward, and resourcing, and bringing them into tangible form. When you have in mind what kind of "right-relationship" you are aiming toward—whether it's a more just world, a healthier relationship, or a deeper connection to yourself—you can start there and work backward to identify the first steps toward that new reality. These steps might involve the creations you bring into the world, the way you carry yourself, how you engage with others, how you spend your time, or the habits you cultivate. Ultimately, manifesting is about what you do with your "one wild and precious life."

How & What to Manifest

There is no "should" in manifesting. It's not about following the "rules of manifesting" or conforming to a particular way of being, speaking, or acting. Instead, it's about taking what you feel when you root, what you hear when you listen, and what you see when you dream—and bringing the pieces of that which are ready to be born into the world. This is really where the process of wayfinding shines. It's about tuning in to your inner compass and letting it guide you toward what feels true and authentic. You move toward right-relationship by manifesting what is uniquely yours—informed by your inner genius that you were born with, your life circumstances, your unique combination of identities, your access and expression of your personal power, and your orientation toward right-relationship.

The key is being intentional. Manifesting is not a passive process; it requires active engagement with your own life and the world around you. It's about making conscious choices that align with your rooted personal power. When you are rooted in your personal power, you can manifest from a place of clarity and confidence, even in the face of uncertainty or resistance. This power allows you to navigate challenges, take risks, and stay committed to your path, even when it feels difficult.

This doesn't mean you need to have everything figured out

or that every step must be perfectly planned. Instead, it's about staying connected to your roots, listening deeply to what is calling you, and taking small, deliberate steps toward the future you envision. When you manifest from this place of intentionality, you honor your unique gifts and contributions. You recognize that your inner genius—the wisdom, creativity, and insight that reside within you—is a vital part of the larger web of life. Your life circumstances, identities, and experiences shape how you see the world and how you engage with it. These are not limitations but sources of strength and perspective that inform how you manifest your vision.

Finally, your orientation toward right-relationship guides how you manifest in the world. When you manifest from this orientation, you consider not only your own needs and desires but also the impact of your actions on others and the world around you. You strive to create a future that benefits not just yourself but the collective whole.

Manifesting with our Scars

Manifesting is not just about creating something new; it's also about how we embody and share the wisdom we've gained through our journeys—and many of us have had plenty of wounds along the way. My friend and colleague, Sarah Buino, has a podcast called, *The Wounded Healer*, where she talks with therapists and healers about their own journeys of being wounded and their journey of healing. Many of us believe that we cannot offer anything if we are wounded, but it is the wounds that lead to the most powerful manifesting—if we are able to have some healing around them.

One of my favorite quotes comes from Rev. Nadia Bolz-Weber who said, "Preach from your scars, not from your wounds." This is such a powerful reminder. When we manifest from our scars, we are drawing on the lessons and resilience that have emerged from our struggles. Scars are evidence of healing; they show that we've faced challenges, endured pain, and come through the other side with newfound strength and understanding. On the other hand, when we're still in the midst of pain or turmoil—manifesting can be more fraught. Wounds are raw and tender; they often carry unresolved emotions like anger, fear, or grief. While it's important to acknowledge and process these feelings, sharing from this place can sometimes lead to projection, reactivity, or unintentional harm. Manifesting from wounds can also leave us vulnerable to re-traumatization, as we may not yet have the clarity or stability to navigate the complexities of sharing our experiences. This doesn't mean we should silence ourselves in times of pain, but it does mean we should be mindful of how and when we share, ensuring that we're not bypassing our own healing in the process.

Ultimately, manifesting from our scars is an act of service. It's about taking the lessons we've learned and using them to create something meaningful—whether that's art, relationships, activism, or simply a more compassionate way of being in the world. It's about showing others that healing is possible, that pain can be transformed, and that we can emerge from our struggles with greater strength and clarity. So, as you move through the spiral of rooting, listening, turning toward, and resourcing, consider how you can manifest from your scars rather than your wounds. Allow yourself the time and space to heal, to reflect, and to integrate your experiences. Trust that when you're ready, your scars will become a source of wisdom and inspiration—not just for yourself, but for the world around you. Manifesting from this place is a powerful way to move toward right-relationship, creating ripples of healing and transformation that extend far beyond your individual life.

Manifesting Situations

Part of what happens when we deepen into our rooted personal power and begin to trust the process of wayfinding toward right-relationship is that we realize we can start to shape experiences, conversations, and situations in ways that are consistent with right-relationship. The concept of situation crafting, as explored in Geoffrey Cohen's book, offers a powerful framework for intentionally shaping our environments to support our goals, values, and sense of belonging. At its core, situation crafting is about designing the conditions around us—whether physical, social, or psychological—to foster the behaviors, mindsets, and relationships that align with our vision.

When we think about manifesting, we often focus on our individual actions—what we do, say, or create. But situation crafting reminds us that context matters. The environments we inhabit—our homes, workplaces, communities, and even our inner worlds—profoundly influence our ability to manifest. By intentionally crafting these environments, we can create spaces that support our growth, amplify our strengths, and make it easier to take aligned action.

For example, if your goal is to manifest a more creative and inspired life, you might craft your physical environment to reflect that intention. This could mean setting up a dedicated workspace filled with art supplies, books, or tools that spark your creativity. It could also involve surrounding yourself with people who encourage and inspire you, or creating routines that prioritize time for creative expression. These small, intentional changes to your environment can make it easier to step into the creative flow and bring your ideas to life.

Situation crafting also plays a crucial role in manifesting right-relationship. If your vision is to build deeper, more meaningful connections with others, you might craft situations that foster vulnerability, trust, and collaboration. This could involve creating spaces for open and honest conversations, organizing gatherings that bring people together, or setting boundaries that protect your energy and allow you to show up fully in your relationships. By shaping your social environment in this way, you create the conditions for authentic connection and mutual support.

On a broader scale, situation crafting can be a tool for manifesting systemic change. If your vision is to create a more just and equitable world, you might craft situations that challenge oppressive systems and promote inclusion and belonging. This could involve advocating for policies that address inequality, creating spaces where marginalized voices are centered and valued, or fostering cultures of accountability and allyship in your community. By intentionally shaping these larger environments, you contribute to the collective manifestation of a more equitable future. And you don't have to do this in big ways. Cohen also talks about the concept of "micronorming" which is "engaging in seemingly small behaviors that establish powerful norms."[1] This is a similar concept of "microintervention strategies[2] " that Derald Wing Sue and his colleagues write about. We are often so dismissive of the little ways we can intervene—when in reality they can have a huge impact. Can you imagine if everyone used their personal power in just a few ways each day that challenged microaggressions, or social norms, or self-doubt? It would be a different world.

1. . Cohen, G. L. (2022). Belonging: The Science of Creating Connection and Bridging Divides. W. W. Norton & Company, p.254.

2. . Sue, D. W. (2021). *Microintervention strategies: What you can do to disarm and dismantle individual and systemic racism and bias.* Wiley.

Ultimately, situation crafting is about accessing your personal power and manifesting your influence in a way that is consistent with your values and inner genius. It's a reminder that we are not passive recipients of our circumstances; we have the power to shape our environments in ways that support our vision and values. Whether it's creating a physical space that reflects your rootedness, designing social interactions that foster deep listening, or crafting situations that allow you to turn toward discomfort with courage, situation crafting helps you bring the spiral to life in practical and impactful ways.

Manifesting as a Practice

It's important to remember that you may not live to see the fruit of the seeds you plant, but that doesn't diminish the importance of planting them. Manifesting is not always about immediate results or tangible outcomes; it's about contributing to a larger vision that extends beyond your individual lifespan. The seeds you plant—whether they're acts of kindness, creative expressions, or efforts toward social change—have the potential to grow and flourish in ways you may never witness. This is the essence of working toward right-relationship: understanding that your actions are part of a greater tapestry, woven together by the collective efforts of many. Even if you don't see the full impact of your work, the act of planting seeds is itself a powerful and necessary step in creating a more just, equitable, and interconnected world. Trust that your contributions matter, and that they will continue to ripple outward, shaping the future in ways you may never fully know.

Manifesting is also not a one-time event; it's an ongoing practice of bringing the insights, visions, and intentions of the spiral into tangible form. It requires patience, persistence, and a willingness to take action, even when the path is unclear. This might involve regularly reflecting on your progress, celebrating small wins, and staying connected to your purpose and values, even when the work feels challenging or slow.

Manifesting is a deeply personal and relational process. It's about bringing forth what is ready to be born, in ways that are true to who you are and aligned with your vision of right-relationship. It's about embodying the insights and dreams of the spiral in a way that honors your unique gifts and contributions. And it's about knowing that even small, imperfect actions can create ripples of change that extend far beyond what we can see.

Reflection Questions:

1. What dreams, visions, or intentions have emerged for you as you've moved through the spiral? What is ready to be born or come forward in your life, relationships or community?

2. What gifts are ready to be shared from your scars? How can your scars become a contribution?

3. What small, intentional actions (micronorming or microinterventions) can you take to move closer to right-relationship?

4. What inspires you to keep planting seeds, even if you may not live to see them grow?

5. What is one small way you can situation-craft or manifest something today?

31

Practicing

"It will take a concerted effort from all of us to raise the level of our personal and collective awareness to fulfill the intention to truly live together in a way that embodies nonharm, nonoppression, and nonexclusion. And it takes time - and a lot more of it than anyone would like." - Larry Yang

"Commitment is the path between your vision and this moment." - Prentis Hemphill

Spirals, in a sense, represent the eternal. They are found everywhere in nature, from the farthest reaches of the universe to the tiniest organisms on Earth. We are meant to keep spiraling. There is no endpoint. So it is with the Right-Relationship Spiral. We are meant to keep making the rounds, learning as we go. It is a constant revolution—we root, we listen, we turn toward, we grieve and resource, we dream a little before we think or act, and then we manifest something, however big or small it is. Then we release it into the world and find our roots again. This is the rhythm of the spiral—a continuous cycle of growth, reflection, and action.

Practicing is a reminder that we are not here to get it "right," as in "perfect" or "correct"—that's not what we mean by right-relationship or *Right* Use of Power. We never arrive at perfection, because it doesn't exist. But what we can do is *practice*. We can learn, observe, become aware, and repair harm when needed. And we can point ourselves toward right-relationship over and over again. If we think about right-relationship like a North Star, we just keep heading in that direction. And if we doze off, mess up, or get off track (which are very human things to do), we can reroute.

Unlike how many of us were taught, there isn't a final destination. And we don't need to hide or be ashamed of finding a different way forward over and over again. In fact, we can celebrate it. Like the Japanese art of Kintsugi, where broken pottery is repaired with gold, we can accentuate the cracks rather than discarding the entire piece. Our mistakes and missteps in the spiral are not failures—they are precious opportunities for exploring our humanness, for growth, and connection. As Rick Rubin writes, "Whatever insecurities we have can be reframed as a guiding force in our creativity. They only become a hindrance when they prevent our ability to share what's closest to our heart."[1] Practicing is about fully embracing the journey of being human and celebrating our ability to create, connect, mess up, and grow. It's about understanding that we are works in progress, constantly evolving and refining our ability to live in right-relationship with ourselves and others. Practice involves several steps: commitment, building muscle memory, and practicing together.

Commitment

Ultimately, practicing is about staying committed to the process, even when it's messy or difficult. It's about trusting that each step of the spiral brings us closer to right-relationship, even if we can't

---

1. Rubin, R. (2023). The Creative Act: A Way of Being. Penguin Press.

yet see the whole picture. Practice takes commitment. It's not a one-time effort or a quick fix; it's a lifelong journey of learning, growing, and aligning with our values. Commitment is what keeps us moving forward, even when the path is unclear or the challenges feel overwhelming.

It's easy to engage in the spiral when things are going well, but the real test of commitment comes when we face setbacks, failures, or moments of doubt. This is where the spiral's cyclical nature becomes so powerful. When we fall out of alignment or make mistakes, we don't have to start over—we simply return to the next step in the spiral. Commitment to practice means showing up consistently, even when it's uncomfortable. Whether it's rooting ourselves again, listening more deeply, or turning toward the discomfort with courage, commitment means we keep going, even when it's hard.

Commitment also means embracing the long game. In a world that often prioritizes quick results and instant gratification, practicing right-relationship requires patience and persistence. Meaningful change—whether in ourselves, our relationships, or the world—takes time. So how do we stay connected to our "why" when we start to drift, or rush, or lose our way? Our *why* becomes the anchor that makes commitment possible.

Building Muscle Memory

By continuing around and around the spiral, we get to deepen into the process of rooting, listening, turning toward, grieving, resourcing, dreaming, imagining, and manifesting. With each revolution, it gets easier and more embodied. With practice, it can become second nature. One of my favorite movies growing up was *The Karate Kid*. It is about Daniel, a new kid in town, who is bullied by a group of karate-trained teens. He turns to the janitor in his apartment building, Mr. Miyagi (who happens to be a karate master), for help. Instead of teaching Daniel flashy karate moves right away, Mr. Miyagi has him do a series of chores: waxing his car, sanding the floor, and painting the fence. Mr. Miyagi has Daniel repeat specific motions over and over, like "Wax on, wax off," "Paint the fence," and "Sand the floor." At first, Daniel is frustrated, thinking he's just being used as a handyman. He finally gets frustrated and tells Mr. Miyagi that he is quitting. Mr. Miyagi responds by throwing a couple of punches at him and saying, "Wax on, wax off." Because it is so ingrained in his muscle memory from the repetition, Daniel is able to block the punches instinctively with the same move he was taught when waxing multiple cars. Waxing the car taught Daniel how to block punches, painting the fence built muscle memory for defensive moves, and sanding the floor strengthened his core and balance.

One of the gifts of practice is that we are building muscle memory so that when life throws us punches, we can respond in ways that are consistent with who we are, what we value, and how we want to live. If we don't practice this, then when things get challenging, we aren't prepared to respond in ways that honor our desire to be in right-relationship. Like Archilochus, and later Bruce Lee said, *"We don't rise to the level of our expectations; we fall to the level of our training."*

Practicing Together

Since the spiral is about right-relationship, practicing is a relational process—whether it's within or outside ourselves. The good news is that we are not alone in this journey toward right-relationship. In fact, we cannot find right-relationship alone.

One of the advantages of practicing together is having others who can help us move when we're stuck or pause when we're rushing ahead. When we don't see that we're failing to connect with our rooted personal power, perhaps others can nudge us in that direction. Learning to be in right-relationship can only happen if we are first willing to be in relationship at all.

When we commit to the spiral, we're also committing to the people and communities around us. This means holding ourselves accountable for our actions, repairing harm when we cause it, and showing up for others in ways that foster trust and connection. And, as mentioned, this will not happen perfectly. When we practice right-relationship together, it is usually a messy endeavor as we learn to attune to one another, to adapt and negotiate. Conflict is a part of the process, and we get to choose whether it is in a generative direction or a destructive one. If we are pointed toward right relationship—when we are attempting to access and honor our own rooted personal power and that of others—we have a greater chance of engaging generatively, even in conflict.

This is just a beginning. It is up to all of us what we do from here. Do we briefly focus on our relational responsibilities and then go back to "business as usual?" Or do we manifest incremental changes in how we show up? Do we feel warm and fuzzy from reading something that supports our beliefs, and then do nothing once we close the book? Or do we put it into practice and create a community of support? There is no right or wrong here. The invitation to practice is an invitation into being intentional. So, as you move through the spiral, remember: you are not here to be perfect. You are here to practice. To learn. To grow. To repair. And to keep spiraling toward right-relationship, one step at a time.

Reflection Questions:

1. What do you want to bring with you? What do you want to leave behind?

2. Where do you think you might get stuck in the spiral? What might you need to keep moving through the spiral?

3. What is your "why" for moving towards right-relationship with yourself? With others? With the Sacred Fifth?

4. What do you need from others to support you in the spiral?

5. What is one thing you can do today to practice moving toward right-relationship?

32

The Art of Shaping
Power for Good

"For to be free is not merely to cast off one's chains, but to live in a way that respects and enhances the freedom of others." - Nelson Mandela

"We can bring down the entire system and have a worldwide revolution, but if we haven't healed our traumas and learned how to be in authentic relationship with each other, we will corrupt any new system we put in its place." - Kazu Haga

"We are the ones we've been waiting for." - June Jordan

Shaping power for good - the art form and practice of integrating power-consciousness (awareness of how power operates across relationships and systems) and wayfinding (navigating complexity with intuitive and ethical intention) to move toward right-relationship and greater liberation in the world.

Have you ever put together a puzzle and one or two pieces were missing? How profoundly frustrating it is to have a hole in something you worked so hard on—carefully putting all the pieces together, only to find that you can't complete the picture without that missing piece. Before we get into this final chapter, I'd like to propose a foundational perspective: that we are each a puzzle piece that has a different shape, color, and purpose—and we are all needed to complete the picture. And yet until we see that bigger picture and understand how we fit together, the pieces can easily become lost. It is like we don't recognize their importance until we see how they fit.

I believe we all have a particular "something" to offer the world—a unique inner wisdom that the world needs. But many of us fail to see this in ourselves or each other. My father would often say, "It takes all kinds." While he sometimes said it in a sarcastic tone, he could have chosen any number of other responses when he encountered something that didn't make sense to him. I really believe that it "takes all kinds" in the truest sense of that expression. This is a paradigm that I think is worth spreading, especially right now when our world is so polarized and divided. This is also the underlying paradigm needed for shaping power for good. It is fundamentally a practice that honors diversity and recognizes its critical importance in sustaining our world. The earth itself and its many ecosystems are perfect expressions of this—diversity is essential, not optional. The more we use power to lessen diversity and partition belonging, the more we put *all* of life at risk.

Shaping power for good is an antidote to this threat to our collective wellbeing. It is an art form that guides the flow of power intentionally to achieve positive social outcomes and relationships that honor our interconnection. It is the responsible engagement of power at every level—from internal self-awareness to interpersonal dynamics, collective action, and systemic structures—while attuning to nuances like privilege, history, and context. We do this by bringing together power-consciousness and wayfinding to right relationship. Ultimately, shaping power for good shifts power from a force of control or harm into one of healing, creativity, and liberation. If we want to see a different world, we have to do this work individually and collectively, and we have to do it continuously according to our capacity.

Even as I write this, I feel exhausted by this very tall order! How do we navigate systems as they are while also recreating them, achieve self-awareness, accommodate diversity, and find right-relationship all at once? While I am still apprenticing in this practice of shaping power for good, I have learned from leaders like adrienne maree brown, that this is much more sustainable work if we view it as an art that can be pleasurable, imperfect, and beautiful, rather than an exacting mandate that adds more duties and to-dos to our already full plates.

Shaping power for good is an invitation to become artists again. I say "again" because we all start as humans with a tendency toward the artistic, don't we? As children, we occupy ourselves mostly with creating and imagining. Children have freedom beyond the conventional world of adults. And artists, even as they grow into adults, have the opportunity to move beyond the bounds of dominant culture. Artists are free to explore, imagine, challenge, and express themselves according to their own inner genius. They can question power, expose injustice, and disrupt comfortable narratives.

Shaping power for good is the art of crafting situations, creating new structures, and exploring relationships in new ways. And it is the investigation into how we can show up differently and connect with ourselves and each other to bring about greater liberation for all of us. In his book, Ginwright cited a quote from Theodor Adorno, a German Jewish philosopher and sociologist, who asked, "How do I have to be as a human being for someone else to be free?" Isn't this the fundamental question? How do we use the power we have access to in a way that creates more liberation for everyone? Ultimately, artists don't just use freedom—they expand it. They remind us that freedom isn't just about individual expression; it's about creating spaces where others can breathe, be seen, and imagine new ways of being together. As Audre Lorde wrote, "Art is not living. It is the use of living." Artists are free to show us what living—fully, boldly, and together—could truly mean.

So how do we become artists of power who wish to see a more just and liberated world? I want to highlight three different realms you could choose to bring your creativity. You could shape power for good: within ourselves, with others, and in systems. Synthesizing what we've discussed throughout the book, let's take a look at each of these realms.

Shaping Power for Good within Ourselves

One of the mantras of this book is the fundamental importance of rooted personal power for navigating the world in ethical and embodied ways. The reason for this mantra is to bring our inner work into focus. It is the very unique and individual healing we must each do to find our wholeness—to contact our inherent belongingness. It is dancing with our shadow, playing in the realm of creativity, and uncovering our basic goodness. This inner work feels more like undressing than it does collecting more skills or perspectives—it's vulnerable business. Part of the vulnerability of this inner work involves the willingness to spend more time with the questions than the answers. And, of course, we have to be willing to *become* an artist, even when it feels intimidating. Rubin said:

"Living life as an artist is a practice. You are either engaging in the practice or you're not. It makes no sense to say you're not good at it. It's like saying, 'I'm not good at being a monk.' You are either living as a monk or you're not. We tend to think of the artist's work as the output. The real work of the artist is a way of being in the world."[1]

That way of being in the world in the art of shaping power for good is, as Dr. Barstow calls it, "standing in your strength, while staying in your heart." It is the art of being firmly rooted yet fully present, receptive to what's around you. It is the ability to have clear boundaries but love deeply, to be responsible and relational at the same time. It is to be in our rooted personal power while pointing ourselves toward right-relationship. This sounds lovely. But, how do we get to this way of being in the world?

Buddhists often use the metaphor of the lotus to describe our human journey toward liberation. The lotus begins its life as a seed that falls into mud at the bottom of a pond or slow-moving river. From there, it sends down roots to anchor itself and begins to grow a stem that must push up through the murky water to reach the sunlight. When it finally breaks the surface of the water, the stem unfurls a pristine leaf which has a microscopic, waxy surface that causes water to bead up and roll off, taking any dirt or contaminants with it—a phenomenon known as the "lotus effect." Soon after, a beautiful flower blooms above the water, untouched by the muddy environment it came from. This entire journey—being rooted from the darkness below and orienting to the light above—makes the lotus a powerful symbol for liberation.

So what is the mud in this metaphor? It is different for all of us, but it ultimately represents unavoidable ways in which our basic goodness and our sense of inherent belongingness get covered over. They get buried through layers of socialization, trauma, shame, and survival skills. And while we cannot avoid the "mud," we *can* anchor ourselves beyond it. Liberation is really about breaking free from the systemic narratives or stories that have kept us in the mud. It is

---

1. . Rubin, R. (2023). The Creative Act: A Way of Being. Penguin Press, p. 48.

only when we root down deep into the earth—even further into the darkness—where there is something more stable to anchor us, that we can begin to grow beyond the mud. It is in that deep, dark place where we find what is sacred to us—where we can access universal power. This is the place that receives our roots, and through the roots, we receive nourishment and resources from that which is sacred. From this rooted place, we have enough personal power to push through the mud and reach the sunlight. Where the darkness and the light touch is where we blossom.

Unfortunately, many of us never *really* know the darkness *or* the light. We stay in the mud and are perpetually frustrated. We have so much invested in the systemic narratives: we've built our identities and lives around them. We believe that if we abandon the stories that systems give us, we would not survive. First, because we don't know any other way of living or organizing ourselves, and second, we might feel that this departure would realize our biggest fear: that we would not belong. The irony is that we end up making the mud feel like a savior instead of a captor keeping us from liberation.

The good news is that systemic narratives are human-constructed and fallible. They do not last. Universal power, on the other hand, is eternal (outside of temporal reality) and not dependent upon any human-constructed system. For me, faith is fundamentally trusting in my inherent belongingness that comes from my contact with universal power through whatever is sacred. And, I would add, there is a lot more that is sacred than that which is human-constructed in the universe.

Like the Buddhist phrase, "we exist in muddy water with purity like the lotus," we cannot escape the human condition and the systems around us. But we can recognize our inherent purity and all that is sacred around us. To do that we must, as Eleanor Roosevelt so simply put it, "do the thing you think you cannot do." Shaping power for good within ourselves means loosening our grip on the realities that were constructed for us, befriending our shadow, and connecting with our sacred birthright to manifest our rooted personal power in the world. Shaping power for good begins with you.

Shaping Power for Good with Others

With power-consciousness, we see the world differently—more comes into view, and our attention to the nuance of power in the room shifts or comes into focus. We see that power is being manipulated and shaped in every relationship, even when people are mostly unaware of that. We also begin to see how we show up in relationships—that we have an impact beyond the moment of interaction, and often beyond our consciousness of it.

Throughout the book, I've pointed to the importance of making power explicit in relationships. With a broader framework and more nuanced language for talking about the complexity of power, we are better able to highlight, challenge, and shift power in any room. And we get to use the various types of power available to us and our allies to do that. This begins with our interpersonal relationships. We can be aware of the power differentials present, explore them together, talk about them, and create structures that support us in navigating them well. For example, as a co-parent in a blended family, I noticed that we had two distinct family cultures coming together, different genders, different ways of relating, different brain structures, and different ages and developmental stages. And, of course, there is the power differential between us as parents and our kids. What I noticed is that everyone was trying to "make do" without talking about our differences or the things that were bothering us. So I used my role power as a parent and

THE ART OF SHAPING POWER FOR GOOD   389

my personal power capabilities to create a family connection circle. Every Sunday night when we're all together, we eat dinner and then one of us volunteers as facilitator. The facilitator chooses some kind of question that is meant to establish connection and learn more about one another, like "What is one thing you didn't get to do this week that you wished you had been able to do?" or "What is one way you showed up this week that you are proud of?" And then we all go around answering the question. And then the next round is usually about something we're grateful for about someone else in the family, or about some other kind of gratitude. And then the final round is something like, "What is something you need support around?" or "What is something you need resolution about?" This offers a structured time for us to connect and to have support in naming tensions in the house or difficulties we are facing. This is also a time when the kids can name things they are disappointed in about us as parents, or say what isn't working for them in the house. Then we get to negotiate those together. Even though the kids are down-power from us, we can creatively craft structures to support them in accessing their own power to let us know what is going on—to offer space for the relationship to be shaped in *both* directions.

Shaping power for good in interpersonal relationships means that we are always holding the question: Am I conscious of the different types of power between us *and* am I showing up in ways that promote everyone's ability to be in their rooted personal power? And if there is a role or status power differential present that might be inhibiting right-relationship, how can we co-create opportunities to navigate around the differential? Ultimately, as Ted Rau said, "shifting the power balance means renegotiating relationships." This is where our creativity must enter. We cannot deny the presence of power differentials, but we can see how they've been constructed and show up differently within them. And when we are in the up-power position, will we recognize that the responsibility to initiate this creative renegotiation lies with us? We must step into responsibility, not as an obligation, but as our ability to respond to the interdependence of our connection and the realities of the power differentials that we must recognize and navigate. Shaping power for good with others is an active collaboration of our powers to be response-able, allow for mistakes, engage in generative conflict, and discover right relationship over and over again.

Shaping power for Good in Systems

While there are ways we can navigate power differentials and our socialization beyond what systems have produced, at the end of the day, the systems will continue to apply pressure to us and our relationships to conform to their shape. The question we have to ask ourselves is—do the shapes of the systems we are in benefit us? And if not, what do we do about it?

I constructed the Systemic Lenses with the understanding that different types of systems have their place in the world. Each creates certain advantages and disadvantages. However, some systemic shapes tend to advantage individuals within the system disproportionately. It is also precisely because each system has positive attributes that make it hard to change. When you look at the outcomes of each type of power through a particular systemic lens, you'll see a self-reinforcing, complex web of attributes that ultimately lead to whole-system outcomes. But it is the systemic *shape* that leads to those outcomes. One of the more controversial and important thoughts I'm chewing on right now is that we focus so much on the players and not enough on the paradigms. We like to think that it is one person or a group of people who is holding the "puppet strings." While certainly those with more role and status power can make decisions that can control others, I think we need to look a little deeper if we are going to make more sustainable change in systems.

There is a theory called Double-Loop learning that could provide a helpful framework for better understanding what I'm pointing to here. Using a systems example, let's imagine a school district grappling with a persistent achievement gap between students of different racial backgrounds. The initial response might involve implementing after-school tutoring programs or providing additional resources to underperforming schools. This is called single-loop learning: a different action or element was implemented to achieve a different result.

But, as many schools have discovered, by adjusting actions or elements to impact racial inequities, they result in little to no improvements. When the core issue or problem persists despite multiple changes to actions or elements, double-loop learning can be engaged to examine the underlying assumptions and beliefs that ultimately shape the elements or actions in the first place. In the context of racial inequities in schools, for example, educators and policymakers would need to question fundamental assumptions and beliefs about race, education, and student success. They might realize that standardized testing, curriculum design, and even the structure of the school day are based on cultural norms that inherently disadvantage certain groups. The school district might discover that its underlying beliefs about education, shaped by historical and systemic racism, are perpetuating the very inequities it's trying to address.

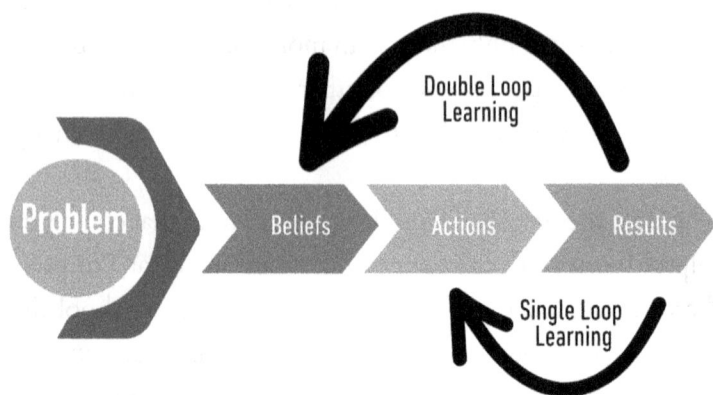

The beauty of double-loop learning is that it goes beyond simply correcting errors or refining strategies—it invites us to question the very assumptions, values, and goals that underlie our actions in the first place. This frees us up to reimagine and create new structures that support the outcomes we say that we want. By addressing their root assumptions and beliefs, the school district in our example can implement more transformative, equity-centered solutions that go beyond surface-level interventions. This might involve completely restructuring how schools are funded, how students are assessed, or even the fundamental goals of education itself.

In organizations and relationships, double-loop learning helps people and groups evolve not just by doing things right, but by rethinking what "right" means. It requires humility, curiosity, and the courage to challenge long-held beliefs. The trouble is, many of us *say* we want certain outcomes but aren't willing to do the work of changing our beliefs and assumptions. Many aren't willing to take the time, energy, and resources to recreate policies, structures, and institutions. So what do we do instead? We target one person or group and sacrifice them so that everyone else can remain comfortable in the idea that they have it "right." We all do this, unfortunately. While it may feel better or easier to blame someone else rather than collectively examine our own assumptions and beliefs, I don't believe this actually helps us shift systems.

Again, it is the shape of systems that makes the puppet strings move in a particular way. And it is the systemic *paradigm* that ultimately does the shaping. What we need to understand is that each systemic paradigm can only make particular shapes or outcomes. However, when we avoid looking at our own beliefs and assumptions, we tend to blame the system generally and wish that it were a different type of system. We can want an Authority System to be an Independent system, but it won't be. It doesn't have the elements or capacity to be that—its shape doesn't allow it. We can protest and give power to different people, but it will always become what it was shaped to be. It cannot change what it fundamentally is—*unless we change the underlying paradigm.*

This scenario of wishing something were different, trying to control elements or actions, but being unwilling to change our beliefs or assumptions, reminds me of a scene in the movie, *Kung Fu Panda*, where Master Oogway was imparting words of wisdom to his apprentice under a peach tree:

Oogway: "My friend, the panda will never fulfill his destiny, nor you yours, until you let go of the illusion of control."

Shifu: "Illusion?"

Oogway: "Yes. Look at this tree, Shifu. I cannot make it blossom when it suits me, nor make it bear fruit before its time."

Shifu: "But there are things we *can* control." [Kicks the tree, causing several peaches to fall.] "I can control when the fruit will fall." [One hits him on the head. Oogway chuckles.] "And I can control... [Tosses the peach in the air and chops it in half.] ...where to plant the seed." [Punches a hole in the ground and catches the seed.] "That is no illusion, Master." [Throws the seed into the hole]

   Oogway: "Ah, yes. But no matter what you do, that seed will grow to be a peach tree. You may wish for an apple or an orange, but you will get a peach."

This brings us right back to shaping power for good within ourselves, doesn't it? Of course, each of us doing our own work before we try to change others or systems is not new information. But it is a reminder. Donella Meadows said,

   "People who cling to paradigms (which means just about all of us) take one look at the spacious possibility that everything they think is guaranteed to be nonsense and pedal rapidly in the opposite direction. Surely there is no power, no control, no understanding, not even a reason for being, much less acting, embodied in the notion that there is no certainty to *any* worldview. But, in fact, everyone who has managed to entertain that idea, for a moment or for a lifetime, has found it to be the basis for radical empowerment. If no paradigm is right, you can choose whatever one will help to achieve your purpose. If you have no idea where to get a purpose, you can listen to the universe."[2]

   Shaping power for good is a choice in every moment. It is an invitation to show up as artists for ourselves and others, so we can create new possibilities rather than chaining ourselves to the same power dynamics and systems that dishonor our interconnection. Shaping power for good is about making micro-revolutionary acts in every moment, relationship, or system we find ourselves in. And it doesn't have to be big or even noticeable to others. We can start with ourselves and create more spaciousness and compassion

---

2. Meadows, D. H. (2008). Thinking in Systems: A Primer. Chelsea Green Publishing, p.164.

for our own shadows and socialization—the mud that can feel like quicksand. With support, we can locate our sacred roots and develop our personal power. We can recognize whatever social power we have been given access to and shape it for good. And we can use our wayfinding skills to co-create right relationship.

Of course, shaping power for good is not something we will have capacity for all the time or without support. It is easier to find that capacity or support when it is an art form—not a battle. This is not a competition or a fight to see who is "right" or "wrong." It is an urgent need to intentionally navigate the "collision of immoral power with powerless morality which constitutes the major crisis of our times," as Dr. King so eloquently put it. When we do have the capacity and support to participate in power in ways that shape power for good, we can "stand in our strength while staying in our hearts"—we can bring love and power together as they were meant to be.

Acknowledgements

This book would have not made it into manifestation without the loving support of several people and, of course, my well-ancestors and Spirit.

First and foremost, to my partner, Steph, who juggled the household, kids and pets, brought me food and words of encouragement, and was my biggest cheerleader throughout the entire process of writing. They pointed me to my own voice again and again when I had doubts or started to follow others' visions instead of my own. Thank you for your belief in me and the many ways you have supported my work. This book would not be here without you.

To my mentor, Dr. Cedar Barstow: All of the contents of this book exist because of the foundation you built over so many years, as well as your willingness to mentor me. Thank you for your generous guidance and support throughout this long journey (that began long before I ever started writing this book). My hope is that this work will amplify yours and honor your legacy.

To the Right Use of Power community: Thank you for continually asking me to "write it all down." I am in deep gratitude for your willingness to learn with me and help me to grow. Your engagement with the Right Use of Power material was the sharpening stone I needed to clarify my thoughts. You were the inspiration to develop this work further than I had ever imagined.

To my Beta Readers, especially Veronica Borgonovi and Cedar:

Thank you for getting through the massive manuscript that was once this book. Thank you for the edits and insights, and most especially for your willingness to challenge me.

And finally, to my well-ancestors and Spirit: For your guidance and patience with me as I avoided this calling and came back to it again and again. Your presence is what gave me the courage to write and publish this book.

Glossary

ACCOUNTABILITY - our ability to account for what happened in the past and answer for the outcomes of our responsibilities.

BINARY THINKING - also known as dualistic thinking or black-and-white thinking, it is a cognitive style characterized by a tendency to categorize things into only two opposing categories: good/bad, right/wrong, us/them, etc. It simplifies complex issues by reducing them to a dichotomy, ignoring the nuances, subtleties, and gradations that exist in reality.

COLLECTIVE POWER - power that comes from gathering strength and influence from multiple sources to promote a common interest.

DOMINANT CULTURE – refers to the cultural values, beliefs, practices, and norms that are most widely accepted and influential within modern Western society.

HOLDING COMPLEXITY - the capacity to acknowledge, understand, and manage multiple, often contradictory, perspectives, factors, and uncertainties simultaneously without resorting to simplification or premature closure. It's about embracing the inherent ambiguity and multifaceted nature of situations rather than seeking easy answers or single explanations.

INTERNALIZED OPPRESSION – the internal oppression that individuals who have experienced down-power often begin to unconsciously accept and live out the negative stereotypes and beliefs that systems create about their identities or attributes. Over time, they might start to doubt their own worth, capabilities, and rights, mirroring the harmful attitudes of the larger society.

INTERNALIZED SUPERIORITY – the sense of superiority that individuals who have experienced up-power often subconsciously absorb via beliefs created by systems. This can manifest as entitlement or an unconscious bias that one's identities, attributes, cultural values and behaviors are the standard.

MORE-THAN-HUMAN BEINGS - plants, animals, insects and all the living organisms who were here before human beings and who co-exist with human beings.

POWER - the ability to have an effect or influence

POWER-CONSCIOUSNESS – an awareness and understanding of how power operates within relationships and systems and how it shapes individuals' and groups' experiences and opportunities. It's not simply acknowledging that power exists, but rather a deep understanding of its mechanisms, its impact on individuals and groups, and its potential for both oppression and liberation.

RESPONSIBILITY - choosing how we respond to situations, people, and challenges in ways that align with our values and the well-being of the relationships involved.

RIGHT-RELATIONSHIP - A temporary state that is reached when everyone in the relationship experiences an active honoring of their rooted personal power and when there is an honest acknowledgment by all of the other types of power at play in the relationship.

ROLE - a set of behaviors, expectations, resources, and responsibilities that are associated with a particular position within a social system or group. Roles are typically awarded, elected, granted, assigned, or hired by a system or collective to an individual. Examples: doctor, facilitator, coach, judge, leader, etc.

ROLE AUTHORITY - the externally sourced access and privileges that accompany a role. Authority is granted by a system and accompanies the role no matter who occupies that role.

ROLE POWER DIFFERENTIAL - a relationship where there is a difference in power between someone who occupies a role that has authority (up-role power) and the person(s) subject to that authority (down-role power).

ROLE POWER - the influence that exists as a direct result of the difference in formal authority between two people and the particular interpersonal relationship between the up-role and down-role person.

SOCIAL POWER DYNAMICS – the complex interplay of power in relationships between individuals and/or groups within a social system. At a systems level, it encompasses the ways in which role, status, collective, and systemic power is distributed, exercised,

- How do you relate with others?

You recognize that independence is really the most important thing because the most efficient way to get to the top is through autonomy. You don't have to worry about bringing anyone with you.

   - How does it feel being in the achievement lens?

• • • ● ● • ● ● • •

Feel free to pause here and jot down any notes you'd like to remember later about any images, sensations, impulses, feelings or thoughts that came up while exploring this lens.

Now shake that lens off and we'll move to the next.

• • • ● ● • ● ● • •

Let's settle again in your body, take a breath, and now we'll explore the Pluralistic Lens.

Imagine you're in a **Pluralistic Lens** and you exist in a globe. You're somewhere on that globe with various other beings. Some are human and some are not human. In this globe, there is diversity everywhere and it feels important to you that there's some level of equality. Imagine for a moment what it would be like to be in a system where diversity is celebrated.

Although there is diversity present and there is movement toward equality and the "common good," there is also conflict and chaos in trying to find what is "right" and determine what equality actually looks like. It is a dynamic and complex system that requires ongoing effort to maintain its balance and to ensure that all groups have a fair opportunity to participate in shaping the system.

1. So as you encounter others in this system, What comes up?

2. What does it feel like in your body to be in this pluralistic system? What sensations arise here?

3. What are your impulses? What are your needs?

4. How do you determine an approach to all of those different kinds of beings and relationships

5. How do you achieve equality while also empowering yourself?

6. How do you figure out what your purpose is? There's no top to get to, so what do you do?

• • • ● ● • ● ● • •

Feel free to pause here and jot down any notes you'd like to remember later about any images, sensations, impulses, feelings or thoughts that came up while exploring this lens.

Now shake that lens off and we'll move to the next.

• • • ● ● • ● ● • •

So again, settle in your body and turn inward. Now we're entering a web of interdependence where you and I are not separate. In the **Interdependent Lens** the connections between us are known and felt. Relationships are about reciprocity and mutuality because there is an understanding that what affects you affects me. Being a part of this web, there's a feeling of belonging like a tree, water, the stars, and the galaxies. You are an inseparable part of it all. However, this interrelated web can create a sense of chaos, with unpredictable, complex behavior arising from interactions and relationships among the system's interdependent components.

- What does it feel like in your body to be in an interdependent system? What sensations arise here?

- How do you show up in relationship in this web?

- What are your impulses?

- What are your needs?

- And how do you go about finding your purpose?

- How do you know that you belong?

• • ● ● • ● ● • • •

Feel free to pause here and jot down any notes you'd like to remember later about any images, sensations, impulses, feelings or thoughts that came up while exploring this lens.

Reflection Questions on the Systemic Lenses:

1. Looking back at your notes, what do you notice as the primary difference between how you felt in each lens?

2. How did your impulses and needs differ?

3. Which lens felt most familiar?

4. While lens felt most comfortable?

5. Which lens felt most confusing or foreign?

6. Based on this exploration, what natural outcomes or consequences do you think might result from each lens?

Appendix B

❖

The Window of Responsibility

I created a framework called *The Window of Responsibility*, which illustrates the many forms responsibility can take depending on our level of engagement (passive to active) and our source of motivation (extrinsic to intrinsic). When I put these along two axes, it creates four distinct quadrants—Obligation, Duty, Reaction, and Response—each reflecting the different ways we show up in responsibility.

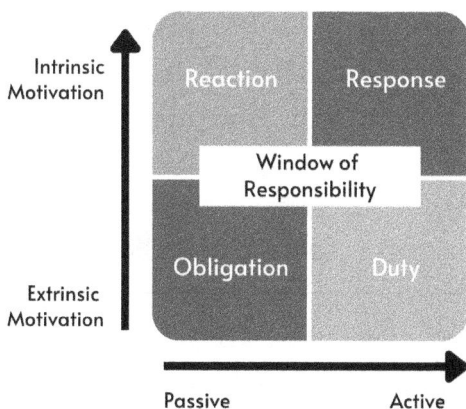

In the bottom left quadrant, we find **Obligation**. Here, responsibility is driven by external pressures or expectations, and we take a passive approach—we do what we are told. We perform what is required, but only because we feel they have to, not because we want to. This is the realm of doing the bare minimum, often out of a sense of societal or relational pressure. For example, someone might attend family gatherings because they feel they should, but they don't actively engage or contribute to the relationships. Obligation is about meeting expectations, but without much personal investment. When we engage from obligation, we often have very little joy, and we count the minutes until we can escape. People often demonstrate regret from this place.

In which relationships or areas of your life do you feel that you engage from obligation? And what kind of return do you get on that type of investment? What is the health of your relationships like when you engage with obligation?

Moving to the bottom right quadrant, we encounter **Duty**. From Duty, we tend toward a more active, engaged approach, but it is still outlined by external expectations. We work hard to meet expectations or fulfill our role, often going above and beyond to do what's required. Duty is about taking responsibility seriously and diligently, even if it's not driven by personal desire. For instance, a partner might take on household chores to avoid conflict or gain approval, even if it's not something they personally value. Duty is characterized by a sense of conscientiousness, but it's still rooted in external validation or pressure. I often see passive-aggression and resentment from people who come from a place of duty in relationship.

In which relationships or areas of your life do you feel that you engage from duty? And what kind of return do you get on that type of investment? What is the health of your relationships like when you engage from a place of duty?

In the top left quadrant, we see **Reaction**. Here, responsibility is driven by internal values, but the we take a more passive or situational approach. From this place we tend to act in alignment with our values when prompted or when a situation arises, but we don't take proactive steps to nurture or strengthen the relationship. Reaction is about responding to situations as they come up, but not initiating action. For example, a friend might offer support when someone is in crisis, but they don't regularly check in or nurture the friendship. Reaction is guided by care and integrity, but it's more reactive than proactive. I often see this kind of responsibility from well-meaning leaders who are overwhelmed, burnt out or who have taken on too much—or those of us who are neurodivergent (all of which are uncomfortably familiar for me).

In which relationships or areas of your life do you feel that you engage from reaction? And what kind of return do you get on that type of investment? What is the health of your relationships like when you engage with reaction?

Finally, in the top right quadrant, we find **Response**. This is the most conscious and intentional form of responsibility. Here, the individual takes proactive steps to nurture and maintain the relationship out of a deep sense of care, respect, and personal integrity. They actively seek to understand and meet the needs of the other person, not because they have to, but because they genuinely value the connection. For instance, a partner might regularly communicate, show appreciation, and work to resolve conflicts because they are committed to the relationship's health and growth. Response is about taking thoughtful, deliberate action to strengthen the relationship, rather than just reacting to situations. When we are rooted in our personal power and have more capacity (i.e. take good care of ourselves and have good boundaries), we are able to respond in alignment with our values.

In which relationships or areas of your life do you feel that you engage from response-ability? And what kind of return do you get on that type of investment? What is the health of your relationships like when you engage with response-ability?

As you reflect on these different origins of responsibility, you might notice that some feel more familiar than others, depending on the context. The purpose of these quadrants isn't to label ourselves as right or wrong, but to help clarify the various influences that shape how we show up in our responsibilities. Understanding what drives our engagement and motivation is a crucial step in learning how to take responsibility in ways that support the co-creation of right-relationship. Let's take a closer look at the two axes to see what they reveal about how responsibility functions in our lives and why we might get stuck in one of the quadrants.

What Makes Us More Extrinsically vs. Intrinsically Motivated in Responsibility?

Understanding the difference between extrinsic and intrinsic motivation can help us approach responsibility in a way that feels more authentic and fulfilling. Both types of motivation have their place, and each influences how we engage with responsibility and relationships—especially when there's a power dynamic at play. While neither is inherently better than the other, they do lead to different outcomes, and it's important to recognize the circumstances that promote one or the other.

Extrinsic Motivation is rooted in external factors—whether it is rewards, punishments, societal expectations, or the desire to avoid conflict. This kind of motivation can provide structure, account-ability, and immediate compliance, which are essential in many contexts. Extrinsic motivators can also help build habits, support social norms, and ensure fairness in systems. However, several factors can make extrinsic motivation less than ideal.

Extrinsic motivation often arises in Authority and Achievement-based systems. In hierarchical organizations that come from one of these power paradigms, employees may feel extrinsically motivated to meet performance targets because their job security and possibility for promotion depend on it. In power–differential relationships, the down-power person may feel compelled to act out of fear of consequences or a need to please an up-power person. When someone outside of a power-differential relationship is evaluating how well and completely you're "checking boxes," it's easy to focus on those boxes instead of the relationship itself. If responsibility is imposed rather than chosen, it's much harder to feel good about it. For example, an employee might work overtime to meet a manager's demands, not because they want to, but because they fear losing their job. Research, such as Deci and Ryan's Self-Determination Theory, has shown that while extrinsic motivation can lead to compliance, it often comes at the cost of personal satisfaction and autonomy. Over time, this can erode trust and create resentment in relationships.

Similarly, in personal relationships, extrinsic motivations may not be the healthiest option. For example, in an intimate partnership, one partner may feel obligated to meet the other's expectations out of fear of conflict or rejection. Or parents might use rewards to encourage their children to be more responsible for their chores.

Alfie Kohn argues in Punished by Rewards[1] , while rewards can produce short-term compliance, they often undermine intrinsic motivation, creativity, and long-term engagement.

While there is nothing inherently wrong with being extrinsically motivated by a paycheck, a smile on someone's face, or the growth of a business, the origin of the extrinsic motivation can have different effects on us and our relationships. Many environments push us into a survival state, where we are perpetually dysregulated and focused on what others want from us. A 2021 study by Gagné et al.[2] found that controlling leadership (which often relies on rewards and punishments) was associated with lower job satisfaction and higher burnout rates. Part of the issue here is a misunderstanding of what responsibility truly means. Some people confuse it with control—feeling they have to micromanage or fix everything —which leads to burnout and a lot of people being annoyed with you!

True responsibility isn't about controlling outcomes but about being accountable and doing your best with what you have. However, it is hard not to be controlling if you are punished for your imperfections and you've become hypervigilant about external cues about your performance. When extrinsic motivations are promoted by control and prompted by fear, they rely on the activation of our nervous systems and the experience of stress in order to "be responsible." No wonder we often avoid responsibility when it's

1. Kohn, A. (1999). Punished by rewards: The trouble with gold stars, incentive plans, A's, praise, and other bribes. Houghton Mifflin Harcourt.

2. Gagné, M., Forest, J., Vansteenkiste, M., Crevier-Braud, L., Van den Broeck, A., Aspeli, A. K., Bellerose, J., Benabou, C., Chemolli, E., Güntert, S. T., Halvari, H., Indiyastuti, D. L., Johnson, P. A., Molstad, M. H., Naudin, M., Ndao, A., Olafsen, A. H., Roussel, P., Wang, Z., & Westbye, C. (2021). The multidimensional work motivation scale: Validation evidence in seven languages and nine countries. Journal of Organizational Behavior, 42(2), 187–210.

extrinsically motivated! Even if we learn to find "success" in those environments, we may eventually face a midlife crisis, broken relationships, or a desperate switch to another career. When we exist in environments that demand constant external engagement and when leadership relies on rewards and punishments to control behavior, we can end up creating systems and situations that take us further away from both responsibility and right-relationship, rather than closer to them.

Intrinsic Motivation, on the other hand, comes from within—it's driven by personal values, care, and a genuine desire to contribute. In power-differential relationships, the up-power person has a unique opportunity to act out of intrinsic motivation by creating an environment where the down-power person feels valued and safe. Research[3] suggests that intrinsic motivation leads to greater engagement, creativity, and long-term satisfaction in relationships. Internally sourced motivation flourishes in environments where individuals feel valued and respected. By shifting our focus to intrinsic motivation, we tap into the internal drive that makes responsibility feel less like an obligation and more like a natural extension of our values and desires. When people are motivated by their own interests, passions, or sense of purpose, they're more likely to take ownership of their actions and feel invested in the outcomes.

Another important source of intrinsic motivation is autonomy—the sense that you have a say in what you take on. Autonomy can shift responsibility from something that feels heavy

---

3. Ryan, R. M., & Deci, E. L. (2019). Supporting autonomy, competence, and relatedness: The optimal conditions for motivation, growth, and well-being. Current Directions in Psychological Science, 28(2), 105–113. DOI: [10.1177/096372141 8807537](https://doi.org/10.1177/0963721418807537)

to something that feels purposeful and meaningful. When people understand how their responsibilities contribute to something larger—whether it's their own growth, the well-being of others, or a greater cause—they're more likely to see them as meaningful and purposeful. This sense of connection can transform responsibilities from a burden into an opportunity to make a positive impact. A 2020 meta-analysis published in the Psychological Bulletin by Howard et al.[4] found that autonomy-supportive environments (where individuals have access to their personal power and feel they have choice and control) significantly enhance intrinsic motivation, while controlling environments (where rewards or punishments are used to manipulate behavior) reduce it. Purpose and autonomy gives responsibility a sense of direction and value, making it easier to engage with it wholeheartedly.

Encouraging the engagement of personal power further transforms responsibility from a weight into a source of strength. Personal power is about recognizing one's ability to influence outcomes and make a difference. When individuals feel empowered, they see responsibility as an opportunity to contribute meaningfully rather than as a chore. This sense of agency fosters confidence and resilience, enabling people to navigate challenges with a proactive mindset. It also strengthens their sense of connection to others, as they recognize their role in co-creating healthy, balanced relationships.

Together, these elements—intrinsic motivation, autonomy, and personal power—create a foundation where responsibility is not just about fulfilling obligations but about actively participating in something larger than oneself. This shift transforms responsibility

---

4. Howard, J. L., Gagné, M., & Bureau, J. S. (2020). Testing a continuum structure of self-determined motivation: A meta-analysis. Psychological Bulletin, 146(6), 511–544. DOI: [10.1037/bul0000225] (https://doi.org/10.1037/bul0000225)

from a passive, often resented duty into a dynamic, meaningful commitment. In relationships, this approach fosters mutual respect, collaboration, and a shared sense of purpose. It allows individuals to contribute in ways that feel authentic and fulfilling while also supporting the collective's well-being. Ultimately, by nurturing these qualities, we can create environments where responsibility is embraced as a pathway to growth, connection, and balance.

What leads to more Passive vs Active Engagement?

The horizontal axis of the Window of Responsibility examines whether we take a passive or active approach to responsibility. This axis is particularly relevant in power-differential relationships, where the distribution of power can influence how responsibility is enacted. Our level of engagement—whether passive or active—is influenced by our sense of agency, the dynamics of the relationship, and the environment in which we operate.

Passive Engagement is characterized by minimal effort or re-action rather than pro-action. In relationships, this often means waiting for someone else to take the lead or only stepping up when prompted. Many factors play a role in our passivity with respon-sibility, but I want to start with the one that is most influential: systemic norms, culture, and context. There are a few systemic contexts that I want to highlight that make passive responsibil-ity particularly ingrained in the culture: punitive or retributive cultures, high economic and other status-based inequalities, and individualistic contexts.

In environments where mistakes are met with punishment, the consequences extend far beyond the immediate reprimand. Punishment often triggers shame, a deeply internalized emotion that can erode self-worth and disconnect us from our sense of personal power. Shame doesn't just make us feel bad about what we've done; it makes us feel bad about who we are. This shift from behavior to identity is particularly damaging because it undermines our confidence and agency, making it harder to take ownership of our actions or learn from our mistakes. Instead of seeing errors as opportunities for growth, we begin to see them as threats to our self-esteem, something to be hidden or denied at all costs. Fear of punishment—and the shame it brings—leads us to avoid accountability until we are forced to confront it, often only when someone else calls us out. In this way, responsibility becomes something we take on reluctantly, out of obligation rather than genuine willingness. We wait to be held accountable rather than stepping forward on our own. This passive approach to responsibility stifles initiative and discourages proactive problem-solving, as people become more focused on avoiding blame than on doing what's right.

Highly retributive systems, where punishment is the primary response to failure, tend to exacerbate this problem. These systems prioritize consequences over learning, creating a culture of fear rather than one of growth. In such environments, people are more likely to disengage, becoming less willing to take risks, innovate, or take ownership of their actions. This passive engagement ultimately produces less actively responsible individuals. When responsibility is imposed rather than embraced, it loses its transformative potential.

Economic pressures add another layer of complexity to how responsibility is experienced and perceived. When people are consumed by the immediate demands of survival—such as paying bills, putting food on the table, or providing for their families—responsibility often shifts from being a moral or noble endeavor to a stark necessity. In these circumstances, responsibility isn't a choice; it's an obligation driven by the urgency of meeting basic needs. This can strip away any sense of purpose or fulfillment that might come from taking on responsibilities, turning it into a relentless grind. The focus narrows to getting through the day, and the broader meaning or impact of one's actions can easily get lost in the struggle to keep up.

When responsibility goes unnoticed or unappreciated, it can breed resentment. This is especially true in environments where people feel their efforts are taken for granted—whether in the workplace, at home, or within a community. When someone is working tirelessly to fulfill their responsibilities but receives no acknowledgment or gratitude, it can lead to feelings of invisibility and frustration. Over time, this lack of recognition can erode motivation, making responsibility feel like a thankless burden rather than a meaningful contribution. The emotional toll of unappreciated responsibility can be significant, leading to burnout, disengagement, or even a sense of bitterness toward the very roles or tasks that once felt important. This dynamic is particularly pronounced in systems where economic inequality is high, and resources are scarce.

In individualistic cultures, responsibility is often framed as a personal obligation, something you carry on your own shoulders. This perspective can foster a sense of independence and self-reliance, but it can also lead to feelings of isolation, especially when challenges arise. When responsibility is viewed as a solo endeavor, the weight of decision-making, problem-solving, and accountability falls squarely on the individual. This can create pressure to "have it all together" and a fear of failure, as there's often an implicit expectation that one should handle everything without needing help.

The emphasis on personal achievement can sometimes overshadow the value of collaboration, leaving people feeling alone in their struggles, even when they're surrounded by others.

Passive responsibility has far reaching effects, particularly when it comes to how we participate in power dynamics. When we tend toward passive engagement, it is more common to ignore the power we do have acess to—which is a misuse of power in its own right. Whether we fail to acknowledge our own personal power, or we are reluctant to step into the up-power we've been given, the diffusion of responsibility is highly detrimental—especially those down-power from us.

Van Kleef et al. (2008)[5] conducted a pivotal study exploring how power dynamics shape people's willingness to intervene in emergencies. In their research, participants were placed in a scenario where they observed someone in distress. Those who were primed in an up-power position were significantly less likely to offer help, even when the need for assistance was evident. This finding suggests that power can create a psychological distance, reducing empathy and diminishing the sense of urgency to act. Similar the bystander effect, the study highlights a phenomenon known as the diffusion of responsibility, where individuals in positions of power may assume that someone else will take charge, leading to inaction even in critical situations. This research underscores the complex and sometimes counterintuitive ways in which power can influence behavior, particularly in contexts requiring compassion or moral courage. It also raises important questions about how power dynamics can impact collective responsibility and the willingness to help others in need.

---

5. van Kleef, G. A., Oveis, C., van der Löwe, I., LuoKogan, A., Goetz, J., & Keltner, D. (2008). Power, distress, and compassion: Turning a blind eye to the suffering of others. Psychological Science, 19(12), 1315-1322.

Active Engagement, in contrast, involves taking initiative and being proactive. In power-differential relationships, the up-power person has a responsibility to encourage active engagement by creating a safe space for the down-power person to contribute. Active engagement is linked to higher levels of trust, satisfaction, and productivity in relationships (Edmondson, 1999). When both parties actively engage, the relationship becomes more equitable and resilient. Active responsibility is encouraged by environments that foster trust, autonomy, and mutual respect. In power-differential relationships, the up-power person can promote active responsibility by creating opportunities for the down-power person to contribute and by validating their efforts. Studies on psychological safety, such as those by Amy Edmondson (1999), show that active engagement thrives in environments where individuals feel safe to take risks and express themselves.

Proactive behavior has been a major focus in organizational psychology, with research distinguishing between passive and active approaches to responsibility. Proactivity involves taking initiative, anticipating problems, and actively shaping one's environment, while passivity involves waiting for instructions or reacting to situations as they arise. A study by Parker, Bindl and Strauss[6] introduces a model of proactive motivation, emphasizing how individuals can move from passive to active responsibility by taking initiative and anticipating future needs. The authors highlight the importance of autonomy, self-efficacy, and a sense of ownership in fostering proactive behavior.

Contexts that foster learning and growth rather than punishment

---

6. Parker, S. K., Bindl, U. K., & Strauss, K. (2010). Making things happen: A model of proactive motivation. Journal of Management, 36(4), 827–856. DOI: 10.1177/014 9206310363732] (https://doi.org/10.1177/0149206310363732)

tend to cultivate more engaged and responsible individuals. When mistakes are seen as opportunities for improvement rather than failures to be punished, people are more likely to take ownership of their actions and learn from their errors. This approach builds resilience, encourages accountability, and helps individuals stay connected to their personal power. Danielle Sered [Kaba, M., & Hassan, S. (2019). Fumbling toward repair: A workbook for community accountability facilitators. Project NIA.]said, "...accountab ility does for those of us who commit harm what the healing process does for us when we are harmed: it gives us a way to recuperate our sense of dignity, of self-worth, of connectedness, and of hope—the things we lost when we caused harm." When someone causes harm, whether intentionally or unintentionally, they often experience a loss of dignity and self-worth. They may feel disconnected from their own sense of morality, from the people they've hurt, and even from their community. This can lead to feelings of shame, guilt, or hopelessness, which can further isolate them and perpetuate cycles of harm. Sered argues that accountability—acknowledging the harm, taking responsibility, and making amends—offers a way to reclaim these lost qualities. It suggests that harm does not have to define a person forever and that change is possible. In essence, Sered is advocating for a restorative approach to justice, where accountability is not just about punishment but about healing and transformation. It's about creating opportunities for those who have caused harm to reintegrate into society as better, more connected individuals, rather than being permanently ostracized or defined by their worst actions. This approach not only benefits the individual but also contributes to a more compassionate and just society.

By engaging in accountability, individuals who have caused harm can begin to reconnect with their own humanity and the humanity of those they've hurt. It allows them to confront their actions honestly, which can be a difficult but ultimately liberating process. This confrontation can restore a sense of dignity, as it demonstrates a willingness to face the consequences and grow from the experience. It also fosters self-worth by showing that they are capable of change and redemption. When we combine active accountability with active responsibility, we are doing the work of protecting our human and relational vulnerabilities. While it may take more effort initially, the outcomes of well-supported active engagement has the potential to transform our relationships and communities.

About the Author

Dr. Amanda Aguilera (she/her/ella) is an author, psychotherapist, consultant, and facilitator passionate about power consciousness and conflict resolution. She currently serves as the Executive Director of the Right Use of Power Institute and is a sought-after speaker and coach, guiding organizations and communities in co-creating structures that support right-relationship and generative communication. Based in Colorado, USA, Dr. Aguilera enjoys hiking, traveling, reading, and spending time with her partner, Steph, as they raise their three kids. You can connect with her online at: www.amandaaguilera.com.

Index

-C-

-J-